SECRETS OF WEALTHY PEOPLE

50 Techniques to Get Rich

David Stevenson

HULL LIBRARIES

SECRETS OF WEALTHY PEOPLE

50 Techniques to Get Rich

David Stevenson

First published in Great Britain in 2014 by Hodder & Stoughton. An Hachette UK company.

First published in US in 2014 by The McGraw-Hill Companies, Inc.

This edition published 2014.

Copyright © David Stevenson

The right of David Stevenson to be identified as the Author of the Work has been asserted by him in accordance with the Copyright, Designs and Patents Act 1988.

Database right Hodder & Stoughton (makers)

The *Teach Yourself* name is a registered trademark of Hachette UK.

All rights reserved. No part of this publication may be reproduced, stored in a retrieval system or transmitted in any form or by any means, electronic, mechanical, photocopying, recording or otherwise, without the prior written permission of the publisher, or as expressly permitted by law, or under terms agreed with the appropriate reprographic rights organization. Enquiries concerning reproduction outside the scope of the above should be sent to the Rights Department, John Murray Learning, at the address below.

You must not circulate this book in any other binding or cover and you must impose this same condition on any acquirer.

British Library Cataloguing in Publication Data: a catalogue record for this title is available from the British Library.

Library of Congress Catalog Card Number: on file.

10 9 8 7 6 5 4 3 2 1

Paperback ISBN 978 1 444 79392 5

eBook ISBN 978 1 444 79393 2

The publisher has used its best endeavours to ensure that any website addresses referred to in this book are correct and active at the time of going to press. However, the publisher and the author have no responsibility for the websites and can make no guarantee that a site will remain live or that the content will remain relevant, decent or appropriate.

The publisher has made every effort to mark as such all words which it believes to be trademarks. The publisher should also like to make it clear that the presence of a word in the book, whether marked or unmarked, in no way affects its legal status as a trademark.

Every reasonable effort has been made by the publisher to trace the copyright holders of material in this book. Any errors or omissions should be notified in writing to the publisher, who will endeavour to rectify the situation for any reprints and future editions.

Typeset by Cenveo Publisher Services.

Printed and bound in Great Britain by CPI Group (UK) Ltd., Croydon, CR0 4YY.

John Murray Learning policy is to use papers that are natural, renewable and recyclable products and made from wood grown in sustainable forests. The logging and manufacturing processes are expected to conform to the environmental regulations of the country of origin.

John Murray Learning
338 Euston Road
London NW1 3BH
www.hodder.co.uk

CONTENTS

Introduction	viii
1. It's an uncertain world	1
2. Debt – the anti-matter of wealth?	6
3. Castles, not pension plans	11
4. Invest in you	16
5. Reading the tea leaves	21
6. Spend wisely	26
7. Spend to accumulate	31
8. Good advice is worth paying for… assuming you can find it!	36
9. Compound it!	41
10. The big number	46
11. Working out the right time horizon	52
12. Regular or lumpy – how do you like your investments?	57
13. Diversification is the best risk control	62
14. Be well behaved!	67
15. Shares: the safest long-term bet?	73
16. From tiny acorns mighty oaks might grow	78
17. Back great companies	83
18. Have you got what it takes?	89
19. Cutting down the risk of failure in business	94
20. Beware the rise of the machine intelligence economy	99
21. Network to build personal capital	104
22. A portfolio approach to your career	109
23. Become a cheapskate – the virtues of value investing	114
24. What type of risk are you willing to take?	119
25. Ride the tech tiger	125
26. Emerging markets?	130
27. The liquidity challenge	135
28. Delight in the humble dividend	140
29. Everyone's favourite – tax!	145
30. On speculation	150
31. The silent killer – inflation	155
32. Future-proofing your investments	160

33.	The property game	165
34.	The Armageddon fallacy	170
35.	The glittering illusion	175
36.	Getting emotional about investments	180
37.	True to your bond	185
38.	Playing catch up?	190
39.	Invest where you have an edge	195
40.	Timing your investments	200
41.	Buying and selling discipline	205
42.	Cash and its uses	210
43.	Think global, beware confiscation	215
44.	Beware the fat pitch	221
45.	How to fight inflation practically	226
46.	Forever blowing bubbles	231
47.	Keep it simple, keep it cheap, use tracker funds	237
48.	Hunting down great investors	242
49.	Taming your debt	247
50.	Be creative	252

This SECRETS book contains a number of special textual features, which have been developed to help you navigate the chapters quickly and easily. Throughout the book, you will find these indicated by the following icons.

Each chapter contains **quotes** from inspiring figures. These will be useful for helping you understand different viewpoints and why each Secret is useful in a practical context.

Also included in each chapter are a number of **strategies** that outline techniques for putting this Secret into practice.

The **putting it all together** box at the end of each chapter provides a summary of each chapter, and a quick way into the core concepts of each Secret

You'll also see a **chapter ribbon** down the right-hand side of each right-hand page, to help you mark your progress through the book and to make it easy to refer back to a particular chapter you found useful or inspiring.

INTRODUCTION

Who said it was easy?

❝ 'It's not whether you're right or wrong that's important, but how much money you make when you're right and how much you lose when you're wrong.' George Soros

❝ 'Business opportunities are like buses, there's always another one coming.' Richard Branson

❝ 'Your life must focus on the maximization of objectivity.' Charlie Munger

❝ 'Many people think that by hoarding money they are gaining safety for themselves. If money is your ONLY hope for independence, you will never have it. The only real security that a person can have in this world is a reserve of knowledge, experience and ability. Without these qualities, money is practically useless.' Henry Ford

❝ 'Intense interest in any subject is indispensable if you're really going to excel in it.' Charlie Munger

No substitute for hard work and worry!

This book is about helping you to think in a more intelligent way about accumulating capital throughout your (hopefully) long life. It's a grounded book, built on hard facts, dismal economics and hundreds of hours talking to successful entrepreneurs and investors. It won't make you rich quick but it might make you think differently and if nothing else it will help you to become more financially secure.

It also accepts that as we grow older our priorities change, which is why the book naturally falls into a number of sections, each focusing on different stages in a person's life:

- The first dozen or so chapters look at the basic guiding ideas that help us build and accumulate wealth.

- We then look at strategies and ideas that will help the younger investor, in their 20s and 30s. We embrace risky, entrepreneurial ideas in these chapters before moving on to chapters that deal with the middle years – the 40s and 50s – where we should (hopefully) be knuckling down and accumulating our wealth at a faster speed. We finish by using a few chapters to explore the challenges facing older investors approaching or in retirement, examining the many risks they face to their wealth.
- Our last chunk of chapters focuses on a set of simple ideas that can be applied to all ages. These are practical ideas and models of behaviour that can help save you money, and focus on what's proven to create capital.

So, that's what you'll get in this book!

You'll notice that each chapter kicks off with a bunch of five sayings, which have some relevance to what follows. You'll also see lots of notions and ambitions bundled up in these fine words, from investors like Charlie Munger and George Soros through to great business legends like Henry Ford. I think I agree with most every sentiment expressed. What you'll notice though is that there aren't many out and out secrets in the list. It's all fairly straightforward, obvious stuff.

So, I'm going to let you into a secret. There are lots and lots of books out there that say they can tell you how to get rich quick. They usually have a cunning plan or two built on a few basic strategies that in turn are usually based on some 'forecast' for the future.

Here's my secret. No one can predict the future, no one can tell how or whether readers of this book will become wealthier.

What I have learnt from bitter experience is that the world we live in is a messy, noisy, chaotic place, largely without shape or structure, and full of utterly terrible ideas that keep re-emerging with grim regularity. Among this noise there are some signals worth focusing on (this book will identify a few), but by and large we are fallible human beings with a whole legion of behavioural tics that fool us into thinking we can make sense of it all. Psychologists have a term for it – excessive self-regard tendency – which roughly means that we think that our view of this messy existence has sense and reason. It doesn't, by and large, although many successful wealthy people are better at playing the game than others.

Yet what I find truly terrifying is that self-regard tendency is most forcefully applied when it comes to one of the most precious things in our existence – money and wealth.

Time for another secret. In my experience, the vast majority of wealthy entrepreneurs and investors that I've talked to and got to know as friends, work their butts off. There is no substitute for sheer hard work, diligence and patience. I'm not sure that's a surprising secret but I think it makes a mockery of the self-help books that claim to divine miraculous pathways to riches. There aren't any, just lots and lots of choices and heaploads of hard work. And the occasional dead end.

But here's yet another secret. Seriously wealthy, successful people make seriously stupid mistakes time and time again. Astonishingly, as they get wealthier they become more self-obsessed, believing their own hype. They come to assert strong views about matters to do with money, built on their vast experience. And then, frequently, they make a mistake, and lose much if not all of that money. Mistakes, powered by a foolish belief that they can see the future, destroy wealth. Years of hard work can be destroyed in just a few clicks by stupid ideas.

Tensions not answers

OK, so how's this book going to help you with that first and most important task mentioned at the beginning of this introduction – slowly accumulating capital and wealth to make you a more financially secure person?

I'm going to attempt to answer that by first articulating a number of basic principles that power this book – three in fact.

1. We all need to think a bit more like economists (yes, really!) and behave in a more utilitarian fashion by facing up to the facts. I was sadly trained as a dismal economist many moons ago and I can't quite shake my background but I passionately believe it offers a valuable insight into the world, like any other science

or social science. It forces us to quantify what 'exists', put a number to it and then think about the use and value of that number.
2. I want us all to slow down, stop behaving impulsively and get planning. Sticking with my utilitarian approach I want us all to recognize that we are far from being rational, that we are plagued by fears and phobias and passions. These need to be understood, largely kept in check and then used to help us build energy and enthusiasm for the things that we really care about. But building for the future requires a plan and making a plan inevitably forces us to slow down, think, put pen to paper (or finger to keyboard) and stop doing things impulsively.
3. Last but by no means least, I want us to objectify our financial situation, because building wealth is – in reality – all about dealing with hard numbers and cash. We need to think about our future in the same way a business would think about its destiny. If this business wanted to succeed over the next decade or so, it would plan, rationalize, work out the strengths and weaknesses and then sit down and understand what it is 'about' i.e. what does the business stand for?

Armed with these principles we're then going to charge off into the real world and try to discover what 'works' and what doesn't. What will help you accumulate capital and what might actively destroy your wealth?

As we navigate our way through the world of business, investment and consumerism we'll discover an unfortunate truth, which is that every opportunity is fraught with danger, that everything is more complicated than we first think.

This book is grounded in reality and I'm not going to lecture you about things like debt being evil or that government is bad or that you must plan for the end of capitalism under a new socialist world government. What I'm interested in is empirically working out why something works and understanding the processes that are lurking in the background. That inevitably leads me to the 'tension' or 'trade-off' challenge, which will keep cropping up in chapter after chapter in this book.

In plain, simple language, everything that is valuable and useful in life involves a trade-off. Here are a few basic trade-offs or challenges that we'll encounter later in this book:

The risk return trade-off. The biggest opportunities in the world of investment, for instance (we're talking shares here), involve equally big risks. There's no way of avoiding this trade-off and if you're unhappy at taking risk, then you need to accept that you won't be making a great return in the future.

The focus versus diversification trade-off. Plenty of books about business and finance suggest you should relentlessly focus on one great opportunity, and ignore anything else. This can be brilliant advice but it sort of assumes that a) you have the right idea; b) you know enough about the opportunity to make a considered judgement; and c) you're lucky.

For a great many people this involves taking far too much risk, which is why they choose to diversify their investments or businesses or properties.

There's no right or wrong answer to this just the constant flux between knowledge (which allows you to reduce risk and increase focus) and risk management (all things being equal, more diversification equals better control of risk).

The thorny old instinct versus delusion debate. Hunches are a great thing and I can personally count a number of brilliant businesses and investments where I've based everything on a deep-seated hunch based on instinct... and then acted on that momentary insight or epiphany. Unfortunately, because I only tend to remember the successes, I also tend to forget the absolute disasters based on that self-same instinct.

This book explores these challenges, debates and trade-offs in explicit detail and acknowledges that we are only human, that we do make mistakes and that there are no easy answers. Sometimes debt or credit, for instance, is a bad thing but sometimes it actually makes sense! Equally, for some investors punting your money on risky equities is the very best thing to do – for others it could be a complete disaster.

Once we understand these tensions we can begin to build plans and develop strategies and hopefully by the time you've finished reading this book you'll be a bit wiser and possibly even a great deal wealthier!

> A note on currencies: Since this book is written for a global audience (by an English writer!) we have made extensive use of both UK, sterling-based examples (£s) and US, dollar-based case studies. In line with usual Anglo-Saxon world views, we haven't detailed many Eurozone, Japanese or even Chinese examples, primarily in an effort to avoid too much confusion about competing currencies.

It's an uncertain world

> 'The name of the game is not to get rich rather it's not to die poor.' William Bernstein

> 'Rule #1: Never lose money. Rule #2: Never forget rule #1.' Warren Buffett

> 'It's not because things are difficult that we dare not venture. It's because we dare not venture that they are difficult.' Seneca

> 'It is always wise to look ahead, but difficult to look further than you can see.' Winston Churchill

> 'The man who goes furthest is generally the one who is willing to do and dare.' Dale Carnegie

Take risks; you have no choice

'Risk' is a scary word, especially to older, wealthier investors. They've laboured long and hard to accumulate wealth and they don't want to lose that money on some hair-brained scheme that is doused in risk. But risk as we'll discover in this book comes in many different shapes and guises and not all of them are obvious!

You must of course be careful of the risks that destroy wealth, but equally alert to the risks of **not doing** anything to grow accumulated wealth. Risks are all around us and a few of them are worth grasping, especially if you have the right amount of time to capitalize on them. Working out the sensible risks (that allow you to accumulate wealth) from the insane risks (that destroy wealth) is the focus of this book.

Not doing anything, sitting in a cave like primordial man, ignoring the great clamour of modern life is frankly not an option for 99.9999 per cent of the readers of this book. You have to accept that you live in this noisy, messy, risky world and make the best of it. If your idea of wealth creation and preservation is to grab as much of it as quickly as possible by any means and then retreat to a cave full of gold bars, armed weapons and a hatred of government as a confiscating, tax-eating monster… turn away now. This book isn't for you! The end is not nigh, you have to pay taxes (though you can absolutely minimize them) and as we'll discover later in this book, gold is probably not the only investment idea worth considering.

The caveman is dead, and the modern man needs to be networking, listening to new ideas, and working out what's a bad idea and what's a great idea that could make you wealthier. You need to be building lots of different pots of capital to protect against stuff that might happen in the future. You need to be honest enough to realize that you don't know what might happen next, and have a plan for it.

In a world of relative truths, and messy realities, we're largely ruled by probabilities and possibilities – this book is about making sure that your odds of winning are increased by sensible, small incremental steps that help improve your odds. Nothing is guaranteed outside of the cave but the fleet of foot and diligent are more likely to be rewarded with greater wealth.

INVEST IN YOURSELF

Ever wondered how the mega corporations got to where they are today? I'd suggest that we can reduce this wealth of research literature based on corporate analysis to just three simple ideas. The first part is luck, largely consisting of being in the right place at the right time with the right idea. The second part is about sheer hard work and discipline, by the entire workforce, carefully co-ordinated using a plan devised by the management. Last, but by no means least, the company's management probably stopped being emotional and started 'objectifying' what 'it' as a business or thing did. In simple language, they got real about the balance sheet, the profit and loss statement, the cash flow and the business's SWOT (its strengths, weaknesses, opportunities and threats) analysis. They might have even thought long and hard about what brand the company stood for, what it appeared to represent to its customers and acquaintances – and how that could change.

I'd like you to think the same way about yourself: objectify yourself, step outside of your own world view and think of yourself as a business. In later chapters we'll build a balance sheet based on your assets. We'll also look at what your brand stands for, and how you might improve your own value to the outside world. We'll examine ideas about building plans to cut debts and create wealth.

But before we can do any of this we need to start with a simple realization, which is that your career is your primary source of future wealth and that means you need to invest in you! In order to grow your housing capital, for instance, you need a better job or improved cashflow. But to get there you need to understand how to grow your own personal capital (your worth in a job or in your own business). That means understanding what makes you tick, and how over your entire working life (which could be more than 50 years if you retire after 70, as most young readers will do) you can constantly evolve, and build up savings.

Ask yourself one simple question every ten years – is there one thing I can invest in now that will make me more valuable ten years hence? If the answer is obvious, and makes sense after you've researched it thoroughly, make a plan to achieve that goal, along the way working out what investment in time and money is required.

TAKE MEASURED RISK – YOU HAVE NO CHOICE IF YOU WANT TO BE WEALTHIER

It is indisputably true that wealth is incredibly easily destroyed by poor judgement, and once lost can take many decades to accumulate again. Yet we shouldn't react by acting like our caveman and abandoning all risk.

You will never become wealthy unless you take measured risks.

This book is entirely about that challenge of understanding risk, measuring it, conceptualizing it and then embracing it. Embracing risk means using carefully thought through strategies that mix facts, instinct and good ideas into practical investment plans that, for instance, focus on companies whose shares are cheap, or businesses that will disrupt and transform entire industries.

PLAN FOR VARYING TIME HORIZONS

Investing in shares if you need cash in five years' time, for instance, is a stupid idea. For those investors with a 30-year time horizon, by contrast, it's potentially a great idea. This process of identifying the right risks involves you working out different time horizons for different forms of capital. We'll explore these time horizons in greater detail very shortly in another chapter.

- As part of the process of looking at yourself like a business, I'd like you to draw up plans and time horizons for the different forms of capital you'll require.
- For personal capital, built around how you can earn more money, you need a 50-year plan.
- It's probably the same time horizon for a young person contemplating their pension using what's called risk capital (shares and bonds).
- Housing capital – your home – might represent a 30-year time horizon.
- Building a sensible pot of emergency capital might need a ten-year plan.
- Last but by no means least, your debt reduction plan (debt is in essence negative capital) might involve a five-year plan.

Different time horizons will work for different pots of capital: in this book we focus on these five: personal capital (you), risk capital (your pension), housing capital (your home), emergency capital (liquid cash) and negative capital (the 'anti-matter' of wealth – debt).

Putting it all together

You PLC or Me Inc. is a complex beast. It'll take many years for us to accumulate sufficient capital and I want to make sure that you don't lose it by taking risks that simply aren't worth taking. More to the point, we want to make sure that any capital accumulated is used to make you even richer over a long time horizon. In other words, it is wisely invested by taking considered risks. This process is best done by thinking like a business and treating yourself like a business, asking yourself what risks am I taking and where do I need extra investment? Yet it absolutely requires you to take a plunge and take risks, where necessary and where measured and researched. The reaction of most people to this noisy, messy world is to retreat to a few simple basics based on personal prejudices and is guaranteed not to make you wealthy. Wealthy people take risks sensibly and listen to the few good, new ideas out there. They pounce on opportunity but always keep an eye on the risks they are taking.

2 Debt – the anti-matter of wealth?

> 'Some debts are fun when you are acquiring them, but none are fun when you set about retiring them.' Ogden Nash

> 'Debts are like children: the smaller they are the more noise they make.' Spanish proverb

> 'The ideas of debtor and creditor as to what constitutes a good time never coincide.' P. G. Wodehouse in *Love Among the Chickens*

> 'Nobody had a credit card when I was a kid. No one had credit card debt. But these big companies and banks wanted to know how to get more money out of people – get them charging things.' Michael Moore

> 'I use debit cards for everyday purchases, as I don't believe in credit cards. But this has caused problems, especially with American touring, because I refuse to have a credit card – and in America you can't pay for anything on a debit card.' Paloma Faith

There's a lot of it about

I think it's fair to say that among investment thinkers and personal finance experts, debt gets a bad name. I have lost track of the thousands of articles in the aftermath of the global financial crisis of 2008 that remind us that global debt levels in the developed world are at all-time highs (true). That we're all in hock to credit card companies and dangerously overstretched with our mortgages (true though getting better). Most of all, we are told that debt is bad. Evil! We should have no part of it and be unburdened by the chains of leverage.

Tell that to the vast corporations that dominate the US and British economies, nearly all of whom have been **increasing** their debt levels in recent years, gorging on cheap loans.

As is always the way with our messy, noisy world, the truth is not binary, neither black nor white. On many levels debt is actually good, if only because our economies collectively need lenders to use their savings to create real world growth. Too much debt that can never be paid back is self-evidently a bad thing, as is debt that is costing a lot more in terms of interest rates.

In simple terms, escalating levels of debt, lent at high interest rates to someone who cannot afford to pay the money back is clearly the financial equivalent of anti-matter for wealth creation – it sucks away cash via the constant motion of negative compounding i.e. every year those interest bills accumulate on top of each other, generating a potential default situation. As we'll discover in our chapter on compounding, if you pay the average credit card interest rate of 18 per cent per year, you'll double the total debt burden in just four years. And debt accumulated by impulse purchases (the subject of another chapter) only makes a bad situation much worse.

High levels of personal debt also expose you to interest rate risk, which means that you are vulnerable in those periods of time when interest rates rise and the economic cycle sags.

But debt is also a necessity, especially for the younger reader. Unless you have rich parents, you maybe have no other choice than to run up debts to fund study. Equally, debt is an essential part of building up housing capital. Last but by no means least, it is sometimes appropriate in the world of business and even investment to take on some form of debt in order to create wealth.

Linking all of these grim realities relating to debt is the fact that the world is becoming a more expensive place. Debt may be the anti-matter of wealth but it is also sometimes necessary to have debts alongside assets in order to hold together our world i.e. someone's debt is usually another person's asset! The trick is to know how and when to use debt in a sensible way.

In this 'relativist' view of financial reality you need to understand the true cost of debt, and then relate it to your cash flow and your own balance sheet of assets and liabilities. Crucially you also need to avoid the undoubted evil of expensive debt, compounding in a negative way over time.

BUILD A BUSINESS PLAN FOR EACH LINE OF DEBT

Sometimes debt is a necessity. Don't be moral about the issue of leverage. Debt is not, in of itself, evil. It is a financial transaction that sometimes makes sense, examined in a rational fashion. Every time you are about to increase your debt levels, stop, think and build a plan for the debt. This should automatically throw up a barrier to using debt for impulse purchases.

Rationally, debt can be examined using three simple measures: its cost, your planned repayment and the values (or even wealth) the debt will help create. Draw up a plan (on a spreadsheet) to analyse each line of debt you take out including a credit card (which is probably the least acceptable form of debt going, outside loan sharks and payday lenders). With a mortgage you might for instance build a plan to save over XX years, at Y interest rates involving Z repayments. Crucially, I want you to look at what costs you save from say renting or what wealth you create (from investing) and then vary the basic building blocks i.e. stress-test this business model by increasing the interest rate to see if you can afford the payments.

This business plan approach forces you to treat debt in its proper role, as a way of deploying capital to generate a future gain.

BECOME COMPULSIVE ABOUT MINIMIZING THE COST OF BORROWED CAPITAL

As I mentioned earlier in this chapter, many large corporations borrow extensively and compulsively – with no obvious downside to their business model. But that relaxed approach to debt management is accompanied by a fierce focus on the cost of capital. The corporate treasurer will relentlessly look at the rates being charged by lenders and then seek cheaper alternatives. You should do the same, with a particular eye on the interest rate cycle and the ability to fix rates at certain points in time, especially as interest rates are falling. When credit is easy, and interest rates low, cheap fixed rate mortgages and personal loans abound. One last point. **Never ever** borrow at a rate of more than 10 per cent per annum unless you have absolutely no choice.

PRACTISE THE SNOWBALL METHOD

We're not all perfect. Many of us can't resist those impulse purchases and we start to use our credit cards to fund those little payments we haven't planned for. It's not evil to borrow in this way but it's dumb in terms of wealth creation. Think what you could have done with that interest you paid on the credit card.

The first step to dealing with this problem of expensive credit is to get the annual cost from your card statement and then think about all the alternative ways you could have spent that credit interest.

Suitably chastised, you should list all your personal (non mortgage) debts and cards, in ascending order from smallest (in terms of balance) to largest. In this 'snowball method' I want you to focus more on the amount owed, not the interest rate, and rank the biggest amounts at the top of the list.

Next up, I want to you to make sure that you make the minimum payment on every debt and then work out how much extra from your budget can be applied towards the smallest debt. Keep paying out until the smallest debt is paid off. Once that small debt has been paid off, add the old minimum payment (plus any extra amount available) from the first debt to the minimum payment on the second smallest debt, and apply the new sum to repaying the second smallest debt. Carry on in this fashion until all the debts have been paid in full.

The logic behind this snowball method? By paying the smaller debts first, you have to put up with fewer bills as more individual debts are paid off, hopefully giving you an emotional and psychological boost as debt is repaid.

Putting it all together

Lurking at the back of this discussion is a central idea in this book, which is to look on yourself in the way a business would examine its own prospects.

Build a personal balance sheet, listing debts (liabilities) and assets (wealth). In particular with the debts I want you to understand the true cost of capital (the interest rate), whereas with your assets I want you to understand what are the realistic rates of return (how much the house might increase in value, for instance).

But this balance sheet is in itself not enough. You also need to link it to your own 'cash flow' statement, your regular budget of incomings and outgoings, and examine whether you can truly afford to make any payments.

The last stage is the most difficult and most important, which is to vary the assumptions about how much money you are paying in interest. Think about how much money you'd save if you reduced the cost, or worry about how you'd fund the mortgage if interest rates were to double.

3 Castles, not pension plans

> 'Our houses are such unwieldy property that we are often imprisoned rather than housed by them.' Henry David Thoreau

> 'So much value has been lost in the housing market that people are now buying. If there's any activity in the housing market, it's because values have plummeted to such depths that the 47 per cent can now afford to live in a government-purchased house, or something like that.' Rush Limbaugh

> 'If the economy grows, housing gets better, quicker.' Jamie Dimon

> 'Bubbles have quite a few things in common, but housing bubbles have a spectacular thing in common, and that is every one of them is considered unique and different.' Jeremy Grantham

> 'You can print money, manufacture diamonds, and people are a dime a dozen, but they'll always need land. It's the one thing they're not making any more of.' Lex Luthor

Your home is not your pension, repeat after me

Here's a worrying observation. Talk to most ordinary folk and they'll probably admit that a) they don't save enough but that; b) they do invest nearly all their available, spare cash, their savings into their home, which will probably serve as their pension.

Worrying as this is, neither of these statements is that shocking or even startling. The self-evident truth is that your home is… well, your home and not your pension! A pension by contrast is designed by its very nature to pay an income in retirement. Unless you are planning to rent out the spare room in your home during said retirement, your home will not produce an income.

What really concerns me is that this obsession with property is not shared by people who are wealthy. If we look at the statistics about these lucky and (largely) hard-working people, what we discover is that their home as a percentage of their total wealth is relatively tiny, whereas with poorer people their home is usually their **only** source of **wealth**. OK, just in case you don't believe me, here are some hard stats about wealth to get you thinking. A recent study (Wolff 2012: referred to at the website http://www2.ucsc.edu/whorulesamerica/power/wealth.html) looked at what the wealthy owned in terms of assets. The bottom line was as follows: wealthier people obviously have greater total marketable assets but what they own is hugely different from the rest of us.

The bottom 90 per cent of the US population, for instance, rarely has more than 20 per cent of its total assets in business equity, stocks and mutual funds and financial securities. Instead, the bottom 90 per cent has the great majority of its wealth tied up in a principal residence, cash deposits and life insurance assets. Once we switch to the top 1 per cent of the US population we discover that 64 per cent have significant concentrations of wealth in financial securities (versus just 6 per cent for the bottom 90 per cent) and business equity (61 per cent versus just 8 per cent among the bottom 90 per cent). In simple language, the majority of the population has taken a big bet on their houses, cash and life insurance while the wealthy elite has invested in risk capital (stocks and shares) and in their businesses.

These numbers hint at a crucial truth. If we exclude those wealthy who have inherited their money (a significant number!), most successful people have followed a predictable route, which is to earn more (by investing in their career or business), then accumulate spare capital and then make **more** money by investing in risky stuff that isn't necessarily your house.

Wealthy people understand the importance of diversification. We'll keep repeating the concept of diversification throughout this book, but it really is hugely important. You need to diversify your wealth and that means multiple forms of capital and potentially even different sources of income. Betting it all on the house you live in is just a risky proposition you shouldn't take – and it's also not one that most wealthy people opt for.

The good news is that you don't have to make the same mistakes, especially if you follow my simple-to-understand 35/35/35 rule – three strategies built around the magic number of 35 that should help you get what you need (a home) but also help diversify your capital.

AIM TO BUY A HOME BY 35

Back in the 1950s and 1960s the average age of the first-time buyer of a house in the US and UK hovered around the mid-20s. Obviously houses were much less expensive in those days, even if interest rates were in many cases somewhat higher. Crucially, many younger people in this era had a reasonable expectation of job security over their working life, making them very happy to take long-term risks.

If we fast-forward to our post-modern era of extortionately expensive houses, limited job security and high costs of living, we discover that the average age for a first-time buyer in the UK is already fast approaching 40 years old, with the US not that far behind.

This sorry state of affairs presents us with a number of challenges, especially if you want to accumulate capital and become wealthy. The first is that many of us are forced to rent. There's nothing wrong with renting whatsoever, especially if you are just moving into a new area or worried about job security. But renting opens you up to an obvious risk which is that rents are only ever likely to go **up**, especially if inflation increases and/or interest rates suddenly start increasing, pushing up the landlord's cost of ownership. Renting also self-evidently involves you giving someone else your precious cash in order to repay their mortgage. There may be many reasons why you are happy with this state of affairs but I would argue that eventually buying your own home is a first small step to accumulating wealth. Housing capital for all its faults represents a great bet against future inflation (an issue we'll discuss in a little more detail in just a few paragraphs). It can also serve as a way of accumulating capital in a tax-free fashion (assuming it is your only property) that could be leveraged to fund a business or a loan to develop your career.

If at all possible, the golden rule should be to scrape together enough money to buy a home (maybe not the perfect dream home) by 35, allowing you another 25 years to repay it – implying your mortgage will be repaid by age 60.

DON'T SPEND MORE THAN 35 PER CENT OF YOUR NET INCOME ON HOME PURCHASE COSTS

My enthusiasm for home ownership shouldn't be seen as an obsession, especially if you really cannot afford to scrape together the necessary deposit or have insufficient income to repay the mortgage. The rough and ready rule is that your total home mortgage servicing costs (interest and capital repayment) should not be more than 35 per cent of your total net after tax income. Anything above that level and you'll not have enough to money to save for any other forms of capital. More problematically, you'll probably not have enough money to sensibly spend on energy, transport and food costs. My guess is that if you do exceed 35 per cent of your net income, you'll start borrowing money on your credit cards in a systematic fashion, pushing you ever deeper into debt.

HAVE PROPERTY AS 35 PER CENT OF YOUR TOTAL WEALTH BY RETIREMENT

We'll keep returning to this last strategy throughout this book, but common sense – and long-term studies of wealth generation – suggests that ultimately you should aim to retire with no more than 35 per cent of your total wealth in property. Between 35 and 45 per cent of your remaining wealth should be in a long-term pension plans of some description (which we call risk capital) while another 20 to 30 per cent should be in a combination of other properties, some cash and other forms of wealth including alternative assets such as art, stamps or maybe even the odd few gold coins!

Putting it all together

I'll conclude this chapter by observing that my scepticism about property as a source of wealth shouldn't be read as an attack on property as an asset class i.e. a way of accumulating wealth using financial assets. My 35/35/35 rules are really designed to make sure you have many different asset classes within your various pots of capital. Housing does in fact offer one wonderful positive for investors focused on the long term – it protects you against the future threat of inflation and is thus what we call a real asset. We'll encounter the scourge of inflation in many parts of this book, but housing and residential property has in the post-war period (after 1945) increased by between 0.5 per cent and 3 per cent per annum on average above long-term inflation rates. That doesn't mean that you won't have bad years where prices go down, nor does it mean that you can't even have an entire decade where prices go down. But over any sensible 30-to-40-year period, housing in most developed world markets has been a good bet against inflation, although not the best! What doesn't make any sense whatsoever, though, is to use your home as the only source of your wealth!

4 Invest in you

> 'The starting point of all achievement is DESIRE. Keep this constantly in mind. Weak desire brings weak results, just as a small fire makes a small amount of heat.' Napoleon Hill

> 'Lack of money is no obstacle. Lack of an idea is an obstacle.' Ken Hakuta

> 'The harder I practise the luckier I get.' Gary Player

> 'Hard work, honesty, if you keep at it, will get you almost anything.' Charlie Munger

> 'The content of your character is your choice. Day by day, what you choose, what you think, and what you do is who you become. Your integrity is your destiny… it is the light that guides your way.' Heraclitus

Invest in your personal capital

In this chapter I want to plant one simple thought in your mind. If you want to get wealthy, or even just wealthier, you'll probably have to work harder and smarter. Sure, some of us will get lucky, many of us might even inherit a bit of money and a lucky few might stumble upon some genius investment idea… but for the vast majority of readers, wealth will be built through investing in your career and building up your personal capital.

Remember in the last chapter we looked at a study (Wolff 2012: referred to at the website http://www2.ucsc.edu/whorulesamerica/power/wealth.html) that examined what wealthy people owned in assets.

We learned that if we exclude those wealthy people who have inherited their money (a significant number!), most successful people have followed a predictable route, which is to earn more (by investing in their career or business), then accumulate spare capital and then make **more** money by investing in risky stuff that isn't necessarily your house.

I'd suggest that three simple principles emerge from this analysis:

1. Invest in your career to allow you to earn more money (allowing an accumulation of surplus capital)
2. Then take risks with that accumulated capital; and then finally
3. Become even richer as that risk capital propels you further ahead.

The key point I want to dwell on for this chapter is the investment in your career – in later chapters we'll explore the necessity of risk-taking in much greater detail, especially with regards to financial assets, also known as risk capital (stocks and shares, for instance). Sitting at a computer betting on the stock market is not going to make you rich. Ignore all those self-help day trader books and give up the dream. It doesn't work.

What will undoubtedly help to make you a wealthier person is your career or your business or whatever combination of the two works for you.

To underline this observation, I have some more hard numbers, this time nabbed from the US income distribution data.

In 2010 the 50 per cent median household income (the dead centre typical income for a household with one or more adults in it) was a shade under US$50,000.

If, by dint of hard work, investment in your personal capital and a hint of good luck you were able to move up to the 80 per cent percentile income (that is, you were in the top 80 per cent of the total distribution of household incomes), you'd be earning at least US$100,000 a year. So moving up the household income distribution charts from 50 per cent to 80 per cent (a not impossible feat) would benefit you by an additional US$50,000 in income per annum.

Now let's further assume that you were able to save 25 per cent of that extra income every year for the next 20 years (and didn't reinvest it in any way, just keeping it in the bank), which would mean that you'd be able to accumulate US$250,000 in capital over just two decades. In reality, my guess is that if you invested that surplus capital in the risky investments I mentioned earlier – as the wealthy do – the real number would be closer to US$500,000! That would be enough to put you in the top 10 per cent in terms of wealth distribution in the US.

The bottom line? Increasing your income, and improving your career prospects, can yield much greater long-term benefits.

THE HIGHEST RATES OF RETURN COME FROM INVESTING IN PERSONAL CAPITAL

Your investment in time and emotional energy is also crucial if you want to work on a project such as building a better career. You need to measure all these inputs and then work out what the likely rewards are. My simple spin through the enormous impact of moving up the income distribution league should focus your mind on the fact that an investment in you – your personal capital as expressed by your career or your business – will produce a huge 'return on investment'. If you are really very lucky, risky stuff like equities might give you, say, a 10 per cent return over the long term, as might an investment in a house. I'd argue that an investment of money and time in your career could produce annual returns well in excess of 20 or even 30 per cent p.a.

DECIDE EARLY ON WHETHER YOU'RE FOCUSING ON YOUR CAREER OR BUILDING A BUSINESS

It's hard to get a firm grip using national data points on what is the actual chief motor of wealth creation in either the US or the UK, but what we do know is that creating significant amounts of wealth probably requires the individual to have a substantial stake in a business of some sort. Business owners tend to be wealthier, though that doesn't mean that all business owners are wealthy! What is probably the case is that owning or being involved in your own business does give you greater flexibility to increase your income levels by simple dint of you being the boss! Work harder, make your business more successful and you can afford to pay yourself more!

For many readers this might suggest that at some point going into business might make sense. And indeed for many that will be the case, but entrepreneurialism isn't for everyone. Not all of us have the required business skills, no matter how many courses you take.

You need to decide fairly early on (in your 20s and 30s) if you have what it takes to set up in business. My advice is to work out whether you want to go into business well before your 40th birthday. There's nothing stopping you suddenly acquiring the passion for business at 50 years old, it's just that the energy required – and possible risks taken – are likely to cause you immense stress. What's even worse is that you may discover rather late in the day that you are not suited to becoming a business person and that you've wasted a huge amount of valuable time later in life learning a bitter lesson.

PORTFOLIO CAREERS AND LIFESTYLES CAN WORK

Many readers might fall into a third, relatively new category – the portfolio career builders, or lifefolio types as I call them. These individuals mix and match elements of a professional career **and** business with self-employment. Crucially, this group might move from a career and then into business and then back again as they get older. My hunch is that more and more of us will be pushed down this road as we're forced to work through from 50 years old to 70. Maybe we'll have a career in our 20s and 30s, start a business in our 40s, sell that business in our 50s, and then start a last career that will take us through to 70. This lifefolio approach requires you to constantly invest in your personal capital as you might have to start an entirely different lifestyle in the future.

Putting it all together

The old world of secure careers with one or maybe two employers who take you through from youth to retirement is long gone, for most of us at least. We now live in a world where you will almost certainly have to chop and change, and constantly invest in your personal capital, in your skills and your knowledge. Every one of us will be uniquely different and the choices we face will be shaped by our own luck, insecurities and hopes, but be under no illusions – investing in increasing your income will only come by investing in your personal capital. A nice home, spending money on bling or a new car or day trading the stock market – none of this will make you wealthy. Building a business or improving your career is for most of us the only option to becoming wealthier. The great news is that it's relatively easy to do. And once you've started accumulating some surplus capital (wealth) you can then start building up your risk capital, which will in turn make you even wealthier.

5 Reading the tea leaves

> 'Credit expansion can bring about a temporary boom. But such a fictitious prosperity must end in a general depression of trade, a slump.' Ludwig von Mises

> 'Business is like riding a bicycle. Either you keep moving or you fall down.' Frank Lloyd Wright

> 'In the business world, the rearview mirror is always clearer than the windshield.' Warren Buffett

> 'Our main business is not to see what lies dimly at a distance but to do what lies clearly at hand.' Thomas Carlyle

> 'Chaos in the world brings uneasiness, but it also allows the opportunity for creativity and growth.' Tom Barrett, US politician

In search of black swans, cycles and signals

Meet one of my more recent acquaintances – Jim. When I met Jim a while back, via a good friend, my first impression was overwhelmingly positive. He'd just crashed past 50 but seemed to have all the energy of a 20-year-old. More to the point, he was super-connected in the world of corporate communications in a giant media corporation. One day he was in New York, the next in London, communing at the very highest level with the gilded occupants of the C Suite world (an acronym that describes the senior executives of the board and near board level of corporations). Critically, he was well paid and modestly wealthy.

And then it all changed, virtually overnight. That secure job was no longer secure; he was made redundant, and he then proceeded to spend the next 12 months out of work, looking for new jobs that weren't too junior for such a senior guy. Jim was the victim of a black swan with very down-to-earth impacts. Black swans are a term developed by hedge fund manager Nassim Nicholas Taleb to describe unpredictable events that produce major political and economic impacts.

These black swans (such as the global financial crisis of 2008) have now entered into common parlance and are generally used to describe broad, nationwide shifts and tectonic movements of economic import. Yet these black swans also have knock-on effects that wreck individuals like Jim. He was actually made redundant from his supposedly super-safe, super-secure high-flying corporate job a few years after the global financial crisis. His employers had survived the economic crash in decent shape, but now wanted to carry on cutting costs relentlessly and in Jim's case decided that they didn't want to spend too much money on his particular form of communications expertise (internal communications).

So Jim was chopped and has never in truth fully recovered. He thought he'd survived the black swan of the 2008 Global Financial Crisis in fine form but that global event produced his own entirely unforeseen personal cataclysm, which was that his employers frankly didn't want to spend money on his professional discipline anymore.

I've laboured the story of Jim because I think too many successful and wealthy people think that their job is secure, that the bad stuff that happens to say freelance people or the self-employed can never happen to them.

Until it does, and then they are woefully unprepared.

My message is simple. We all need to think like freelancers and self-employed people do – as do entrepreneurs. They look at their job like any other business and constantly watch for signs of big structural changes, of sudden downturns, of panics that can destroy cash flows. They're 'economically aware' in a hypersensitive way because they realize that the path to building wealth can be delayed/destroyed by the changing business and economic cycle. That awareness means that they watch and they listen… and they prepare. They think through contingency plans, build reserves and, most importantly, watch for opportunities. They watch the broad business cycles.

The good news is that watching for these cycles – this ebb and flow of confidence and fear – isn't as difficult as it sounds. These cycles are predictable. Busts tend to follow booms, which are in turn buoyed up by excessive optimism and too much debt – all detailed in much more detail towards the end of this book. But busts also present opportunity and eventually that fear is quelled, and confidence returns. Watch, listen, learn and start to make adjustments to the various plans outlined in this book.

STRESS-TEST EVERYTHING

Start to stress-test your own career, finances and portfolios. Identify three big risks that could emerge if there were a sudden downturn or a massive change in the economy. Could your mortgage survive a sudden increase in interest rates for instance? If the economy dipped would your job be in the firing line – if not, which other parts of the business will go first? In your portfolio, analyse whether you're taking big bets on intrinsically risky stuff that could get walloped in a downturn? But don't stop there. Properly stress-test your life in the way an engineer would examine a bridge for dangerous weaknesses. What's the one key risk that could completely derail all your plans and what would you do about it… or what can you do about it if you are so minded?

WATCH FOR THE SIGNALS

The world of dismal economics has focused for many years on identifying key signals that warn of impending economic and financial trouble. Many of these 'macro' signals as they're called are a little technical and nerdy but they are useful in giving you a hint that trouble or change could be on its way. The great news is that there are lots and lots of them but I'd keep a beady eye on just four signals.

Be very wary about rising interest rates and a sudden spike in inflation. You can find this data easily on the web, and in this book we talk about them in much more detail in later chapters, but a sudden and unexpected spike in both of these rates is a bad sign. If they start moving upwards, think about taking risk off the table and start preparing for the worst. Another more technical indicator is to look at the yields on offer from investing in bonds issued by the US government via its Treasury – called T Bonds. Look at what 'interest rates' or 'income' these bonds pay for a one-year duration and then compare those for 5- and 10-year versions of the same bond i.e. bonds issued with a duration of 5 or 10 years. This yield curve as it's called (plotting income rates versus number of years on the bond) should slope upwards. But if the yield on short-term, say one year (or less), bonds is **below** 10-year rates, run for the hills – this is a great leading indicator for a recession!

LISTEN TO THE CROWD

One of my favourite strategies for utilizing key signals is to harness the wisdom of the crowd via online tools such as Google Trends. This wonderful service allows you to see what the world is searching for in real time. Amazingly, it is incredibly powerful and very telling and entirely free! Medical researchers have discovered, for instance, that searches for influenza on Google are sometimes a better leading indicator of flu outbreaks than more traditional screening methodologies.

I'd apply the same thinking to business and economic cycles. Look for what's charting and see if people are beginning to search for key words like inflation, rising interest rates or recession. Most of the time you'll probably have to wade past endless celebrity junk but when economic key words start cropping up more regularly, take note and watch the trend like a hawk. Maybe these searches are telling you something. They might be a warning or an opportunity.

Putting it all together

My invitation to 'economy watch' is not a cue to become obsessed by the daily noise of news and comment and then suddenly market time like crazy. In fact I'd argue quite the opposite, as the over-attentive news- and trend-watcher can become deafened by this noise and then end up believing everything they read!

This warning not to become too obsessed by news flow and trends is especially important for investors in financial assets like shares. Many ordinary investors become so obsessed by signal watching and web crawling (for news) that they constantly try to second-guess what happens next. This is called market timing and it's a mug's game. Hardly anyone ever does it properly and I can guarantee you won't. Your magic crystal ball is just as useless as mine!

The smart investor by contrast makes sure that they understand where the risks are in their portfolio generated by booms and busts, watch out for key signals and then pounce on opportunities. This same thinking can be applied to your personal capital and your career. Watch for the tell-tale signals that my friend Jim missed. Constantly understand how big, broad changes can affect your career and always have a plan… even if you think you're totally secure, which you won't be!

6 Spend wisely

> 'Anyone who lives within their means suffers from a lack of imagination.' Oscar Wilde

> 'If you buy things you don't need, you will soon sell things you need.' Warren Buffett

> 'Too many people spend money they earned… to buy things they don't want… to impress people that they don't like.' Will Rogers

> 'If you know how to spend less than you get, you have the philosopher's stone.' Benjamin Franklin

> 'One must choose, in life, between making money and spending it. There's no time to do both.' Édouard Bourdet

Necessity is not always the mother of spending

We all live in a consumerist society in which messages about spending are blasted at us night and day. You can of course escape this real world by hiding in a cave and ignoring everything around you but I'm guessing that for most of us that isn't a great option!

Another alternative is to get all moral and judgemental about spending money, rather like a couple of relatives of mine whose parents believed that modern society was evil – both my cousins as kids were drilled into thinking spending was bad and materialism even worse. Every time we met up with them, these boys looked fairly miserable to me, a fact that was confirmed many years later when both decided to over-indulge in drugs, alcohol, fast cars and fast women – coincidentally both ended up working in high finance and both nearly went bust from over-spending!

I'm fairly certain that in many personal finance textbooks there's a line that says something along the lines of abstinence (in the matter of spending) is a virtue but I can't help but think this is lousy – and obvious – advice. Over-consumption is an intrinsic, structural flaw within modern capitalist society and criticizing it is a bit like saying that democracy has flaws.

The important challenge is to understand that consumption, though necessary, is in of itself only a means to an end. To use language borrowed from psychologist Abraham Maslow's pyramid/hierarchy of needs, at its most basic of course consumption is about survival, in that we must consume food. Next up in the order of priorities and needs, we consume in order to participate in modern society, using cars for instance to get from A to B. We also, very importantly, consume for enjoyment, buying the odd bottle of red wine, say, to relax of an evening. And let us be honest here about wealth, which is that we accumulate in order to spend money on things we really like. Wealth is merely an aid to making you a happier person, not a means unto itself. Consumption, like debt, is not an evil, just a necessity that can end up dominating your life unless you're careful.

But let's also put down a few markers or should we say warnings about the subject of spending. The first is that you must self-evidently never spend more money than you earn.

The next golden rule of spending is not to spend so much that you trap yourself in a lifestyle that might one day become frankly unaffordable. Many Wall Street high-flyers lock themselves into a self-indulgent, self-reverential lifestyle powered by bling and societal status. This is all fine and dandy until they are knocked for six by changes in the business cycle or those black swans and they lose their job. Or – much worse – they become divorced. Using excessive consumption to power a lifestyle choice invariably ends in disaster and extreme wealth destruction.

Crucially, spending and consuming in order to cover up a gaping emotional or psychological hole in your life is also a recipe for disaster. We all need cheering up once in a while, and that might mean going to see a favourite film or having a nice meal but that should be the exception not the rule. Many psychologists have discovered that the most troubled people use consumption and spending as a way of dealing with immense personal trauma, landing them in debt and even more misery.

A research report by two academics from Minnesota found that 'respondents' feeling states' was a huge factor in deciding spending patterns and that 'both positive and negative affective states appear to be potential triggers for impulse buying. This supports claims that impulsive buyers are more prone to buy on impulse when experiencing mood states of either positive or negative hedonic tone.'

Quite.

Learn the lesson, which is that spending to enjoy is fine, but spending to avoid being miserable is a disaster.

THE IMPULSE PURCHASE TEST

Here are two small tests, designed to spot whether you have a spending problem based on impulse buying.

The first test is as follows – do you use a debit card/cash to make small purchases like crisps, snacks or lunch or a credit card? Recent research suggests that those who use a credit card tend to spend an additional US$10 on each purchase! We've all fallen for this particular trap. We think that in order to use the card, it makes more sense to spend a tiny bit more. By my own estimates, during one 12-month period in which I used a credit card to pay for 'ordinary' impulse items, I overspent by £2,000.

The second test is what I call the 'I want' test. You see something in a shop that you really, really want, based on a strong impulse. What do you tend to do next?

Will you:

- go and buy it?
- compare the price against other shops, or
- wait for one week to see if the impulse passes?

Now, there are no awards for guessing that I want you to say both the second and third options and not the first. Impulse buying is deadly and is to be discouraged.

BUY THE BEST

Sometimes, even surmounting the various barriers suggested in my first strategy, you may discover that you absolutely have to buy something that is expensive, something that you really, really want and need, and you may even have to buy it using a credit card.

These things happen in the real world and it's not worth beating yourself up about it either emotionally or intellectually. But always buy the best quality option you can sensibly afford. If we look at the behaviour patterns of many impoverished consumers, they hunt down discount shops promising to sell you a cornucopia of stuff for a few dollars or pounds. They're tempted to buy the cheaper version of something that is essential. Therein lies the danger. If you need to spend money on something that is really important to you, don't waste it on low-quality rubbish. Buy the option with the very best quality reputation, and the best 'social review' buzz. If it costs the extra 10 per cent for quality, then spend it.

BUY IN BULK AT SALE TIME

Another key idea is that if you really, really need to spend money on a key item, or even items on a regular basis, buy them in bulk during the sales. This talks again to my core concern, which is to delay or even stop impulse spending, and focus spending only on those items that you really need. Do everything in your power to delay these emotionally driven purchases and act rationally. Waiting until the right time of the year can frequently save well over a third off the price of a wide range of items.

With your priority spending, buy in bulk when things are on sale… be patient.

Putting it all together

Wealth without happiness is pointless and for many of us the pleasure of spending on what we need is an essential part of life. But that doesn't mean that you can't spend wisely and sensibly. The key is to take the emotion out of purchases and spending money and not use it as a prop to help manage an emotional problem. That means avoiding impulse purchases, planning and researching big expenditures (especially at the right time of the year).

If you are an impulse buyer, I want you to carry around cash as a basic necessity for all ordinary purchases. Here's how it could work. Set your budget for the week and withdraw the money from your bank account or debit account i.e. walk around with some hard cash in your pockets.

Use that cash to buy all normal impulse items and stick to that weekly/monthly cash spend come heaven and hell! If you do want a bigger impulse purchase, I want you to go away and think about the idea. Review the different prices charged by different businesses and then wait for seven days, hoping that the psychological impulse will wear off. If, after that time and the suggested research, you still absolutely **need** the item, buy it but make sure you avoid using a credit card.

Crucially, remember the golden rule, which is to always try to live within your means and avoid using those credit cards wherever possible.

7 Spend to accumulate

> 'Want what you have and you will always get what you want.'
> Buddha

> 'Never buy a thing you don't want merely because it is dear.'
> Oscar Wilde

> 'When I get a little money I buy books; and if any is left I buy food and clothes.' Desiderius Erasmus

> 'Never buy what you do not want, because it is cheap; it will be dear to you.' Thomas Jefferson

> 'Money is the representative of a certain quantity of corn or other commodity. It is so much warmth, so much bread.'
> Ralph Waldo Emerson

Think rationally!

Spending can sometimes make a huge amount of sense. In particular, spending that unlocks relationships and a network based around skills and opportunities is hugely valuable. We live in a world that gives value to interlocking networks and shared knowledge.

Our open, information technology based society has over time begun to openly reward those most open to sharing information and ideas – the better networked a professional, the higher their earning capacity. Or, in other words, the more valuable you are to other people, the more value you can potentially capture for your own wealth creation.

Sometimes that need to network and connect with others requires spending money. And sometimes spending money in a wise way makes absolute sense.

My simple demand is that you first understand what you spend your money on, and then prioritize that expenditure. Add up what you think you spend every year on each on your main spending lines, both non-discretionary and discretionary products and services (stuff you could live without). The next difficult step is to attach a value to the spending activity. I want you to use two methodologies: the first is based on opportunity cost and time you'd have to spend by **not** spending money on that opportunity; the second is decided by whether that spending makes you a happier, more contented and valuable person.

In simple terms, everywhere we go we are presented with myriad spending opportunities, aided and abetted by a financial system that is keen to load us up on debt. In a simple, black-and-white world you'd only ever spend what you can afford and then only have bought what you needed. Maybe unfortunately, we don't live in that world and the constant bombardment and noise of consumer choice can create inactivity, confusion and debt. So we need to adopt a utilitarian perspective and put a value on what we spend our money on. Simple happiness derived from buying a good or service is a perfectly acceptable answer, which means that if, for instance, chocolate or whisky makes you happy, so be it. But I also want you to think if a spending activity helps you create future 'value' i.e. wealth. Does it make you a more knowledgeable person, for instance, in which case some spending may be virtuous?

INVEST TIME AND MONEY IN PEOPLE

Our modern economic cornucopia values both knowledge **and** communication. I'm sure we've all run into lots of clever people jam-packed full of fascinating knowledge who are stony-broke poor. Their challenge? Communicating that immense knowledge to an outside world, which will then put value on that skill. Equally, I think we're all aware of many people who are far from being clever but who have positioned themselves brilliantly by dint of luck and networking to take advantage of opportunities that present themselves. Maybe they are great communicators, or maybe they're just very connected people?

In my experience, luck and being in the right place at the right time and then being able to communicate to a broad network of people who can help you build wealth is more important (in most cases) than pure knowledge. In that case I think it hugely important that you spend money in meeting people and opening yourself to opportunity. You might for instance invest in joining some kind of business or professional club. Alternatively, you might force yourself to go to the endless number of seemingly pointless business events that nevertheless allow you to network and understand future opportunities. See my later chapter on networking.

Personally, I think the biggest opportunity comes from constantly meeting and working with younger people, in whatever professional-, business-, social- or sports-based structure that makes sense. The vibrant optimism of young people and their sense of constant opportunity and willingness to change the world is, I would argue, infectious.

DITCH THE BLING

In Thomas J. Stanley and William D. Danko's excellent book *The Millionaire Next Door* they identify an all-too-common stereotype, the hyperconsumer. These are the apparently 'go-getting' types who would appear to prioritize spending over meeting people and networking. Yet these wealthy hyperconsumers also spend vast amounts of money on status-based activities and obvious signs of wealth and sophistication, aka bling. These are fashion-conscious types who want to communicate to the outside world that they are super-successful and that wealth deserves respect.

Unfortunately, spending these vast amounts of money on bling and obvious status symbols is a fool's errand. Usually, high expense hyperconsumer items involving a substantial amount of 'brand value' (you buy a product for its brand name, at an extra price tag) usually bring with them almost instant depreciation. For every high margin German car that supposedly depreciates slowly in value after purchase I can cite a much longer list of vanity cars that lose their buyers a vast amount within the space of just a few months. Bling-based items also send out the wrong signal, which is that you demand respect. If you need that kind of recognition, you'll end up poor at some stage, loaded down with debt. Respect should be based on either your success with work and family or your public service or contributions to public knowledge or creativity.

If you really feel the need to invest in obvious consumer statements then at the very least buy valuable and rare real assets such as old cars or exclusive art, both of which cost an absolute fortune and look good in front of your friends but also tend to retain their value over the very long term.

THE ONE THING NOT TO SPEND YOUR MONEY ON... DIVORCE

Recent longitudinal-based wealth studies (research looking into the accumulation of wealth over time) have revealed that:

- we're becoming a more unequal society, and
- that mobility between different socio-economic groups has either stalled or is in active decline.

Yet there is one notable exception to this trend for declining social mobility – divorced men and women (especially the latter). Study after study suggests that women who are divorced (especially mothers with children) can very easily drop down the social ladder at a truly alarming speed. It's also true that divorced men, especially those in middle age, are particularly vulnerable to downward social mobility.

In simple terms there is one form of spending that is **entirely** ruinous and destructive towards wealth – divorce and separation. The vast amount of expense on not only lawyers but also on establishing two new households (where there was once just one) is economically destructive. It also goes without saying that this expenditure also tends to result in dire consequences for the children in relationships.

Divorce is thus the real enemy of wealth creation; a vast black hole of spending that should be avoided wherever possible. This may sound a horribly utilitarian approach to what should be a relationship issue, but we need to call a spade a spade in our liberated society. Frequently, separation cannot be avoided – nor should it be – and of course happiness within a relationship is absolutely vital, but divorce and separation is almost certainly going to make you very much poorer and quite possibly very unhappy for a long period of time.

Putting it all together

I make no apologies for my utilitarian approach to activities that might be regarded as issues of the heart or desire. Spending is not bad if it enriches us and makes us happier, but happiness always comes at a price. All that I ask is that you put a price on that happiness and then value it against other outcomes. Utilitarianism is a valuable tool in the fight against modern consumerism, which is itself largely designed to make **you** poorer.

You are constantly encouraged to spend money and fall deeper into debt and the only way of avoiding this usurious impulse is to measure and attach value to goods and services. Lots of things will make you happy in life but I'd be willing to bet that most of these pleasurable outcomes won't actually involve the spending of money directly (although going to see a fabulous sci-fi film for me is one such costly indulgence!).

Spending money should be about a few small, happiness-inducing luxuries, a wider bevvy of essential purchases you simply cannot avoid and a handful of expenditures that help to make you a more knowledgeable, better-connected individual.

8 Good advice is worth paying for... assuming you can find it!

> 'If a man will begin with certainties, he shall end in doubts; but if he will be content to begin with doubts, he shall end in certainties.' Francis Bacon, English philosopher/scientist

> 'The only good thing to do with good advice is pass it on; it is never of any use to oneself.' Oscar Wilde

> 'Give a man a fish, and you'll feed him for a day. Teach a man to fish, and he'll buy a funny hat. Talk to a hungry man about fish, and you're a consultant.' Scott Walker, US politician

> 'A word to the wise ain't necessary – it's the stupid ones that need the advice.' Bill Cosby

> 'Wise men don't need advice. Fools won't take it.' Benjamin Franklin

You are a target

Time to share a dirty secret. As you build up your pot of investment-based risk capital you become a target for a vast wealth management industry. Endless market research reports suggest that the size of your capital pot dictates whether you're a target for private banks, wealth management firms, independent financial advisers or just high street banks.

The dirty truth is that, by and large, this industry is set up to extract excessive fees from you, based on the mystique of financial expertise, helped along by the soothing message that 'we can take all the pain and hassle out of money' by just leaving your risk (investment) capital with us!

In reality, many of the supposed experts within this huge and growing industry are far from being experts. Even more worryingly, many of the frontline staff working with customers are in effect glorified salespeople, who simply pass along the received wisdom of a small handful of (genuine) experts at the provider who rarely ever talk directly to customers.

The brutal truth is that very few of these institutions really provide the expertise you require at a sensible price. They're mostly following fairly standard financial-based models that you as an investor can access using a bit of research and a modicum of hard work. In my humble opinion, although most of us will struggle with doing it all by ourselves, we can do a huge amount on our own account.

But that doesn't mean that we don't need expert advice – simply that the basis by which you pay for it needs to be transparent and honest. You will need advice at varying points in life and if you do for instance have to pay a proper professional a few thousand pounds to set up an investment plan that will help you over the next 20 years, so be it! It's good money well spent.

So good advice is worth tracking down, but you need to find a proper, independent expert who understands all the technicalities and your own financial position and you need to establish a sensible price for that advice.

Recent research suggests that the average investor in the UK would only put a value of between £300 and £500 on the ideas and hard work provided by a financial adviser. This number is frankly delusional – we'd pay far more for a landscape designer to shape our garden or a plumber to fit a new heating system. What price a financial plan for your entire life? Good financial experts need paying properly, and it is precisely because they will be expensive, that we thus need to use them sparingly and intelligently.

IF YOU DO WANT GOOD ADVICE, PAY AN AGREED FEE PER HOUR

There are many circumstances where good financial advice in particular is worth paying for. Despite my earlier scathing comments about financial 'experts' I'd accept that you probably do need some help in building a portfolio structure and process, especially when it comes to making full use of your tax allowances and setting up the right pension.

Specialist advice around tax planning or maybe working out how to transfer your business wealth to a future generation self-evidently need specialist help, particularly as the law can be hugely complicated.

So contracting in a financial adviser can make sense, but it needs to be done on your terms. Too much financial expertise is actually a series of spreadsheets tied up by simple common sense, all presented in a bill that has a nice company heading and scary looking regulatory jargon.

My simple rule is to always get an independent adviser if you need expert help and never ever use an adviser based at a big bank. Once you have selected your adviser then sit down and ask them what skills they have and how they'll make a charge. Make sure you like working with them and respect their intelligence. Then agree a charging structure, which in my humble opinion should be based on an agreed fee per hour, with the number of projected hours stated in advance (this may of course vary, depending on what you discover as you and your adviser work together). Many advisers try to encourage you to move to a per cent charge based on your assets under management but I think that this system isn't a smart choice for you, largely because I think this charging structure encourages a certain laziness among advisers as they try to scale up the number of customers and minimize their personal service.

In particular, I think paying a fixed fee up front to set up, say, a pension plan that you can then monitor over time makes a huge amount of sense. Maybe agree a yearly review, again at a fixed fee, and then accept that if you need extra services you'll pay for them on an ad hoc basis.

ALWAYS BENCHMARK YOUR ADVISER

If you do use an independent financial adviser on a regular basis, I strongly recommend benchmarking their performance. This could be based on the returns from their portfolio advice over a few years, or simply based on equivalent customer service from other peers.

Talk to your friends and colleagues about what they get from their adviser, in terms of both service and investment returns. Keep monitoring what your adviser is up to and always make sure you understand why they've taken a certain course of action – get them to explain their strategy to you, and then go away and research what they've said. This constant benchmarking is not an invitation to 'doubt' the wisdom of their knowledge, just an acceptance that even great professionals can sometimes make bad decisions. And as these advisers are managing your accumulated wealth, you can't afford for them to make lots of mistakes with your money.

AVOID ANY INSTITUTION THAT SHOUTS TOO LOUDLY

If you do succeed in building up a sizeable pot of risk capital, avoid going anywhere near a big bank, especially a private bank. In my experience, with a few honourable exceptions, they are a racket from start to finish. These banks are focused on treating wealthy customers like the 'flow' emerging from their supremely overpaid investment trading desks i.e. numbers that need to be maximized in order to hit profit targets.

This business model built on scale is of course completely understandable, as they are simply trying to make a profit, but it usually involves compromising standards. I'm also very cautious about trusting my money to huge transnational institutions who use their resulting balance sheets to leverage even higher returns. No amount of amazing special offers to select customers or exclusive invites to customer-only sporting events is going to dispel the idea that you are working with institutions who will ultimately take advantage of you.

Putting it all together

Talk to most financial experts and they tend to slide into a disparaging tone when it comes to DIY (Do it Yourself) investing. The subtext is usually that most people can't be trusted to make the right financial moves. With many investors there is some truth to this assertion but I'd hope that if you are reading this book and using its ideas as the basis for personal self-improvement, you are not going to be completely financially illiterate.

If that is the case I'd argue that you can do a huge amount of financial planning and investment practice on your own account, helped along by some specialist advice where necessary, provided by an independent expert and billed appropriately. I'd also strongly argue that the online 'crowd' does possess some wisdom, and can be used to help shape some of your ideas – use the Internet and especially sites such as Seeking Alpha that offer up great ideas for free. Crucially, your own networks of friends and business acquaintances probably contain within them some of the most powerful insights.

9 Compound it!

> 'Youth is wasted on the young.' George Bernard Shaw

> 'Money makes money. And the money that makes, makes more money.' Benjamin Franklin

> 'Compound interest is the eighth wonder of the world. He who understands it, earns it… he who doesn't… pays it.' Albert Einstein

> 'If people do not believe that mathematics is simple, it is only because they do not realize how complicated life is.' John von Neumann

> 'The ability to simplify means to eliminate the unnecessary so that the necessary may speak.' Hans Hofmann

The majesty of numbers

Numbers are funny old things. I think it's fair to say that we're all brought up to respect the fact that life is messy, that things don't quite go to plan, and that there is no great scheme of things, no great order to the chaos of life — except what we make of it!

Yet numbers do respect a certain order, a curious hierarchy comprising rules that can actually work in your favour when it comes to building wealth.

Take for instance the 80/20 rule otherwise known as the law of the vital few or the Pareto principle. This roughly states that for most events or outcomes (or investments for that matter) roughly 80 per cent of the results come from 20 per cent of the causes i.e. 80 per cent of the land in Italy in 1906 (as observed by Mr Pareto, an Italian economist) was owned by 20 per cent of the population. To use a more modern example, most business people tend to cite the idea that 80 per cent of their profits come from 20 per cent of their customers.

What's lurking behind this principle is an even more powerful concept, of exponential success. This is the idea that as something becomes ever more successful (those few enterprising landowners in Italy, say, in the centuries leading up to 1906), its power exponentially grows and compounds. In simple terms, success breeds success, and eventually 'compounds' on top of itself, producing a very 'skewed' result or set of numbers… which is all very predictable of course!

This order in numbers is of course no accident – as we've just observed success breeds success, and that success keeps compounding exponentially over time. Numbers and maths respects outcomes, and in the world of wealth there is one certainty that is powered by this force – compounding income and returns.

We all sort of understand intuitively this power of compounding, this regularity in numbers growing ever bigger over time. Take the small savings account we forgot about a very long time ago. We assumed we'd left almost no money in that account, say 10 years ago, at most a notional £1 or two. Yet when we look again many moons later we discover that our money has multiplied over time to a few pounds (say 5 or even 10 over a few decades), especially as interest is paid into the account, which then earns more interest in coming years. Perhaps a more common occurrence is the power of negative compounding accompanying those annoying unpaid credit card bills. We swear blind that the last time we looked a few years ago we only had £100 left in debt on the card, yet we suddenly discover to our horror that this wretched bill has mushroomed exponentially.

Compounding contains within it three interrelated elements. The first is a period of time, which is usually extended over many years. The second element is that of inactivity, simply leaving alone for something – money in this case – to grow over time. The last element is that something begets something, money produces more money by the power of interest. Add these three elements together, mix with the predictable power of exponentially increasing numbers and then shake – to either produce wealth or to mire you in debt.

Compound interest is, in this humble author's opinion, quite the most powerful force for the creation of wealth conceivable for the busy person and the even better news for readers is that working out exactly how compounding weaves its special magic via numbers is as simple as typing into a search engine 'compound interest calculator' and then using an online calculator to work out how much money you can make over the long term.

If, for some perverse reason, that doesn't work you could always visit the excellent compound interest calculator online at http://www.moneychimp.com/calculator/compound_interest_calculator.htm

THE RULE OF 72

Websites that calculate for you the impact of compounding are all fine and good but it probably makes sense to also understand the logic at work – maybe without the aid of a mechanical device! The simplest way to grasp compound interest is to use the rule of 72, a wonderfully simplified way to work out how long an investment will take to double in value, given a fixed rate of interest.

The rule goes something like this: divide 72 by the annual rate of return you're expecting (interest or capital growth). The resulting number will give an estimate (not exact it must be said) of how many years it will take for the initial investment to double in value!

For example, the rule of 72 says that that £1 invested at 20 per cent would take 3.6 years ((72/20) = 3.6) to turn into £2. Actually if you use an online calculator you'll discover the truth which is that it takes 3.80 years to double that £1 (to be wonderfully exact) but the point is that the Rule of 72 is a simple way of working out how to build your wealth without the aid of computers or calculators.

AVOID NEGATIVE COMPOUNDING

We've already mentioned that compounding works in reverse, to devastating effect especially when it comes to high-interest credit cards. For instance, a debt that incurs 18 per cent interest doubles in just four years!

That should make any reader stop dead in their tracks i.e. in just four years a singular £1 debt has doubled to £2. Four years is likely to be between 3 and 5 per cent of our likely total life span (not very much at all) and yet it's enough time to double a debt! Just think what could happen if you left that original £1 debt to compound over ten years, a simple decade? The answer would be that our £1 debt has turned into £5.23 at the end of those ten short years!

Now before any reader laughs at my exponential jiggery-pokery, consider the fact that many credit cards charge around 18 per cent per annum in interest, applied monthly. In fact I'm fairly certain that most readers of this book probably have had direct and bitter experience of these interest rates in the past few years.

The good news is that you can absolutely do something about this negative compounding state of affairs. For instance, simply reducing the interest rate to 9 per cent means that our notional £1 takes a full 8 years to double, rather just 4 years. Reduce it further to 4.5 per cent and we're suddenly into 16 years!

USE THE POWER OF LITTLE NUMBERS AND COMPOUNDING

Get compound interest working for you in a positive way, using small numbers first. The strategy here is to find something you spend money on on a regular basis that you could do without! I'll give my own example, namely a bottle of red wine every week.

Man can live without red wine (or so I've been told), and given my predilection for expensive bottles that cost £10 each, I reckon I could save £10 a week simply by drinking less (and helping my liver!). If I were to save that £10 a week in the piggy bank, and then invest it every year in a share investment scheme that gave an average long-term positive return of

6.5 per cent per annum, I'd be looking at building a savings pot of £20,276 in just 20 short years… all from abstaining from one bottle of wine a week!

Putting it all together

Compounding matters for all of us because it is one of the few things that financial institutions 'gift' to us. They allow us to keep building up our interest in savings accounts or reinvesting our dividends via our share reinvestment plans at zero cost! They positively encourage us to be sloth like and lazy but, in this example, that can work to our favour. As long as we are disciplined and keep away from using that money we can leave it alone to grow steadily.

The trick then to really make compounding work for us is to make sure that either the negative interest rate you pay is as **low as possible** or the positive rate of return is as **high as possible** i.e. we want an above-average rate of interest or capital growth.

But to find that bountiful supplier of bumper returns means that we need to find a financial institution we can trust our money with over the very long term, and the right financial product or investment to put our money into!

Use compounding interest as a positive, be patient and get the right savings or investment opportunity.

10 The big number

> 'The rich man plans for tomorrow, the poor man for today.'
> Chinese proverb

> 'Let our advance worrying become advanced thinking and planning.' Winston Churchill

> 'I don't have a dime left. I am dependent on my friends for food and a small old-age pension.' Bela Lugosi

> 'Son, that number you've got in your mind is only ever going to get bigger as you get older, especially for what you're going to need!' My great-uncle Fred on my plans for wealth, aged 13

> 'Time is more value than money. You can get more money, but you cannot get more time.' Jim Rohn

What's your number... the number that will take you comfortably into retirement?

A couple of years back a large American-owned investment bank asked its London-based researchers to talk to private investors about their 'future'. The particular 'future' this bank had in mind was our collective, national retirement and the questions centred on how much these lucky folks in the survey reckoned that they needed to enjoy a half-decent retirement.

The US$64 million question was what was the number (a big one but not US$64m hopefully) that would make us comfortable in retirement.

£100k? £200k? £1m? How much is enough to last you through your retirement?

Lo and behold the bank discovered that for an average 40-year-old male, they'd probably need a pot of about £435,000 come 65 to prosper and enjoy retirement. With that number out in the open, the challenge for the investors in the survey was to guess the number, bingo style!

Of course, only a tiny percentage of smart alecs even got remotely near in the survey.

The banks' logic for publicly revealing this collective ignorance?

We'll all need a great deal of money on our retirement and most of us consistently underestimate just **how** much we'll need.

But I actually happen to think that this survey was a tad optimistic, as one of its basic assumptions for working out the magic number for a retirement pot was based on average life expectancy for a 65-year-old male of 17 years.

In fact, based on recent trends powered by modern and radical improvements in healthcare, we can sensibly estimate that that longevity number has been increasing by 0.5 years for each year of the last decade. By my estimates, by the middle of the 21st century the average life expectancy for a healthy middle-class male who manages to live past his 65th birthday, will be an additional 30 years!

If we plug this number back into a long-term planning model, the size of the nest egg or retirement pot grows **massively**, shooting past £750,000 if we use the same assumptions as our friends from the large global bank.

But do not despair at the sight of this seemingly impossible-to-hit big number.

Three simple strategies can help you work, save and invest your way to the right number (eventually), but all involve a spot of simple maths and some lateral thinking.

WORK OUT THE NUMBER

Extra longevity is a demographic fact and you can plan for it. In fact you can track down simple spreadsheets that do the work for you. There are also some great web-based tools that will perform the same task including ones at the wonderful www.moneychimp.com.

Alternatively, you can do the maths yourself, and see what happens when you start fiddling around with the assumptions.

Start by opening up a spreadsheet on your computer, learn a few basics to do with equations and then work out your likely annual income needed in retirement to cover the basics. Itemize those basics and add them up. This gives your annual income required from that big lump sum!

The next step involves a choice. Either you could work out your likely years in retirement and then multiply by the annual income required. So if you have an annual retirement income of say £17k and you think you'll need to plan for 30 years, you'd need 17 × 30 = £510,000.

Alternatively, see what income you could get every year from a very safe investment like 30-year government securities.

Search online for Government Bond Rates and you'll probably see the *Financial Times's* Market Bonds Data section. This will show the range of yields you'd make if you invested in varying long-term gilts, maturing over a range of just 1 year through to 50 years. Look for the 30-year bonds, and then use that annual yield as your benchmark.

The last time I looked, this was at 3.5 per cent but will have undoubtedly changed by the time you read this book. Next, we divide our annual income required in retirement by the percentage – 3.5 – and then multiply by 100. The final figure is £485,000.

Whichever method you end up using, you'll probably figure out that a sensible minimum target is something like £500,000.

Hallelujah! – you have a first big number to start planning towards.

FACTOR IN INFLATION

Whatever number you come up with also has to account for a beastie you'll become very familiar with in this book, inflation. For all sorts of reasons, prices go up over time. Sometimes we can blame governments, other times the rising cost of materials such as energy. Occasionally, we should also blame ourselves for our craving of nice, big houses that keep rising in cost every year, stoking the inflationary flames.

Whoever is to blame, we all feel the effects.

Whatever number you come up with now in terms of retirement target lump sum will need to account for inflation rates over the next 10/20/30/40/50 years – pick your time frame dependent on how long you have until you plan to retire.

Luckily, we can easily model for this number, depending on your country of origin, with the UK at between 2.5 per cent and 5 per cent p.a. and the US between 2 and 4 per cent p.a.

But what to do with this number once you have it on paper and incorporated into your big number-busting model? Cue an elegantly simple solution – just increase your annual payments into your pensions stash by that inflation rate.

If you expect 2.5 per cent inflation and you start off paying £100 a month into the plot, plan to increase that annual payment next year by 2.5 per cent (to £102.50). And then keep doing that every year by your presumed inflation rate for the foreseeable future, compounding as you go along.

WORK OUT A SENSIBLE RATE OF RETURN

Whatever number you'll have come up with for your pensions target, it will look truly immense after allowing for inflation. But do not despair! You now need to work out how much to save on a regular basis and also allow for a likely return rate from that regular saving over the next 30 or more years.

A wildly optimistic investor might start with an average annual compound return over the next few decades of 7 per cent per annum (before costs) whereas a more cautious type might notch that estimate down to 5.5 per cent per annum.

But these return rates are just gross numbers and don't include costs. Unfortunately, we all collectively pay far too many costs for financial services and bitter experience teaches us that in reality these nasty charges and fees will eat up at least 2 per cent of your savings per annum. For the cautious investor our net return has now sunk to 3.5 per cent annum – or 5 per cent for our more adventurous investor.

Putting it all together

Don't despair about the big number!

Apologies for the blizzard of numbers but the point of this exercise is deadly serious. Whatever number you think you might need, it probably underestimates likely longevity, increased costs and woeful returns from bad investment decision-making.

How can we hope to approach that number by smart saving? Factoring in net returns of 3.5 per cent per annum, our 40-year-old investor would need to be shovelling £25,000 per annum into their long-term savings plan, assuming they hadn't already saved anything before this date.

Bottom line? You'll need to save a heck of a lot more money than you first thought.

But these numbers change dramatically if you:

- relentlessly cut down on costs, and
- focus on increasing returns (maybe pushing up to 8 per cent p.a. before costs, giving a net return of 7 per cent p.a. after costs).

For instance, if we fiddle around with our numbers, target higher net returns of 7 per cent p.a., we can make our net annual contributions collapse from £25,000 to just over £12,500 p.a. A much more sensible number.

Maybe you could also assume that you'll retire later, work a bit in your retirement, drive down your living costs – many factors can help reduce the financial task of saving.

And to help with the savings bit, here's a neat idea – automatically set up your pension payments and direct debits so that at least 25 per cent of any **increase** (and only the increased bit) in your salary from now on goes straight into your pensions savings account.

But whatever you do, face the reality and start planning now.

11 Working out the right time horizon

> 'They always say time changes things, but you actually have to change them yourself.' Andy Warhol

> 'You may delay, but time will not.' Benjamin Franklin

> 'Time is what we want most, but what we use worst.' William Penn

> 'Time is a created thing. To say "I don't have time" is like saying, "I don't want to".' Laozi

> 'Someone's sitting in the shade today because someone planted a tree a long time ago.' Warren Buffett

How long is enough?

Humans are myopic creatures. Through virtually every element of society and our economy we can see that short termism is both prevalent and a curse. We're quick to jump on short-term risks that are almost staring us in the face but slow to register long-term challenges that require a complex answer. It's not really worth debating this issue in any more depth but there is one vital dimension of this challenge that has a huge impact on all of us.

Psychologists are increasingly beginning to recognize a phenomenon called tunnelling, especially in both stressful situations and those environments where humans are experiencing scarcity. Hopefully, no one reading this book will be afflicted by these pernicious processes but we need to be honest – tunnelling is pervasive. Stress and the lack of resource (money) causes us all to focus on the only thing that matters – less 'stress' and more money.

There are a great many ways of coping with this tunnelling but I think the single biggest way out is to plan, and to carefully map out – in a clear-headed fashion – a way of dealing with various challenges over time. Of course, most of us would concur about the need to plan, but I really do think that building multiple plans and then attempting to stick with them is not only essential but will make you both a happier and wealthier person.

Which leads us nicely back to the subject of this chapter – time horizons. To build wealth will be stressful and may at varying times cause you immense financial stress. If you don't take risk you won't accumulate wealth. But risk brings with it stress and sometimes short-term poverty. That causes the very best of us to lose track of the longer-term perspective and focus on the tunnelling phenomenon I have just described.

Plans by contrast, on paper, and preferably involving hard numbers are a commitment. But you'll need multiple plans, over different time horizons, for different 'end games' i.e. the accumulation of wealth. I have no doubt that you'll frequently break your plans and then revise them.

The very existence of a plan allows you to step out of tunnelling and escape into the longer term.

MULTIPLE PLANS FOR MULTIPLE CAPITALS

I'd suggest that the first really important step is to identify different forms of capital you want to accumulate over your life span. We've already mentioned this concept of multiple capitals in an earlier chapter, but they should consist of:

- personal capital (investment in your career or business)
- savings or emergency capital (short-term reserves designed to keep you afloat in the worst of circumstances, usually consisting of between 6 and 12 months of living expenses)
- housing capital (your home)

- risk capital (your long-term savings plans, including pensions)
- and possibly a very small amount of 'end of the world' fall-back capital tucked away under the bed in case of real societal level challenges.

Each of these pots of capital will require varying time horizons – we'll come to that next – but **each** and **every** one will require a spreadsheet on a computer with some hard numbers attached over many years. That means sitting down with a pen and paper, making some assumptions about reasonable contributions, sensible rates of return or interest, and the transferring of these to a spreadsheet for each pot of capital. I fully expect you to miss every one of those plans and I'm also willing to bet that over time you'll revise them up or down, depending on your circumstances. Fine, plans are there to be broken, but without a reference table you are simply being myopic and short-termist.

THE SHORT-TERM PLAN

A number of these pots of capital will need to be addressed over what I call the short term, which is anything up to 20 years. Building up your savings capital is the first and immediate challenge, especially for younger readers. Building a reserve fund that can keep you going for, say, six months will be no easy task but it's necessary. I'd also expect a plan to reduce and ultimately eliminate all your debts over a five-to-ten-year time frame (if not even quicker). You should also be making a start on building a deposit to fund the purchase of your home, which ideally should happen before you are 40 (at very most) and before 35 ideally. We'll come to the home repayment plan in the next strategy, but you need to realize that with property as expensive as it is, the chances of you paying off your mortgage within 20 years are low. Last, but by no means least, you should also start building a plan to accumulate some money to pay for you improving your person capital. In my humble opinion every single one of us needs to be looking at renewing and improving our career skills set every ten years – look on it as a refresh on your personal capital. That might mean taking an MBA, looking at building some vocational skills or start thinking about another career later in life. If you don't invest in your career, you'll miss the essential foundation for creating accumulated wealth.

THE LONG-TERM PLAN

When I use the term 'long term' I mean plans that will come to fruition over a 20-to-40-year time-span – that means lots of lines on your spreadsheet.

In this exercise, three pots of capital stand out.

First, you need to focus on paying that mortgage off over a period of between 20 and 30 years, unless you are already in your 40s, in which case we're probably talking about building a plan for less than 20 years. Once you've paid off the mortgage on the first home, I'd be strongly tempted to consider buying a second home or property – but that's for another chapter on property as a real asset.

Next up you need to continue funding investment in personal capital. In particular, I'm increasingly concerned that as we live longer – and longevity post-65 increases steadily – we face a long 'third age' that is neither retirement nor our original career. Most readers in their 20s will have to work all through their 60s. The challenge is that for most of us our main career will probably be difficult to perform at that age (though there will of course be huge variations). We might need to consider a new career, downsizing or simply making ends meet. I think it best to plan for that near-certainty and not condemn yourself to a miserable 'third age'. Look at the broad societal trends and see what kind of jobs you can sensibly do in your 60s and build a plan to develop the skills required over the coming years.

My last pot of capital is for risk capital, which I define as your pension plan for retirement post-70 (or 65 if you are lucky). This will necessarily involve you taking risks with your capital in order to accumulate wealth. As we'll discover in this book, you can take measured risk by understanding how investment works but you need to be honest about time horizons. Investing in things like shares and bonds is a 20-to-40-year process, and requires focus, dedication and a tolerance of risk. It is risk capital and you need to be willing to ride out the wild ups and downs of stock markets.

> **Putting it all together**
>
> Getting the right time horizon for each of our pots of capital requires you to think long term, avoid myopia and tunnelling and setting up reference benchmarks (in spreadsheets) that you can refer to later when you feel stressed or lacking in resources. And of course these plans are to be broken and you shouldn't live your life by them, but you need some way of measuring your progress and advancement. I absolutely believe that a spreadsheet with its scary looking series of hard numbers is the only way to be objective — writing downs words as in a business plan mission statement is just too vague and impossible to quantify. Numbers tell a story and if your numbers don't add up or compare to what's in the plan, you know you need to do something fast. Start with a plan, put numbers to it, work out the right time horizon and then get back to what you are good at, which is creating accumulated savings.

12 Regular or lumpy – how do you like your investments?

> 'Little and often can do you good.' Traditional saying

> 'The regularity of a habit is generally in proportion to its absurdity.' Marcel Proust

> 'Time divided, is never long, and regularity abridges all things.' Madame de Staël

> 'The safest way to double your money is to fold it over once and put it in your pocket.' Kin Hubbard

> 'Money, says the proverb, makes money. When you have got a little, it is often easy to get more.' Charles Dickens

Be regular, be predictable and be lazy

Financial experts agree on very few things but on the subject of pound-cost averaging the consensus view is probably that it is one of the seven great wonders of the economic world, a veritable godsend that should help us all invest with discipline over the long term.

What exactly is this amazing financial discipline? In simple terms, pound-cost averaging describes the practice of buying shares of a stock or fund in equal pound amounts, and at regular intervals, rather than scrunching all our savings up into one lump sum and then investing all in one go.

The precise definition for pound-cost averaging is a little more technical of course, as you'd expect from the economists who devised the term – it is a 'method of accumulating capital by investing a fixed sum in a particular security at regular intervals, in order to achieve an average purchase price below the arithmetic average of the market prices on the purchase dates' as one economics textbook puts it.

Here's how it works in practice. Let's say you have £1,200 in cash to invest. Rather than invest all £1,200 at once, you could invest £100 per month for a year. Now let's say the fund you're investing in sells for £10 a share in the first month but drops to £5 a share in the second. Using the pound-cost averaging method, you would end up buying 10 shares in the first month, before the market drop, but 20 shares in the second, after the drop. Had you invested the entire £1,200 in the first month you would have owned 120 shares, which, in month two, would have declined in value to £600. In this way, pound-cost averaging helps reduce an investor's exposure to a potential market downturn, a danger inherent if you invest in things like stocks and bonds using a lump sum – all in one go – approach.

Does pound-cost averaging actually work?

This pound-cost averaging approach sounds great doesn't it – what's not to like about a regular, thorough way of saving over the long term? In reality the closer one looks at this approach, the more obvious the potential flaws, not least the opportunity-cost to be paid for holding money in cash while you wait to invest in the market at one of your regular payment times. If the market goes up while you're pound-cost averaging into it, you've lost out on any gains you would have had by investing the entire amount right away.

Researchers from US fund management group Vanguard looked at these issues in much more detail for a recent study and discovered that actually investing via a lump sum resulted in higher returns than pound-cost averaging about two-thirds of the time. The authors examined historical monthly returns for £1 million invested (!) as a lump sum as well as for pound-cost averaging. The researchers looked at periods as short as 6 months and as long as 36 months, and then tested these numbers over rolling 10-year periods from 1926–2011.

Their analysis revealed that the lump-sum method delivered higher returns compared with the 12-month pound-cost averaging method about 66 per cent of the time regardless of whether an all-equities, all-bond or 60 per cent equity/40 per cent bond allocation was used. The researchers also found that the longer the time frame used, the greater the chance of the lump-sum method outperforming. For example, pound-cost averaging over 36 months lost out to the lump-sum method 90 per cent of the time for US markets.

POUND-COST AVERAGING WORKS BEST IN FALLING MARKETS

Let's be honest, in falling markets it is extremely difficult to predict the bottom of the market in order to invest at the cheapest point. As a result, many investors miss the bottom and end up kicking off an investment plan once the market has started rising.

Cue pound-cost averaging. During market declines, the pound-cost averaging method often performs better because it helps mitigate the effects of falling share prices, whereas the lump-sum method puts all the capital at risk in the market at once. This analysis was confirmed by our friendly Vanguard researchers who looked at a huge range of rolling 12-month periods for investing in US shares and found that lump-sum investors would have seen their investment decline in value 22.4 per cent of the time versus 17.6 per cent for pound-cost averaging. The bottom line? If you expect a market downturn in the near future, pound-cost averaging is the better choice. By spreading out contributions at regular intervals, you are essentially limiting your exposure by keeping some of your money in cash.

USE POUND-COST AVERAGING IF YOU'RE BUSY

The Vanguard research is all well and good but in reality most readers probably need the discipline provided by this methodical, regular method of saving. Economists in particular like pound-cost averaging because it goes with the behavioural flow i.e. it accepts that we are sometimes lazy and don't necessarily always do everything we promise! Rather than trying to figure out the best time to invest using a lump sum, this pound-cost averaging approach is much more systematic and helps investors conquer bad habits such as buying shares only when the market is on its way up.

I'd suggest that for most of us the modest disadvantage of pound-cost averaging (based on that Vanguard research) is probably a small price to pay for peace of mind that comes from leaving alone a regular savings plan. To my mind, pound-cost averaging offers a number of advantages for the lazy investor who wants to focus their time and bother on other things like cutting down debts and building up their personal capital. These advantages include:

- reducing your risk and potential losses in volatile markets
- less pressure to try to 'call the bottom' or 'time' the market
- less frustration from potentially investing a lump sum at the 'wrong' time and watching its value decline
- encouraging investment discipline and a long-term view.

In sum, pound-cost averaging, especially through an automatic contribution mechanism like a pension, offers a level of investing discipline that lump-sum investing does not. The lump-sum approach, by its nature, involves market timing, and that's a dangerous game to play, especially during times of volatility. Pound-cost averaging provides a smoother, more consistent entry into the market.

KEEP POUND-COST AVERAGING COSTS TO A MINIMUM

Pound-cost averaging does run one big risk however, which is that you're clearly signing yourself up to regular payments which means, in turn, that your adviser or pension fund manager will be trading more often, running up additional costs that you have to pay for one way or another. For example, if you do use pound-cost averaging you'll end up paying multiple brokerage fees to buy shares of a stock in several lots rather than just once, which may further erode your returns as compared with the lump-sum method. If this is a real concern hunt down stockbrokers who will only charge you a small fee of no more than US$1.50 a trade per month to run these regular savings plans or, if possible, use a fund provider who won't make any extra charges for regular payments.

Putting it all together

I think that pound-cost averaging does make a huge amount of sense for most readers, largely because I don't want most of you turning into market speculators, endlessly trying to second-guess in which direction the investment herd will charge next. Market timing is potentially deadly and encourages an exaggerated sense of your own investing skills, traits that are pretty much guaranteed to make you poorer over the long term. As we'll discover in later chapters, if you do have the right skills and experience to focus on tactical, speculative investing, it might make some sense for a small minority but for most of us we should be focused on building up our personal capital and that means not becoming too fixated on the ebb and flow of the stock market! By the way, it goes without saying that if you do want to be speculative and tactical, pound-cost averaging absolutely sucks!

13 Diversification is the best risk control

> 'Diversification and globalization are the keys to the future.'
> Fujio Mitarai

> 'Career diversification ain't a bad thing.' Vin Diesel

> 'Mutual funds have historically offered safety and diversification. And they spare you the responsibility of picking individual stocks.' Ron Chernow

> 'Strength lies in differences, not in similarities.' Stephen R. Covey

> 'Diversification is protection against ignorance. It makes little sense if you know what you are doing.' Warren Buffett

It's that risk word again

Whenever we discuss risk in this book we're also referring to the complex interrelationship that exists between opportunity and knowledge. We've already established that you won't get very far without taking risks, yet it's also true that excessive risk can destroy many years of hard work simply by blowing your hard-earned savings on a daft investment!

One of the ways that this tension between risk and opportunity is managed is through knowledge. Where you know a great deal about something in particular you should look to exploit that opportunity, focusing on a particular idea and then relentlessly working out every angle that can benefit you i.e. focus and concentrate on taking one particular risk in order to reap a (hopefully) substantial reward.

But by its nature this focus on a particular opportunity cannot exist alongside a very broad knowledge of absolutely everything else. In simple terms, you can't be an expert at everything. For the opportunities where your knowledge is shallow you need to manage your risk, and that very simply means diversifying across lots of different ideas.

Of course this concept of diversification makes intuitive sense. We instinctively know that holding a little bit of lots of things reduces our chances of being wiped out by one big thing. Yet that common sense application of diversification has also been transformed into a formal language within the weird and wonderful world of investment economics. Study after study has shown that those investors who diversify across different investments – called asset classes – stand a better chance of building a less risky portfolio. The resulting framework is called asset allocation theory and it reminds us that different assets within our portfolio move in entirely different ways as the wider global economy ebbs and flows. And I would argue that what's true for investments can also apply to our careers and our personal capital.

For every form of endeavour connected with creating capital I want you to understand this tension between diversification and focus, between risk and opportunity. Where you have real in-depth expertise I think the smart thing to do is to focus down, increase your risk levels and really understand the opportunity – and 'go for it'!

For everything else, including most of your pension pot, minimize risk and diversify your capital.

Three simple strategies should help you diversify.

MAKE SURE YOU HAVE A DIVERSIFIED PORTFOLIO OF INVESTMENT ASSETS

Unless you are willing to invest a large amount of time, hard work and due diligence to the process of investing in risky stuff like equities (see the next strategy if you are), my advice is to make sure you are properly diversified in portfolio terms.

If we're 100 per cent invested in US equities, for instance, we're likely to see our risk capital go up and down in line with the US economy i.e. it'll be relatively volatile. But bonds, especially those issued by the US government, tend to go in the **opposite** direction to those equities, so that as the economy slows down, bond prices start to creep up. It doesn't take a genius to understand that a portfolio that mixes bonds with equities might be more diversified than one which has just one asset class.

This same analysis has been applied to huge pension funds and academic researchers have discovered that intelligent diversification between assets is in fact the **primary** driver of long-term returns – one study by a team of academics led by Gary Brinson suggested that more than 90 per cent of long-term returns from investing is derived from building a diversified portfolio.

What might sensible diversification look like? Diversification works at a number of levels. You could for instance be diversified:

- between different countries
- between different kinds of assets classes including equities and bonds
- using alternative assets, such as gold or property, both of which are what's called real assets that tend to offer some inflation protection
- between income-producing assets (bonds and high-yielding stocks) and capital gains orientated investments
- between assets that move in different ways based on the rate of economic growth or the direction of interest rate – this kind of diversification is called diversification between economic 'sensitivities'.

DEVELOP A CORE OF FOCUSED INVESTMENT IDEAS

More experienced investors might be tempted to follow the advice of Warren Buffett, who was quoted at the beginning of this chapter. He argues that: 'Diversification is protection against ignorance. It makes little sense if you know what you are doing.' In Buffett's world view, you only make the really big profits by focusing on a small number of very concentrated bets, every one of which you have carefully analysed. This due diligence is your insurance against risk, not diversification.

One way this could work for you is to figure out if a particular 'style' of investing resonates with your own deeply held beliefs. In another chapter we discuss the idea of value investing, which attempts to buy high-quality assets cheaply – this is an approach that Buffett has in the past taken.

Another approach is to focus on the blue-chip businesses of tomorrow by investing in them now – the subject of yet another chapter! A last, more speculative style is to find great businesses that are growing gangbusters and hope that they'll be the tenbaggers of your portfolio, i.e. smaller companies that grow tenfold in size to become bigger companies, making you a huge profit. This last approach is called growth investing and is usually applied to smaller company stocks.

Whatever individual 'style' makes sense for you should be applied to a satellite portfolio of more concentrated bets where you've clearly done your homework. In simple terms, you'd then go overweight with the sectors that have the best chance of outperforming in your view. With the remaining core of your portfolio – where your specialist knowledge is more limited – I'd suggest indexing the 'hard to know' stuff using a low-cost exchange-traded fund.

DIVERSIFY YOUR PERSONAL AND HOUSING CAPITAL

Last, but by no means least, what's true for your investment or risk capital should also be true for the rest of your investments including in your career and in housing.

Maybe if you've spent many years training for a very specialized career in say medicine or law, a focus on one particular skill might make sense. But for many of us boasting more – how can I put it politely – 'general' skills, we might find demand for our services moves with the ebb and flow of wider economies. If that is the case, maybe the smart thing to do might be to take a more diversified approach to our work. Maybe we should look to build what I called a portfolio or should I say lifefolio approach, looking to move between different occupations and skill-sets over different time frames – or even during the same time frame if we want to keep ourselves incredibly busy!

> **Putting it all together**
>
> I think diversification is a fabulous protection against two great dangers – the first and most important danger is that we're all much more vulnerable than we think to the ebb and flow of the business cycle. In other chapters we discuss how badly we can be hit by the changing dynamics of three hugely important 'economic' rates: the growth rate, the interest rate and the inflation rate. As each of these changes, different sets of investors and employees feel the pain. Diversification helps soothe some of that 'economic' risk.
>
> Yet I also think that diversification and its acceptance that we can't possibly know everything, is also a great protection against our own behavioural vices, especially hubris. We examine these vices in much more detail in another chapter but my own worry is that we're all quick to jump to conclusions and then commit vast amounts of money and time to a project/job/business/investment that could end up becoming a total disaster. Sometimes we have no other choice than to make those 'blink-of-an-eye' decisions but its inherently dangerous and this book is about slowing down everything you do so that you consider its potential impact on your wealth. Diversification is a natural extension of this discipline and is a subtle way of saying 'I don't know, so I'm going to protect myself against that unknown'.

14 Be well behaved!

> 'It's not that I'm so smart, it's just that I stay with problems longer.' Albert Einstein

> 'Las Vegas is busy every day, so we know that not everyone is rational.' Charles Ellis, US engineer

> 'Nothing in life is quite as important as you think it is while you're thinking about it.' Daniel Kahneman

> 'Overconfidence is a very serious problem. If you don't think it affects you, that's probably because you're overconfident.' Carl Richards

> 'The irony of obsessive loss aversion is that our worst fears become realized in our attempts to manage them.' Daniel Crosby

The seven deadly sins of behavioural economics

No self-respecting book about wealth could possibly avoid the prickly subject of behavioural biases. Over the past few decades dismal economists have fundamentally changed their view of the humble human being. In the bad old days we were all supposed to be eminently rational beings, constantly looking to maximize our individual 'utility'.

Except that we weren't.

What psychologists and their cousins in behavioural economics discovered is that we are in fact a walking disaster as a species, constantly about to slide into an irrational world, dominated by a very long list of syndromes and biases. The last time I looked, behavioural economists had managed to list at least 50 different ways in which we are anything but rational. I'm not about to list all those tics and manias, just seven, deadly behavioural vices that need to be identified and then acted upon.

Let's kick off with the most familiar challenge, the sunken cost fallacy. We'd all like to think that we make rational decisions based on the future value of objects, investments and experiences. The reality is that your decisions are actually shaped by the emotional investments you accumulate, and the more you invest in something the harder it becomes to abandon it.

Our second deadly sin is a familiar chap called over-confidence bias. I don't know a single investor or business person who hasn't suffered from this at some point, me included. This all-too-common syndrome involves someone (you) having greater confidence in their judgements than their actual accuracy.

Next up is my favourite high finance syndrome, called 'group think' as well as the cascade model, which is at epidemic levels on Wall Street and in the City of London.

The term group think was originally devised by psychologist Irving Janis to describe a situation where individuals strive for consensus within a group, abandoning their own deeply held (and sometimes rational) beliefs in order to build that consensus.

This group think syndrome can then start to fan out across space, time and markets by what's called the cascade momentum effect in which everyone else believes this 'select' group of experts. The end game is what's called the bandwagon effect, where we all jump on board the good ship group think… and then proceed to hurtle off into the financial abyss!

Another favourite of Wall Street and frankly most business leaders involves seeing patterns in random distributions, an affliction otherwise known as apophenia.

Researcher Klaus Conrad described this as the 'unmotivated seeing of connections' accompanied by a 'specific experience of an abnormal meaningfulness'. Gamblers are the worst offenders in this pattern-seeking behaviour, and investors (especially traders) are not far behind.

Turning to risk, I think we should all be careful about disaster myopia!

Imagine everyone has jumped onboard our earlier bandwagon effect (propagated by the cascade effect and started by group think). We're suddenly all relentlessly optimistic and we start to disregard small bits of relevant information that suggest that risk is starting to increase. Lurking beneath this very familiar situation (anyone care to guess what happened at the Wall Street bank Lehman Brothers back in 2008?) is that investors have a high propensity to underestimate the probability of adverse outcomes from the distant past, especially if that event occurred a long time ago!

I'm also especially concerned by something called base rate fallacy – also prevalent among nearly every investor and business person I've encountered. This describes the situation where we collectively start to ignore core, important base data (risk levels rising, interest rates starting to increase), choosing instead to focus on specific information (information only pertaining to a certain case).

Last but by no means least, we need to watch out for what's called the availability heuristic. This classic whopper is where we all make mental shortcuts based on judgements of recent, easy-to-hand examples. In sum, if something can be easily recalled, then it must be important. The net effect is that we end up giving a larger weighting to more recent news, ignoring everything from base rate information through to past historical disasters.

Ok, so now we've got these seven deadly vices out in the open, what can we do about them?

BUY RIGHT AND HOLD TIGHT

Many of the biases and tics detailed above have a physical manifestation in activity i.e. trading, buying and selling. The interplay between risk and return is constantly being played out in our caveman-like minds and the net result is that we 'do' too much.

- We think
- We get greedy
- We react
- We trade
- And then we lose money.

By and large, the most important defence is to use the discipline of research and due diligence to find something that's interesting, examine the opportunity rationally, buy it and then leave it alone! Unless you want to become a speculator – and potentially lose very large amounts of money – you should find business and investment opportunities, decide how many years you'll stick with it and then stop looking. If you do feel the desperate need to be more short-termist in nature, then make sure you see my later chapter on market timing systems towards the end of this book.

HAVE REALISTIC EXPECTATIONS ABOUT RETURNS

The next great defence against your inner self speaks to that constant risk/return trade-off that is whizzing away in your mind.

You see something that you think might make you a large amount of profit and you get greedy. You ignore the risks (because you can't see them and they might not have popped up recently) and thus have a faulty risk/return trade-off.

The best corrective to this danger (called greed) is to have a realistic estimate of both the time scale (see the chapter on time horizons) and the likely return from using your capital. In my experience, anything that returns double-digit percentages is probably a fat pitch that should be avoided largely because it will involve too much (unacknowledged) risk.

Investing in stock markets – in stocks and shares – for instance is unlikely to reward you with much more than 6 to 8 per cent per annum over the very long term. Bonds will be closer to 5 per cent and cash under 3 per cent. Investing in your career and your personal capital will probably give you double-digit returns but it's intrinsically difficult to measure, so we don't tend to do very much of it!

EVERYTHING REVERTS TO MEAN, EVENTUALLY

Whenever I see an opportunity, especially one that has enormous potential, I like to remember the importance of the mean reversion argument. This suggests that markets, people and economies are largely without 'meaning'. Markets are random creatures although we, the participants in these markets, are largely irrational. Maybe all that irrationality adds up to randomness?

Nothing really happens for a reason, it simply happens because it can and usually will. Randomness is the dominant economic motor of our society, i.e. luck. That doesn't mean that cycles don't play out and trends emerge, just that eventually randomness crushes everything in its path and we all revert back to the long-term average.

This 'mean reversion' theory works very nicely in practice and can be both a positive and a negative. When you see enormous wealth created by say social media companies, for instance, remember that eventually most of the capital created in this sector will be destroyed by another wave of innovation – although that doesn't mean that it can't make money while the going is good!

Putting it all together

Lurking in the background of my third strategy is a slightly scary idea, which is that change is constant and that much of that change is random – cold, without meaning and a potential risk to your capital. Yet we as humans approach this reality with a trainload of prejudices, biases and frankly irrational stupidity. The cold, hard world of economic and financial outcomes is as random, constantly changing and, heartless as it seems, no amount of believing otherwise will change it!

The good news is that once you understand this challenge, the remedies are easy.

Don't take yourself too seriously, admit your weaknesses and embrace your mistakes so that you can learn from them. Just because you are emotionally driven (a given) doesn't mean you can't aspire to be more rational in pursuit of advancement and wealth. And always remember that mean reversion can provide opportunity and that just because everything is overwhelmingly random and without meaning, doesn't mean that there isn't constant opportunity.

15 Shares: the safest long-term bet?

> 'Investing should be more like watching paint dry or watching grass grow. If you want excitement, take US$800 and go to Las Vegas.' Paul Samuelson

> 'The main purpose of the stock market is to make fools of as many men as possible.' Bernard Baruch

> 'It takes 20 years to build a reputation and five minutes to ruin it. If you think about that, you'll do things differently.' Warren Buffett

> 'The way to make money is to buy when blood is running in the streets.' John D. Rockefeller

> 'To achieve long-term success over many financial market and economic cycles, observing a few rules is not enough. Too many things change too quickly in the investment world for that approach to succeed. It is necessary instead to understand the rationale behind the rules in order to appreciate why they work when they do and don't when they don't.' Seth Klarman

Equities have delivered on the extra risk

Investing in the stock market – in shares or stocks – is a self-evidently risky business. In fact it's so clearly risky that equities (stocks and shares) are actually called 'risk' assets (i.e. they are risky!) by economists who also wax lyrically about the trade-off between risk and return. This relationship is in fact so central to much of investment-related economic and financial theory that academics have spent entire dissertations drawing up complex graphics and graphs that chart this constantly evolving relationship.

Put simply, the basic financial message is that the more risk you take, the greater your reasonable expectation of return, but only if you are willing to be patient and wait a long time.

Economists may be a generally pretty dismal bunch but when it comes to stocks and shares they are spot on and insightful – equities make sense because they are risky!

There's very little in the manmade world apart from extraordinary luck and sheer hard work that can give you a return of between 5 and 10 per cent per annum over many years, but shares are one of those unique opportunities. This remarkable promise is almost entirely a consequence of the fact that shares (equities) are risky and that by putting your money into a share or a fund you are taking the not inconsiderable risk that you could lose anything between 10 and 50 per cent in a single year.

But that trade-off – and the possibility of massive losses – produces what's technically called an equity risk premium, which sounds complicated but is simply an estimate for the long-term return from investing in shares compared with a 'risk-free' asset like cash or a government bond.

Generally over the long term, historical studies show that this 'premium' – the excess return over cash expressed as a percentage – is anything between 2 and 5 per cent per annum although that percentage can be much, much greater in a good decade and is sometimes considerably smaller (and even negative) in dismal years! Obviously much depends on what's the risk-free rate from cash or government bonds, but if we assume a long-term average of between 0.5 and 3 per cent per annum, that would suggest shares are capable of producing between 2.5 per cent and 8 per cent per annum. And in fact the past analysis of US stock market data suggests a long-term average of around 6 to 8 per cent per annum is possible, a return echoed by similar UK and European studies.

Adventurous types, especially those who are young and patient, can reap this premium by dint of simply being patient i.e. waiting for the average return to emerge. How long might these patient adventurous types have to wait? The general ready reckoner is that anyone looking to invest over just 5 years is taking too many risks with shares, whereas over 10 years they might feel a little more comfortable. But there have been ten-year periods where shares have underperformed and barely returned even positive numbers, so even the patient investor waiting over a decade might end up being frustrated.

The consensus seems to be that a period of between 10 and 30 years is sensible with an emphasis on more than 20 years. If you can afford to invest for this length of time in order to build up your risk capital, you should be rewarded by a decent return – though there is **absolutely** no guarantee!

Given this reward for taking risk what should a young investor do, especially one in their 20s or 30s? My radical suggestion is to invest 100 per cent of all your savings allocated to the risk capital pot (pensions) into equities.

CAPTURE THE RISK PREMIUM AT LOW COST

Nothing in the world of investment is certain **except** for the fact that excessive costs will destroy your capital. Every extra 0.50 per cent per annum in fees compounds over time and eventually deprives you of a more prosperous retirement.

The good news is that within the noisy and expensive world of investment there are some lower cost ways of managing things like shares and funds. In recent years we've seen an explosion of new funds and stockbroking dealing services that have shaved down fees and trading expenses, almost to the point at which I'm not entirely sure that they're not competitive to offer into the market. But someone else's business challenge is your great advantage. Look at the annual fees charged on funds and if possible hunt down a measure called the total expense ratio, which includes nearly all the key costs of managing a fund. If that fund is charging more than 1 per cent per annum in total fees, you better have an insanely good reason for selecting it!

The same goes for stockbroking charges. Every extra few dollars or pounds per trade adds to your costs and should be avoided. Maybe your broker for instance offers a monthly, flat fee dealing charge of just a few dollars/pounds if you send your purchase orders in advance and are willing to trade with everyone else on one day a week/month. If this service (usually called a regular investment service) is offered, use it and cut costs.

CAPTURE THE EQUITY RISK PREMIUM IN A DIVERSIFIED WAY

When investors first approach the weird and wonderful world of financial markets they sometimes make the bold assumption that frankly every share or bond is pretty much the same i.e. risky and a tad confusing! But there is in fact huge diversity within the global stock and bond markets, both at a 'sector' level (what the company does) and at the international level.

REBALANCE ANNUALLY

We'll look at some practical portfolio ideas in related chapters, but one precaution should figure prominently in your calculations, which is to look at your assets every year and rebalance back to your original plan. This idea of rebalancing can sound a bit daunting but actually it's a very simple concept. Let's assume that you had a 50/50 split within your portfolio between a fund that invests in global bonds and a global equities fund (in practical terms let's assume that equates to £50 in each investment). After year one let's say that the global equities fund goes up by 20 per cent but the bonds fund falls in value by 10 per cent. Our equities would now be worth £60 while our bond fund would be worth £45. Overall we're up by £5 in one year. In order to rebalance we want both investments to be worth £52.50, implying that you sell £7.50 of those equities in order to invest the money in the bonds. Lurking within this rebalancing exercise is a simple strategy – that you need to take profits on your successful investments in order to invest in the losers, which in turn stand a decent chance of rebounding in value in the future. Rebalancing effectively forces you to take a contrarian approach to financial assets, investing in the losers, using proceeds from your successful bets!

Putting it all together

Investing in risky equities (stocks and shares) is potentially **the** single biggest way of building wealth over the long term besides investing in your own career and personal capital – it is also, if done badly, the single easiest way to destroy your hard-earned wealth. That opportunity/jeopardy is well understood and many readers might choose to take a less risky approach to their capital, pumping all their money for instance into their house. Yet, as we discuss in this book, virtually every form of wealth accumulation also comes with its own (perhaps less obvious) risk, not least that you can't live off the income produced by your home.

I think if you are serious about building your wealth, and your options as regards accumulating personal capital are limited, you **need** to take the risks that come with investing in equities – and that's especially important if you are young with a time horizon that stretches into the next 30 years. In fact, I'd go so far as to suggest that if you don't take the risk of investing in equities you'll make a huge mistake.

16 From tiny acorns mighty oaks might grow

> 'I find it quite useful to think of a free market economy – or partly free market economy – as sort of the equivalent of an ecosystem. Just as animals flourish in niches, people who specialize in some narrow niche can do very well.' Charlie Munger

> 'The simpler it is, the better I like it.' Peter Lynch

> 'Small cap companies complain constantly that they are neglected. They have a very tough time getting Wall Street research analysts to follow them, to pay attention to them. There are small companies that will say that I have grown my earning at 20 per cent over the last five years and no one will pay attention to me.' Bethany McLean

> 'All you need for a lifetime of successful investing is a few big winners, and the pluses from those will overwhelm the minuses from the stocks that don't work out.' Peter Lynch

> 'If you're looking for a home run – a great investment for five years or 10 years or more – then the only way to beat this enormous fog that covers the future is to identify a long-term trend that will give a particular business some sort of edge.'
> Ralph Wanger

Smaller companies are worth the risk

For most people in this world investing in the stock markets is largely about buying shares in big companies. Big institutions and big fund management groups focus their efforts on the very biggest companies because they're easy to watch and the choice of stocks and companies is not completely overwhelming (hundreds rather than thousands).

That focus on what's called 'large cap' stocks – companies whose market capitalization is likely to be above at least US$1 billion, if not US$10 billion – produces a steady flow of money into the space, making investing in smaller companies something of a 'niche' pursuit.

To understand just how much money is invested on the large caps consider the main UK stock market index called the FTSE All-Share index. This index captures 98 per cent of the total value of all stocks quoted on the London Stock Exchange. The 100 largest companies by market capitalization within this broad market measure account for between 80 and 85 per cent of the total value of the index, followed by what are called mid-cap stocks – which as the name implies are smaller than the very biggest companies but still very large. These mid-caps (numbering 250 in the UK) account for around 10 per cent of the total value of the FTSE All-Share index, which implies that between 90 and 95 per cent of the total value of the index is accounted for by just 350 companies. The remainder (between 5 and 10 per cent depending on market conditions) of this total market index comprises the thousands of smaller companies whose market value in the UK is below about £450m.

So to repeat, 350 companies account for around 95 per cent of the value of the index, while the other 2,000-plus account for 5 per cent to 10 per cent. And just in case you wondered, this asymmetry is also true for trading volumes and institutional interest. Talk to most huge hedge funds and massive investment banks and they'll probably have dozens of analysts looking at mid and large caps and barely a handful examining the prospects for smaller companies. Transaction flows will also parallel this interest, with billions in turnover for the very largest stocks on a good day, whereas a smaller company might be lucky to see a few small trades in the low hundreds of thousands of dollars.

You might think that this vast discrepancy between small and large companies is entirely rational because large companies are likely to produce greater profits and probably boast less risk. In reality, the truth is very different.

Large caps are indeed easier to research but the hard numbers tell us that investing in smaller company shares actually produces a much bigger long-term return. The definitive study of stock market historical data comes from a duo of London-based academics called Professors Elroy Dimson and Paul Marsh. They've long been running their own version of a small company stock market index and they've exhaustively crunched the numbers.

The results are startling.

Their version of a UK small cap index (which is similar to many other similar indices tracking small company shares) has produced a compound annual return of 15.5 per cent per annum since 1955 (through to the end of 2012) compared to 11.9 per cent for the whole London stock market as measured by the FTSE All-Share index (that's the broad index we mentioned earlier).

There is of course an obvious downside, which I'm guessing virtually any sentient reader can spot – investing in smaller companies' shares is risky! One of the most striking things about these small cap indices is to see the huge turnover in company names within the list every ten years.

Yet although investing in smaller companies is self-evidently risky, the hard numbers from study after study tell us that it is worth the anxiety, worry and fear, especially if you can afford to be patient.

A SMALL CAP SATELLITE PORTFOLIO

No one (except perhaps the very bravest soul) is suggesting that you invest **all** your risk capital for the next 20 to 30 years in smaller company stocks, but it does seem to me an eminently sensible idea to allocate **some** money to these smaller caps. In a later chapter we'll encounter the humble dividend stock as well as the cheapskate value share – alongside small caps, these are different styles of investing that have been shown to deliver superior returns to the patient investor. My suggestion is that you should run two types of equity-based portfolio: one a core of about 50 per cent that comprises relatively straightforward large cap stocks (familiar names) in a fund. With the remaining 50 per cent I'd think about splitting it into a series of satellite portfolios, which will comprise smaller caps, value stocks and dividend friendly companies. My core suggestion is that somewhere between 10 and 25 per cent of your total equity wealth should be invested in small caps.

USE A FUND AND MAKE SURE YOU GO INTERNATIONAL

You absolutely can invest directly in smaller company shares but unless you are willing to put in the time for detailed research and due diligence I'd probably stick with a fund manager who specializes in this area. There are some cheap index tracking funds (ETFs or exchange-traded funds) that invest in smaller cap stocks but I think in reality you need an expert who can go out and meet the companies in their portfolio, understand the obvious risks and then make sure they trade the shares efficiently (by narrowing down any trading transaction costs, especially between the selling and buying price).

I'd also think seriously about making sure you have not one but a few small cap fund managers, with a nice international spread of market coverage. In particular, my sense is that over the next 30 years, smaller companies in emerging markets will be a remarkable story and could produce some stunning numbers, although there might also be a fair amount of volatility on this particular journey.

HAVE A BIT OF FUN

Although I do recommend using a fund manager, I also think it is worth having the odd punt or two on small caps – not as a surrogate form of gambling but as a way of learning about the opportunities on offer. My suggestion would be to put aside a tiny pot of your risk capital that can be used to take specific small cap bets. You need to understand the risks you are taking and this should be money you are happy to entirely lose! But if you are lucky and you find that stock that will be tomorrow's Google or Apple, your returns could be absolutely huge. Investors have even developed a term called the tenbagger to describe these shooting stars that get us all terrifically excited. A tenbagger is that legendary stock that increases by more than tenfold in value, hopefully more than making up for all the other deadbeat small cap stocks in your speculative portfolio that will almost certainly crash and burn. But the real purpose of this fun portfolio is to watch, listen and learn (especially from your mistakes).

Putting it all together

In this chapter I've introduced an absolutely crucial distinction between a core portfolio of (hopefully) less risky large company stocks and a string of satellite portfolios that can be much more focused and niche. In later chapters we'll pick up on this theme but I really want readers to take this idea to heart. As we constantly reiterate throughout this book, diversification between different risk profiles, sectors and themes is **absolutely** crucial and small caps are all about dosing up on higher risk opportunity – but in an informed manner. And that word 'informed' is the important one in this discussion, because in my experience nearly everything I have learned from investing has been in the world of small cap investing. Failure is common among these minnows and failure teaches us all the most valuable lessons. Larger investment institutions hate to take that risk, which is why so many avoid this niche, but you, the private investor, can afford to take the hit to your reputation, learn the lesson and then make sure you are smarter next time. Small cap investing is one of the very few areas where you, the ordinary investor, have the advantage. Use it to make yourself wealthier!

17 Back great companies

> 'There's more money to be made in finding tomorrow's winners than chasing yesterday's.' Foster Friess

> 'Profits are supposed to be higher in fast-growing industries. Myth! They're not because everyone else knows they are fast growing. Returns are often higher in unfashionable activities like tobacco. Best are industries that grow faster than expected, whether expectations are high or low.' John Kay

> 'If you want something new, you have to do something old.' Peter Drucker

> 'Great investment opportunities come around when excellent companies are surrounded by unusual circumstances that cause the stock to be misappraised.' Warren Buffett

> 'As time goes on, I get more and more convinced that the right method in investment is to put fairly large sums into enterprises which one thinks one knows something about and in the management of which one thoroughly believes.' John Maynard Keynes

Bet big on the blue chips of tomorrow

Access to capital seems to me to be the chief determinant of enormous success in this unequal world. Luck, hard work and knowledge of course play a huge role in generating business success but if you want to make it really, really big (and I mean in the billion dollar league) it would increasingly appear to be the case that you need cheap access to capital.

Of course amazing businesses do appear literally out of nowhere and then go on to make their creators and investors huge fortunes, but my guess is that 8/10 of these success stories have had access in shape or form early on to significant amounts of working capital, probably provided either by the wealthy entrepreneurs lurking in the shadows or by venture capitalists with deep pockets who invested countless millions in the business.

Consider the challenge facing a business in a globalized marketplace, where barriers to entry (many of them based on rules and regulations) are growing ever higher by the day and many competitors in markets as diverse and far flung as China and India seem to have privileged access to cheap credit.

Who do you think will succeed in this unequal playing field – the scrappy start-up with loads of great ideas but poor access to capital or the bigger company with established shareholders, an open credit line at the bank and the ability to tap bond markets?

Look at it another way, through the prism of debt, the flipside of capital. Since the global financial crisis of 2008/2009, access to credit for smaller and medium-sized enterprises (SMEs) has quite literally fallen off a cliff throughout the developed world – and in China even! Yet access to capital for bigger companies – many of them listed on a stock market or owned by private equity – has never been easier. These companies can tap investors for huge amounts of money at relatively (in historic terms at least) low interest rates.

My point here is that we live in a world that gives massive structural advantages to bigger business – maybe the great capitalist cry of our era should be that the blue chips of tomorrow will inherit the world!

This structural inequality (of which I for one heartily disapprove) has enormous implications for readers of this book.

I am all for smart, dynamic types starting their own business and investing for growth – the greatest wealth is usually made by business owners who've hit upon a great opportunity. But I equally don't want to fool readers into thinking that this isn't risky, and that this kind of success is arguably growing riskier by the day!

Maybe the smarter strategy might be to try to find the next great businesses and then either:

- invest in these businesses via their shares, or
- go and work for these businesses and enjoy the ride as these surging behemoths help you to create enormous personal capital.

The twist in my strategy is not to invest your capital (personal or risk) in today's existing blue chips but to hunt down tomorrow's new stars, the next decade's blue chips!

It seems to me that today's blue chips are already a known quantity. Personally I'd always ignore the top five companies in an industry or sector and focus instead on the second division of up-and-coming businesses, the companies that are straining at the leash to smash the big guys. But how do we go about finding these companies?

In the world of stocks and shares – investing in businesses – there's always a second tier of what are called mid-cap-sized companies that tend to feature an interesting collection of corporate wannabes.

In the UK these companies can usually be found in an index like the FTSE 250 or even the FTSE SmallCap Index, while in the US a good place to start would be to look at the companies that are between 200 and 500 in terms of market capitalization within the S&P 500 stock market index.

In terms of actually working for tomorrow's blue chips, I'd maybe look at smaller companies that haven't quite made it on to the stock markets but are privately owned and absolutely going places because of their access to capital.

My own favourite strategy for spotting great places to work is to look out for the regular deluge of surveys hoping to pinpoint the hot 'up and coming' companies of tomorrow – these lists usually go by the name of something like the Hot/Fastest Growing/Sexy/100 start-ups/growth businesses.

LOOK FOR ABOVE-AVERAGE EARNINGS GROWTH

How do we know if a fast-growing business of today is going to be a corporate leviathan of tomorrow? A good place to start is with the corporate Profit & Loss account i.e. is it generating enough capital through its own business operations to invest for tomorrow?

If possible, try to hunt down these numbers for at least the past three to five years and then carefully analyse key metrics such as the operating margin, as well as the rate of sales growth. For a bit more depth, switch to the balance sheet and look at two key lines – the growth in cash produced by the business and the change in debt levels.

BET BIG ON GOOD MANAGEMENT

Businesses are not faceless machines that run without people! They're led by chief executives and management teams and it's these senior people who give a business its 'texture' and 'feel'. One can quite easily research this management team and the messages they're giving the wider workforce by going online, hunting down interviews with the bosses, and understanding what makes them tick.

See whether these business leaders are winning awards for their management style and see whether the company is picking up prizes for its investment in people and training. In particular, I'd watch out very carefully for a clear sense that the company knows where it's going, has a sense of its mission with a clear corporate worldview about what's possible. Great managers usually help make great businesses, and that should filter down to the shareholders (through a surging share price) and to the employees (through higher wages, better training and a pool of valuable share options).

LOOK FOR A BIG MOAT OF COMPETITIVE ADVANTAGE

Great business leaders and a strong profit and loss account are wonderful positives but they're not quite enough on their own. I can think of a long list of businesses I've respected that have slowly lost their way as competition has intensified, in large part because the company doesn't have what's called a 'moat of competitive advantage'. Quite simply, an economic moat is a long-term competitive advantage that allows a company to earn oversized profits over time. The concept was actually developed by a certain Warren Buffett, who realized that companies that reward investors over the long term have a durable competitive advantage. Assessing that advantage involves understanding what kind of defence, or competitive barrier, the company has been able to build for itself in its industry. The best businesses are those that have a great product, good management, access to enough capital to grow and a moat that makes it difficult for competitors to enter the market and make a profit.

Putting it all together

With each of my three strategies, I think it's immediately obvious that access to capital is a key consideration. Businesses that can keep on growing their profits usually require additional working capital to sustain growth. Equally, hiring a brilliant management team necessitates paying them well, which in turn needs lots and lots of money. Last but by no means least, building a moat of competitive advantage usually requires patient investment in either a piece of intellectual property like a brand or in technology; alternatively, the business has an advantage based on both brand and technology but is also investing like crazy in new capex (capital expenditure) spending to keep boosting productivity.

Capital is king and that means that businesses that want to scale up quickly need access to the global financial markets either through a listing on the stock market or via backing from private equity investors. That in turn favours companies that are already growing fast, have that moat of advantage and are big enough to attract the best talent.

To me this suggests carefully focusing your investment strategies – both personal and risk investment – on finding the best companies and then betting big on their success. But always remember that this is nevertheless a risky strategy. No matter how careful your due diligence, you could end up picking tomorrow's Xerox – itself a great business in its day but now a very pale shadow of its former self.

Shooting stars have a tendency to light up our collective skies and then come crashing down. The trick is to find the business that can just keep on growing.

18 Have you got what it takes?

> 'The best way to predict the future is to create it.' Peter Drucker

> 'Winners never quit and quitters never win.' Vince Lombardi

> 'My biggest motivation? Just to keep challenging myself. I see life like one long university education that I never had – everyday I'm learning something new.' Richard Branson

> 'Opportunity is missed by most people because it is dressed in overalls and looks like work.' Thomas Edison

> 'He who begins many things finishes but few.' German proverb

The entrepreneurial mindset

Investing in your personal capital – your job, profession or business – is likely to be the single biggest means of boosting your wealth over the long term. For a growing number of readers that wealth creation focus increasingly means taking the plunge into some sort of business activity, maybe involving a start-up of some variety. That plunge into entrepreneurial dynamism is probably the single biggest factor for explaining why some people are wealthy... and others are not! Look deep enough at wealth statistics for both the UK and the US and you'll find that those who are 'wealthier' are disproportionately likely to own their own business. That doesn't mean that sticking with a profession such as law or moving up the career ladder at a big international company isn't an alternative route to riches but the hard fact of the matter is that your chances of becoming seriously wealthy increase exponentially if you own your own business. Unfortunately – as we're about to discover – we also have to be honest about the chances of success for the average start-up, which are very low. Start your own business for sure if you want to build your wealth, just don't assume it'll be a success.

If after this soul searching you do decide that the business life is for you, you next need to face the facts about who and what succeeds – and what personal skills you'll need to build that business capital. I'm constantly fascinated by the guff that is printed in the endless series of books by entrepreneur coaches, full of gushing adjectives about how you need to be creative, and have the right financial mindset… or whatever it is that is in fashion at any particular moment in time.

I prefer to mine the rich literature of research about who these entrepreneurs are and what makes them successful, especially focusing on their 'mindset'! Bill J. Bonnstetter, for instance, at the *Harvard Business Review* has also focused on these personality traits. Based on a 17,000 respondent survey of business people and entrepreneurs (plus a control group of ordinary employees), he puts something called 'persuasion' at the top of his list. According to Bonnstetter this trait is defined as 'the ability to persuade others to join the mission'. In the study, this was uncovered by ranking on a scale of 1 to 6 prompts such as: 'I have been recognized for my ability to get others to say yes' or 'I have a reputation for delivering powerful presentations'. Next up comes 'leadership', which was defined as 'having a compelling vision for the future', i.e., surveyors who highly ranked prompts such as: 'In the past, people have taken risks to support my vision, mission or goals' or 'I have been criticized for being too competitive'. Serial entrepreneurs ranked both of these prompts highly. For people with an entrepreneurial mindset, their strength of vision is usually tied to a product or service that provides solutions to challenges, even when the general public is not aware the challenge exists.

Other skills include personal accountability, which is 'demonstrating initiative, self-confidence, resiliency and a willingness to take responsibility for personal actions… individuals who blame others for their failures display a significant lack of personal accountability and will most likely stall in any entrepreneurial effort'. Then there's also goal orientation, where the entrepreneur is 'energetically focusing efforts on meeting a goal, mission or objective'.

Finally, there's also the obvious strength in interpersonal skills, 'the glue that holds the other four skills together. They include effectively communicating, building rapport and relating well to all people, from all backgrounds and communication styles'.

This researcher concludes that 'entrepreneurially successful people are successful for a reason – that many of them highly display certain personal skills. And while this research identifies these skills, it should be pointed out these five attributes are not inherent. They can be learned and developed, especially early in life, and further honed throughout an entrepreneur's career.'

FOCUS ON QUALITY AND EXECUTION… THINK KAIZEN

Many successful entrepreneurs are intensely creative and boast amazing interpersonal skills but once we dig a bit deeper we discover another hugely important trait – an obsession with detail based on extensive knowledge of the opportunity. This suggests a ferocious focus on quality and a clearly mapped out plan for executing the business strategy, hopefully built around some sort of business plan (although you don't always need one straight from the get-go!). Sometimes this precision thinking takes on a more structured approach with more and more successful businesses learning from a Japanese concept called kaizen. This hugely popular idea features a whole world view that consists of thinking about systematically capturing continuous improvement in quality, technology, processes, company culture, productivity, safety and leadership. Nearly every business I've encountered that uses kaizen is a success!

BE HONEST ABOUT YOUR MISTAKES AND WEAKNESSES

As we'll discover in the next chapter, businesses fail, all the time. Many entrepreneurs in fact have at least a few failed businesses on their CV. I personally know of not one veteran entrepreneur who has never failed in business. Not one! Mistakes happen and you need to know – and understand – what can go wrong and why! Luckily those entrepreneurial academics (this time at the University of Tennessee) have been asking lots of business people why their start-up failed. The number one factor appears to be incompetence (near to half of all cases) with particular issues being 'emotional pricing', 'living too high for the business', 'non-payment of taxes', 'lack of planning' and 'no experience of book-keeping'.

Next up as a contributor to failure was unbalanced experience (at 30 per cent) with poor 'credit granting practices' and too 'rapid expansion'. Touchingly, the Tennessee-based academics conclude their analysis with a wishlist of avoidable errors including 'going into business for the wrong reasons' and 'family pressure on time and money commitments'. I was especially drawn to the observation of one respondent who suggested that their business had failed by 'being in the wrong place at the wrong time'!

IF AT FIRST YOU FAIL, THEN TRY, TRY AGAIN!

Now that we've admitted that business starts-ups can and do fail with great frequency and those entrepreneurs should learn from their mistakes, we can also admit that serial entrepreneurs are also more likely to succeed. One Harvard Business School analysis examining the success of serial entrepreneurs concluded that everything being equal 'a venture-capital-backed entrepreneur who succeeds in a venture (by our definition, starts a company that goes public) has a 30 per cent chance of succeeding in his next venture. By contrast, first-time entrepreneurs have only an 18 per cent chance of succeeding and entrepreneurs who previously failed have a 20 per cent chance of succeeding.' Moral of the story, keep trying until you get it exactly right.

Putting it all together

If the entrepreneurial way is for you, I have a final practical thought about planning, a favourite subject of this book! Earlier on in this chapter I mentioned in passing that you don't always have to have a business plan for every new start-up. In my humble experience too many clever, industrious people obsess about these detailed documents and never quite spend the right amount of time 'feeling out the opportunity' i.e. actually getting something like a product to market.

What I think can work though is that you write your own 'entrepreneurial plan', where you establish a bunch of simple goals over the next few decades, such as acquiring the right experience over the next X years in someone else's business for instance! Then you might set another target to acquire knowledge about your chosen opportunity and maybe you might also give some thought to a financial plan that involves building up a small pot of capital to invest in your start-up and maybe build a first prototype. Most importantly, with this plan I want you to set some realistic targets for success, identify the long list of risks (a subject we'll discuss in the next chapter) and be honest with yourself regarding at what stage you identify that 'enough is enough' i.e. when you need to admit that the campaign to start a business is just not going to succeed. Not everyone is destined to be a successful entrepreneur! Let's be honest about business: if wealth accumulation is your target, wasting money on a series of failed businesses is hardly going to make you rich!

19 Cutting down the risk of failure in business

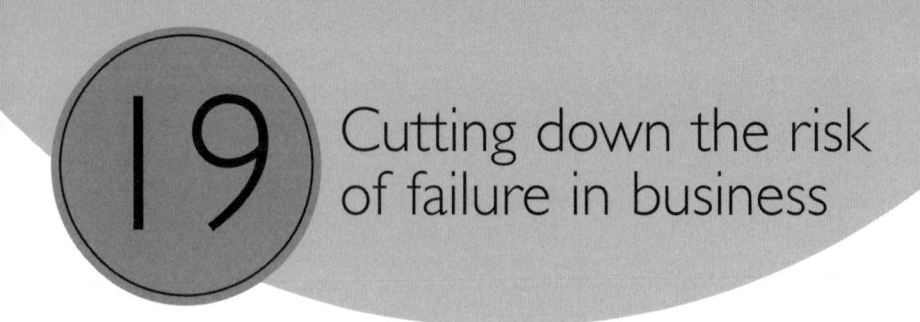

> 'I have not failed. I have just found 10,000 ways that won't work.' Thomas Edison

> 'Don't fear failure so much that you refuse to try new things.' Louis Boone

> 'Failure is the condiment that gives success its flavour.' Truman Capote

> 'Failure can either be a stepping stone to success or a stumbling to defeat.' Ron Holland

> 'Every failure is a step to success.' William Whewell

Improve the odds on your business succeeding

In the last chapter we explored the personal skills and traits that are needed in order to build up your personal capital by starting a business, with a strong emphasis on learning from your mistakes. In this chapter we're going to pick up again on the risks of starting a business, this time focusing rather less on your personal skills, and more on the sheer brute facts of what succeeds in enterprise… and what doesn't! The key thought we'll explore is how you can minimize your risk of failure by thinking and acting smarter.

Let's start by injecting a few facts into the debate about successful entrepreneurs. Perhaps the most basic question is what does the average, successful 'still-in-business' entrepreneur actually look like in the flesh? The answer is that if nothing else they are likely to have substantial experience from an earlier job, be aged around 40 and have a university education. That at least is the conclusion of research by a US organization called the Ewing Marion Kauffman Foundation, which looks at what exactly defines an average entrepreneur. In a report from 2013 they suggested that most US-based businesspeople:

- are an average age of 40
- boast a BA degree (or equivalent) education or more (more than 95 per cent); many have an advanced degree (47 per cent)
- used own savings to start their business (more than 70 per cent)
- were usually the first in their family to start a business (52 per cent)
- admitted to benefiting greatly from simply being lucky (73 per cent)
- were more likely to live in Arizona, Texas or California
- had an average of two business start-ups on their résumé.

Of course, these stats don't mean that there aren't any entrepreneurs out there who are 25-year-old females with no university education, and living in West Virginia! It's just that the odds are probably stacked against them, which for some, of course, is a major part of the challenge of starting a business – proving those white middle-aged university men living in California that they're wrong!

Our next encounter with the dry world of statistics is to look at how many entrepreneurs and their start-ups actually succeed. Here the news is – being honest – fairly grim! Most businesses fail. One study, for instance, for a hugely successful business incubator called Y Combinator found that of the 511 companies that entered the programme over a five-year period (it's worth bearing in mind about 10,000 actually applied to join this fast-track programme), only 37 then went on to a 'successful exit', which was defined (somewhat optimistically in my opinion) as a sale for over US$40m. That implied that 97 per cent failed even after an acceptance rate that was only 5 per cent at very best! Another report from academics at the University of Tennessee (the illuminating paper is called 'Startup Business Failure Rates') suggested that overall 25 per cent of businesses failed by year one, increasing to 55 per cent by year five and a tragic 71 per cent by year ten. OK, so armed with this data, what are the next steps for our aspiring entrepreneur?

FIRST MOVERS DON'T ALWAYS HAVE THE ADVANTAGE

Talk to many business 'gurus' and they'll excitedly tell you that you need to rush to market, capturing the elusive 'first mover advantage'. This term was first popularized in a 1988 paper by a Stanford Business School professor, David Montgomery, and his co-author, Marvin Lieberman. It sounds a great idea. Come up with that killer idea, develop a product, conquer the world and define the category – and get rich! Unfortunately, a host of academic studies tells a rather different story. While some well-known first movers, such as Gillette in safety razors and Sony in personal stereos, have enjoyed considerable success, others, such as Xerox in fax machines and eToys (remember them?... thought not) in Internet retailing, have failed. Personally, my favourite example is that of Netscape, which was first to market with an Internet browser, boasted an amazing share price that made tens of millions of dollars for its backers before plummeting like a lead balloon in 1997 following the rise of Microsoft's browser, Internet Explorer.

Academics Peter N. Golder and Gerard J. Tellis have in fact found that 47 per cent of market pioneers fail and only 11 per cent of current market leaders were actually what's called pioneers. They argued that 'our results show that being first in the market may not confer automatic long-term rewards... Indeed, early pioneers who entered an average of 13 years after the pioneer are more likely to be lead markets today'. My advice? Wait for someone else to prove the model first and then build a better version!

PICK THE RIGHT POINT IN THE BUSINESS CYCLE!

My next strategy is based on the brutal assessment of nearly every business person I've ever known as a good friend. To a man and woman these veterans believe that good old-fashioned luck is absolutely essential as is a good sense of business timing. In simple terms, start your business when confidence is slowly returning to an economy after a slowdown.

And if you don't believe me, here's a bunch of Harvard Business School academics on the subject – they looked at successful start-ups and serial entrepreneurs and found that 'the industry-year success rate in the first venture is the best predictor of success in the subsequent venture. Entrepreneurs who succeeded by investing in a good industry and year (e.g., computers in 1983) are far more likely to succeed in their subsequent ventures than those who succeeded by doing better than other firms founded in the same industry and year (e.g., succeeding in computers in 1985)… Thus, it appears that market timing ability is an attribute of entrepreneurs.' Watch out for bubbles (the subject of a later chapter) and avoid starting a business when everyone is totally overexcited!

GET THE RIGHT EXPERIENCE, IN SOMEONE ELSE'S BUSINESS

My last strategy for minimizing the risk of failure in a business is perhaps the most important. Whatever business or product you decide to launch, make sure you've learned everything you need about running a company at someone else's expense! One recent study of UK businesses, for instance, found that almost two-thirds of entrepreneurs admitted that they had no prior experience of owning or managing a business, though half of these active entrepreneurs had previously worked in the sector they started a business in. This confirms a 2000 study by an academic researcher called Amar Bhide, which found that 'a substantial fraction of the Inc. 500 [the fastest growing private companies in the US] got their idea for their new company while working at their prior employer'. The Kaufman Foundation – mentioned at the beginning of this article – also notes that 75 per cent of entrepreneurs worked at another company for at least six years before starting their own business.

Putting it all together

Time for honesty at the conclusion of this chapter. Sometimes starting a business isn't the right thing to do. Maybe, despite your best efforts, you can't quite tick all the boxes in this chapter (and the last) and are forced to conclude that business is not for you! There's no shame in that admission and frankly in my humble opinion (as someone who has invested in business start-ups) there's rather too much money wasted on businesses that were always destined to fail! Entrepreneurs are certainly not born but equally there are more than a few of us who were absolutely never born to be entrepreneurs!

Yet just because you haven't got what it takes to be a business person, doesn't mean that you can't use some of the ideas in these two chapters to help shape a more portfolio-based career. In my experience, many successful people don't want to employ lots of staff but are willing to treat their career and their knowledge base as a business in of itself. Great! The opportunities to accumulate wealth via a portfolio approach may never make you super-rich in the style of Google or Facebook's founders but it may produce a better 'risk adjusted' return i.e. after accounting for the likelihood of a business start-up failing – and costing you a heap of money – a portfolio approach might be more profitable in the longer term.

20 Beware the rise of the machine intelligence economy

> 'At some point we'll arrive at a future where a lot of people have stagnant real incomes but they won't count as poor in the contemporary sense. You will neither be correct to say that they are well-off – but they will have a lot of free stuff, not much money in the bank.' Tyler Cowen

> 'Accountants, machinists, medical technicians, even software writers that write the software for "machines" are being displaced without upscaled replacement jobs. Retrain, rehire into higher paying and value-added jobs? That may be the political myth of the modern era. There aren't enough of those jobs.' Bill Gross

> 'We believe that if men have the talent to invent new machines that put men out of work, they have the talent to put those men back to work.' John F. Kennedy

> 'Machines were, it may be said, the weapon employed by the capitalists to quell the revolt of specialized labour.' Karl Marx

> 'The future masters of technology will have to be light-hearted and intelligent. The machine easily masters the grim and the dumb.' Marshall McLuhan

How vulnerable is your career to machine intelligence?

No other recent American economist has generated quite the same level of anxiety and downright panic as Tyler Cowen. Paul Krugman may constantly bang the drum for radical new economic policies in his widely read op-ed pieces for major US broadsheets and Steve Levitt may constantly enthral us with his original insights into behavioural economics but Cowen has mastered the dismal skill of scaring the heck out of us! He's tapped into a slightly fearful sense that the world as we know it is subtly changing… and not necessarily for the good! He's highlighted trends such as the progressive impoverishment of the middle classes (a fact attested to in study after study of US household incomes over the past few decades) but then worked out what's actually producing these powerful new forces.

Perhaps the most powerful analysis comes in a book called *Average is Over*, in which Cowen does his level best to scare the hell out of the professional middle classes. We've all become painfully aware over the past few decades that globalization has slowly but surely hollowed out the industrial base of many (though not all) Western societies. Offshoring to places such as China and India has destroyed countless millions of once well-paid industrial jobs that kept a large part of the working class (and middle classes as well) off benefits and in meaningful work. What's followed in the wake of this offshoring is a progressive lowering of the median (most common) wage rate for the lower working class (defined by economists as the bottom 10 to 20 per cent of the income rankings in the US and the UK).

The good news is that we've created huge numbers of new, largely service-based, jobs for those once industrially focused workforces. The bad news is that their salaries are much lower, with greater job insecurity.

But the middle classes have until recently been insulated from these changes, safely ensconced in jobs that depended on a new knowledge economy. But Tyler Cowen reckons change is coming to this group as well, picking up on the work of many leading economists who've spotted a new trend, which is that even knowledge-based jobs are beginning to vanish.

Some of these jobs are also being offshored to places like India, helped along by globalization. But many economists have begun to worry about how the Internet, and new IT-based processes built around machine intelligence, are slowly but surely eating into middle-class careers.

Cowen's core argument is that we're entering a new age of machine intelligence, where clever programs can do much if not most of the work of many middle-class jobs. Great swathes of the professional and white-collar classes will see their salaries at first lowered and then eliminated entirely as the machines plus their offshore helpers get to work. It's a hugely powerful argument and it contains within it a paradoxically positive message, which is that as this wave of economic disruption gets to work, we might see some big jumps in national productivity, which in turn will help make us all wealthier. Maybe this new technology is precisely what's required to kick-start our relatively anaemic recent national economic growth numbers.

But the challenge for you and me is, I think, evident, especially if one's aim is to work out how to build up our wealth from personal capital. That the middle classes aren't safe anymore, especially if they do a job that already involves a large amount of working with computers (which funnily enough many do!). My own suspicion is that Cowen slightly overeggs the potential for economic and social disruption but in big picture terms I think he's dead right in pinpointing a threat to the personal capital of a great many readers of this book. In simple terms, you've invested in your personal capital by focusing on your knowledge economy skills, especially those based around computers.

WORK OUT HOW EASILY REPLICABLE YOUR SKILLS ARE

You need to understand how vulnerable you are to change. How long will it take for smart AI or software programs to do the majority of your well-paid, knowledge-intensive job? Cocky professionals in medicine and the law, for instance, may decide that they are completely immune but I'd suggest that their arrogance is largely misplaced. I'm fairly sure that a highly skilled court-based advocate or a heart surgeon is probably fairly safe for many decades to come, but my guess is that the average solicitor or general practitioner is already having to contend with a host of clients who claim to know more than they do after having looked things up on the Internet.

This will only get worse.

In order to survive and build up your personal capital you need to understand the risk. My suggestion would be to talk to any nerdish 18-year-old who has spent far too long on both the Internet and their games console and ask them what they think! These kids instinctively have a better sense for where technology is heading. Listen to them. Ask them questions like 'do you really think that a computer could do dad's job eventually'? If they answer yes, start to think about developing a new career or look to improve your set of skills pronto!

STICK WITH THE WEALTHY

Tyler Cowen's work hasn't just focused on the rise of machine-based, AI intelligence. He's also looked at slow rates of recent national economic growth and the progressive increase in income inequalities within developed world societies via books like *The Age of Stagnation*. His suspicion is that the growing inequality of wealth is being fuelled by modern technologies, which are rewarding those who own businesses that benefit from all these new systems. The good news is that the number of beneficiaries of this new technology wave will grow and grow. But overall he also suspects that the wealthier will simply become even wealthier! That creates an immense opportunity based around servicing the needs of the time-poor, asset-rich super-wealthy. We've already seen the remorseless rise of the wealth adviser industry comprising legions of overpaid financial advisers who will supposedly provide all the financial alchemy required for the new global wealth elite. But that wealth services economy is now beginning to broaden out at an astonishing speed. The wealthy also require other skills, ranging from advice on how to keep fit through to mentoring either for their own careers or developing their kids' wellbeing.

LEARN TO WORK WITH THE MACHINES

The other excellent bit of news from Tyler Cowen's analysis is that the number of people who will need to work with machines on an intensive basis will inexorably increase. To use my example of journalism under threat, my guess is that IT-heavy content generators will still require some senior staff to help shape content and work with the programs to fine-tune new articles, comments or even videos. The good news then is that technology constantly creates jobs for those who know how to think in a smarter, more intuitive way than the computers… and then work with them. Clearly, it'll also create a constantly growing army of programmers and developers who will work with these AI and machine intelligence assistants. Constantly invest in your IT-based personal capital and make sure you are riding the next wave of change.

Putting it all together

Terminators are not about to roam the Earth, set to destroy the last remnants of the human civilization that created them. Robotics is also still probably at least one if not two generations away from having a genuinely disruptive impact on ordinary human society, although manufacturing industry may feel the impact sooner. I think it's also true that genuine machine-based artificial intelligence is still low key and restricted to specialist areas around engineering and maybe aeronautics. But a machine intelligence revolution is nevertheless fast approaching and ordinary, knowledge-based skills that required repetitive tasks are about to be comprehensively uprooted and changed. As more and more of us work all the way through to our 70s, the impact on every one of us will be immense. We won't be able to simply opt out of this change and say it doesn't have any impact on me – unless of course we want to make do with low-skilled, low-wage service economy jobs that will absolutely **not** make you wealthier! Be on the right side of the coming changes and invest in your personal capital now.

21 Network to build personal capital

> 'You have to dig a well before you can draw water from it.'
> Richie Norton

> 'Networking is not about just connecting people. It's about connecting people with people, people with ideas, and people with opportunities.' Michele Jennae

> 'Today, the lines between mentoring and networking are blurring. Welcome to the world of mentworking.' Julie Winkle Giulioni

> 'Networking is an essential part of building wealth.'
> Armstrong Williams

> 'My Golden Rule of Networking is simple: Don't keep score.'
> Harvey Mackay

The new networked world

The stunning revelations by former US security consultant and now whistleblower Edward Snowden have prompted an increasingly frenzied and anxious debate about how 'private' we can possibly hope to be in our 24/7, 'always on', technologically enabled world. This debate – with the consensus coalescing around the increasing impossibility of privacy – opens up all sorts of questions and worries but I think it also opens up all sorts of possibilities and opportunities, many of which can be used to help build your personal capital.

At its most basic I would contend that the Internet and information technology generally is making us more 'social' as creatures and forcing us to become more collaborative, although I'm not sure everyone would agree with that contention especially if they – like me – have teenagers whose idea of 'communicating' with each other is to text or Facebook each other while sitting in the same room together!

But social doesn't have to be about talking, merely about sharing and then using those titbits of information to develop something new, something better. Those titbits of information might actually end up sitting on the NSA's servers or they might spark a debate among friends. That debate might then spin out to a wider circle and before we know it a new 'collective' idea (or meme as some have called it) has emerged almost out of nowhere.

I think it's no coincidence that every phase of massive societal wealth accumulation through history has been accompanied by some new form of communication, usually involving communicating an idea of some sort, be it religious or one based on prices!

Many moons ago I looked at the rise of the coffee shop in the early modern London of the 17th century. These entrepôts of hot coffee served as talking shops for the new entrepreneurial elites emerging off the back of mercantile trade routes that spanned the world. Eventually these meeting-places turned into exchanges and the rest is financial history.

In each phase of the Industrial Revolution we see similar patterns, involving postal services, telegraphs, telephones, and then the Internet and computers. And in each phase of innovation the sharing of ideas has become easier, more instantaneous and more global. Now we stand on the edge of another era in which every thought can be shared and discussed – and dissected – instantaneously.

This abundance of communication possibilities and channels puts us in a difficult position though. Increasingly, we need to choose which channel we'll use to communicate. Also, it forces us to be more sparing with our communications, choosing which type of 'interaction' to use in order to develop our personal brand. Maybe one might use blogs to develop our 'thought leadership' skills whereas we might use networking events to hone our personal skills and develop a marketing strategy.

In my humble opinion, networking is now one of the biggest challenges facing any smart person looking to build up their personal capital. They can't remain utterly private anymore and nor should they if they want to succeed. They have to choose to open themselves up, but they also have to choose their moments, their channels/forums and they have to shape their message.

For me, networking is about many things, not least about accelerating luck and serendipity. It's about putting oneself about in an intelligent manner, meeting people who will help create opportunity for you, allowing you in turn to develop your personal capital. But it's also crucially a collaborative affair; it's about giving as well as taking. In simple terms, repeated interaction encourages cooperation. People who repeatedly come into contact with each other tend to develop positive relationships, especially when they share a common goal.

It is absolutely not about immediate gratification and instant sales wins. Make yourself more valuable to others and you create your own value in an increasingly networked, globalized marketplace. And as your network expands, so your network of contacts and their contacts in turn become immensely larger and more valuable. Remember that the average professional knows 3,500 people directly… and each of those people has a similar number of contacts.

The power of networking operates in a similar fashion to compounding, an endlessly increasing power law that makes you wealthier. Your challenge is to work out the gaps in your own personal capital, and then understand how to use networks to make you wealthier.

DITCH THE PITCH

If you do decide to focus on physical events (a sensible move in my opinion), remember that these are not sales pitches. Great networking is all about constant collaboration and sharing of ideas. Indirectly it is also about discrete personal marketing, especially around your personal brand. What it is not is an opportunity to thrust your latest business plan into the hands of some poor unsuspecting acquaintance you've just met over coffee. Unless you've been specifically told to bring along a PowerPoint brochure detailing your latest brilliant idea, I'd leave it at home! If you do discover someone who will be enormously useful for your career, I'd also go out of my way never to be too forward on the first meeting. Get to know them first, let them understand who you are and then talk properly to them on the second meeting – between the two of you over a coffee!

WATCH THAT BODY LANGUAGE

In my experience body language and voice pitch account for more than two-thirds of the battle when it comes to networking events. Tone counts as does a handshake, a smile and being polite and empathetic. What doesn't count is a) how you dress unless it says something really important about you; b) how much you generally brown nose; and c) how important you make yourself sound.

Networking events accentuate the physical and behavioural traits that most of us keep hidden away! To combat this you need to be relaxed, go in to these events confident but not cocky and be open to listening to other people. The last thing anyone wants to meet at these events is some crushing bore who constantly talks everyone else under the table.

One last secret on behaviour – humour usually goes down a storm. Remember everyone else is probably as nervous/anxious as you are, so a smart joke loosens everyone up.

THE FOLLOW-UP

Remember the follow-up and cherish the business card. It's a simple rule but so many people make a big mistake by not being prepared for the follow-up. Make sure you have enough cards going in, and then make sure you carefully collect the cards of acquaintances and contacts afterwards. When you get back to work or home, copy in (or scan in) the details of the people you like and then make a note to reach out to those who you clicked with most. But don't do it the next day. Wait a day and then just send them a short greeting (not some long rambling email detailing your life history) and where relevant always try to get them to meet up for a coffee at some later stage. Crucially, don't expect those follow-up meetings to generate any 'wins' or 'marketing successes' for at least a few weeks, if not months. You have to invest time in networking and a sensible strategy of building your personal capital through better contacts takes years to pay off!

Putting it all together

I'm a great believer in networking and have found it enormously valuable in my own career and business, although I sometimes also suffer from networking fatigue. That occasional weariness has made me much more selective about how I meet people. I've increasingly tried to define my own network and focus more on face to face through events. I also think that networking works best if you combine it with associated strategies such as developing your own brand built around thought leadership i.e. you're the go-to person if acquaintances have a specific problem or challenge that you are very knowledgeable about.

As you become more discriminating about networking you also become demanding of your 'friends', 'contacts' and 'acquaintances'. We all need to be very aware that people tend to associate with others similar to themselves. That's both good (we can all be useful) and bad (we all speak and think the same way). I also can't help but think that it's better to hang out with people better than you… as one friend once said to me 'you'll drift in their direction'. Crucially, I also think we need to think about networking relationships in three directions, those above you, those below and with your peers. They all matter!

22 A portfolio approach to your career

❝ *'The finest souls are those that have the most variety and suppleness.'* Michel de Montaigne

❝ *'Accept what life offers you and try to drink from every cup. All wines should be tasted; some should only be sipped, but with others, drink the whole bottle.'* Paulo Coelho

❝ *'Variety's the very spice of life, that gives it all its flavour.'* William Cowper

❝ *'A change is as good as a rest.'* Winston Churchill

❝ *'Sour, sweet, bitter, pungent, all must be tasted.'* Chinese proverb

Just one career?

A long time ago in the last century the great British economist John Maynard Keynes imagined a new age of Aquarius where by the end of the 20th century productivity would have increased by so much that we'd all be benefiting from an excess of leisure time **and** an excess of wealth and money.

Unfortunately, a rather more distressing scenario has heaved into view, which is that although the productivity of many core workers has substantially increased, we're actually midway through an 'under-employment' revolution where large numbers of people have shifted from a conventional career with regular 9 to 5 working hours into an irregular, increasingly informal, economy where the terms 'self-employed' and 'in business' are increasingly euphemisms for under-employment, lots of enforced 'down time' and very irregular working patterns where famine tends to follow feast.

This under-employment revolution has been taken to extreme lengths by some employers as they enforce zero hours contracts on their staff, while some younger members of the workforce have never, ever, had a proper full-time job but haphazardly move from one 'freelance' gig to another, barely earning enough to pay their bills… let alone save money for the future.

This shift in employment patterns – accompanied by the structural growth in the numbers of long-term unemployed, usually in their 50s and 60s – is a conscious part of government-sponsored labour market reform throughout the West (with France perhaps being the notable exception).

In many respects it's helped provide some enormous benefits for us all, including more leisure time (not that everyone has wanted it), lower overall short-term unemployment rates (fewer claiming benefits) and greater economic flexibility within the labour force generally.

The flip side of this flexible work revolution is also all-too obvious, especially for young workers (low wages, lack of training) and much older workers (gradual detachment from the labour market for want of appropriate work).

This huge transformation is not about to end any time soon, so we all have to decide how we're individually going to go with the grain of this revolution.

At the core is a challenge that keeps cropping up in this book, time and time again. Do we lower our overall risk levels by diversifying our capital (in this case our personal capital via multiple careers) or do we focus on a particular opportunity and then bet everything on that one job/career, running the risk that you might fail catastrophically?

The tension between diversification and focus is all about personal risk management and if you really want to build your wealth, you need to decide on one or the other. In my experience the **very** richest people have tended to be those who've bet big on one career and one opportunity – and then focused laser-like for many years on battling to achieve success. But by its very nature we only hear about the huge successes and my guess is that for every winner, there's probably at least another ten bitter failures out there who no one has ever heard about. I'd also contend that this unceasing focus on one outcome shouldn't be your only option. In fact, in my experience many wealthy people have taken a diverging approach and built what's called a portfolio career.

This form of work can come in two formats.

The first is a classic portfolio approach as defined by management thinker and writer Charles Handy in his seminal book *The Empty Raincoat*. In this form of portfolio work one might juggle a number of jobs at the same time, with maybe one core 'occupation' and then a number of more entrepreneurial activities on the side.

Yet there is another way of building a portfolio career, familiar to anyone who's ever been in the army – the lifefolio approach, which involves lots of different occupations that change over the duration of your working career. You might for instance sign up for the army in your 20s then leave the forces and work as a security consultant in your 30s and 40s. Maybe in your 40s you're quietly developing a business idea, which you launch and then as that becomes successful you maybe switch over to becoming a consultant in your 50s or 60s or maybe even completely retrain and go into, say, teaching in your later years. In this 'lifefolio' approach you'll be switching between careers as you get older, constantly building up skills, in order to make sure you are as employable as possible when you hit your 50s and 60s – and not left behind in the under-employed segment I described earlier.

Regardless of whether you follow a portfolio approach or my lifefolio approach, most labour market economists think that there'll be a great deal more of it about in the coming decades. The whole jobs-for-life concept is – by and large – well and truly dead, replaced by more part-time jobs and employers looking for flexibility.

HAVE YOU GOT THE SKILLS REQUIRED?

A portfolio approach is absolutely not for everyone. Before you even think about adopting this approach to work and personal capital, draw up a proper analysis or audit of your skills and weaknesses – a sort of personal SWOT analysis (strengths, weaknesses, opportunities, and threats assessment). What should go on your list of personal skills needed to prosper? You need to have a high-risk tolerance level, high self-motivation and personal resilience. You need to be able to self-manage your time, and be constantly curious and always willing to invest in continuous personal development i.e. your personal capital. It goes without saying that you'll be doing a great deal more selling and marketing (of yourself), so be comfortable trumpeting your skills. You also, crucially, need to be willing to seek help from others to help develop your own skills, be open to criticism and new challenges and… above all… be a great multi-tasker.

HAVE AN ANCHOR

Marci Alboher, author of the book *One Person/Multiple Careers*, has developed a smart term that can also be used to describe those practising the portfolio approach – she calls those with multiple work identities 'slashers'. Crucially though, Alboher applauds these entrepreneurial types, she also thinks that they need one or two anchor jobs, which are steady bits of work that allow you to develop new opportunities and services. The other ideas and opportunities orbit around this central anchor, keeping you in business and in food! These anchor jobs also give you enough self-confidence to say no to the time-wasting 'opportunities' that could end up costing you a fortune in time and money.

HAVE A RAINY DAY FUND AND MAKE SURE YOU ARE PROPERLY INSURED

Last but by no means least, before you consider charging down this portfolio approach make sure you have a rainy day fund, aka an emergency capital pot. I'd repeat my central advice, which is that you should aim to have at least a six months' spending money capital reserve, and if you have a separate business account try to make sure that there's an additional reserve there as well, plus an all-important business overdraft facility (in case you really, really need it). Also make sure you have adequate insurance in place to cope with any serious medical ailments or accidents. My suggestion is to take out some form of medical insurance, mortgage protection and critical illness insurance.

Putting it all together

I'm going to finish off this chapter by going back to the words and ideas of Charles Handy, who first developed the idea of the portfolio approach. According to Handy: 'Going portfolio means exchanging full-time employment for independence… I told my children when they were leaving education that they would be well advised to look for customers not bosses… They have "gone portfolio" out of choice, for a time. Others are forced into it, when they get pushed outside by their organization. If they are lucky, their old organization will be the first client in their new portfolio. The important difference is that the price-tag now goes on their produce, not their time.'

I think those twin concepts of independence and focusing on your 'produce' are hugely important. The independence concept is about containing and managing your own risk levels and then seeking your own fate, which I would argue is what characterizes most wealthy people. But I would add one coda to this claim, which is that while it's great to be independent you still need to be social and network like crazy. These interdependent relationships help you source new business and check out new ideas.

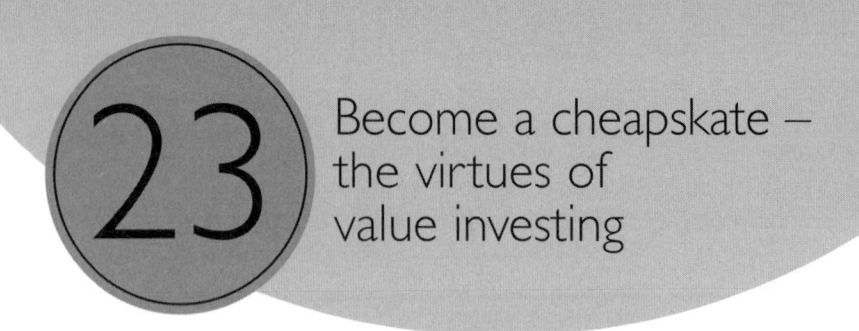

23 Become a cheapskate – the virtues of value investing

> 'The number one idea is to view a stock as an ownership of the business and to judge the staying quality of the business in terms of its competitive advantage. Look for more value in terms of discounted future cash flow than you are paying for. Move only when you have an advantage.' Charlie Munger

> 'Out of clutter, find simplicity. From discord, find harmony. In the middle of difficulty lies opportunity.' Albert Einstein

> 'Value investing is risk aversion.' Seth Klarman

> 'Price is what you pay; value is what you get. Whether we're talking about socks or stocks, I like buying quality merchandise when it is marked down.' Warren Buffett

> 'The pessimist complains about the wind; the optimist expects it to change; the realist adjusts the sails.' William Arthur Ward

Buying a decent quality asset on the cheap

Hedge funds are the new masters of the universe. Now that we can all officially hate the big investment banks, the real movers and shakers of the financial world seem to have moved over into the rarefied world of speculative hedge funds. As we consider these seriously wealthy people most of us probably start to feel a little confused about what these men (and occasional woman!) actually get up to in their day jobs.

What on Earth could justify their huge fees? Aren't some of these hedgies basically rocket scientists who run huge super-computers looking for patterns in the stock market, just as they would search for extraterrestrial life in space? It also seems to be the case that many hedgies are just great traders who watch every ebb and flow of the global financial market and then bet big on the key trends.

Yet there's a secret truth about **the** most successful hedge funds that stands in direct contrast to this master of the universe stuff. Cut away the jargon, and one discovers that many of the most successful hedgies are actually the investing equivalent of cheapskates. If you don't believe me, ponder the world's greatest hedge fund, Berkshire Hathaway and its boss – a certain Warren Buffett. You'll know that Mr Buffett is a) stupendously wealthy; b) probably one of the world's greatest living investors; and c) damned smart in a very humble way. But I'm willing to bet that you didn't think he ran what is in effect a hedge fund. You might say instead 'doesn't Warren run a big insurance company with lots of different industrial businesses and a big portfolio?' Yet scratch away the corporate veneer and one discovers that Buffett and his partner Charlie Munger are really just old-fashioned hedge-fund guys, who use an insurance business to help fund their various investment activities via the cashflow of premiums. It's bog-standard, back to basics investing for the patient contrarian type who is willing to take some super-sized bets on sound businesses.

And the good news is that the academics who've studied this cheapskate investing back up the central message, which is that this 'value' investing works, most of the time. In another chapter we encountered two London-based academics called Professors Elroy Dimson and Paul Marsh who crunched the data and found superior returns from small caps. They've also looked at the returns from cheapskate value investing over the past 50 to 100 years and their results are startling – value investing delivers superior returns with a value strategy kicking in between 1 and 3 per cent per annum consistent annual outperformance over the long term, although those numbers do hide a huge variation in returns with some years producing only mediocre numbers.

And what is the secret of this long-term success? In a nutshell, it's all about buying shares in a good-quality business that has a decent balance sheet, produces decent cash flow, perhaps pays a dividend and is unloved by the market. That's it.

USE A STOCK SCREEN

Hopefully, the reader is scratching his or her head at this point wondering 'why if it's so easy, don't we all do it?'. The first answer is that most investors, especially in big institutions that run things like pension funds, aren't paid to invest in beaten-up stuff that everyone hates.

They also like shiny, sexy businesses that everyone rates highly. Market trends have a strange way of powering big momentum trades and these eddies and currents tend to leave lots of decent businesses in the shallow end with no one watching or caring.

The next bit of good news is that most investors don't really like doing the hard work to track these businesses down. It may, for instance, mean going online, tapping in the word 'stock screen' and then using an automated system that uses key company fundamentals to search for an opportunity – in the UK there's a great one online at www.stockopedia.co.uk.

You might for instance use these quantitative 'stock screens' as they are called to look for businesses with a low share price, lots of cash on the balance sheet, decent profit margins and little debt. These are all what are called fundamental measures that can be inputted into an online system, and then used to spew out a bunch of potential opportunities.

Now comes the bad news!

You have to sift through these lists to find real gems. But for every three or four hopeless candidates you'll find a company whose shares have been unfairly trashed.

FOCUS ON THE CASH FLOW

OK, I'm cutting a few corners as I explain how these screening systems work online (most of them are free by the way!), but in truth they're not really that complicated. They basically take stacks of data from two different sources. The first looks at the business operation through the prism of the profit and loss statement and the related cash flow summary. Basically you are looking to see how much cash this business is producing and whether it's enough to pay the bills, the shareholders and the bank. This analysis needs to be fairly dynamic and you're focusing on the 'flow' of cash through the business and trends over time. It goes without saying that you are looking for a positive dynamic i.e. the business is churning out more and more cash.

The next step involves the balance sheet analysis, which is slightly more about a series of snapshots in time. You'll be looking at the assets (are they really worth what they say they are or are the auditors missing some hidden value) and then comparing them to the liabilities, notably the debts. Hopefully, the assets will be much greater than debts (if the cash reserves are very high, that's even better news). Your last exercise is to then see how the market values this business. Is it underestimating the potential? Or has the market probably got it about right?

BE CONTRARIAN

You'll also need to be patient. Years might go by before the market spots the potential of your chosen share or company. The shares might bob up and down and you'll be worried about your judgement.

But you need to be patient, sure in the knowledge that you've made the right choice.

Understand now why so few professional investors stick with this style of investing?

Thought so! Value investing is all about hard work, measuring the potential for risk and then waiting until your opportunity comes. It's a tough old business and very few institutions can afford to tie up the experts, the money and their collective time in a strategy that can produce terrible returns in bad years. That's why the likes of Warren Buffett are trusted old men who've been doing this kind of stuff for decades. It also explains why some of the greatest hedge fund managers are value investors. They've been at this game for decades, are trusted, have deep reservoirs of knowledge and skill and are left alone to get on to do what they are brilliant at. Crucially, they nearly all have to be deep-seated contrarians who are willing to turn their faces to the market and stick with what they believe in.

The good news is that the institutional barriers to running a value-based strategy aren't as relevant for the ordinary private investor looking to accumulate wealth. You can afford to be contrarian and patient but only if you've done your homework and properly researched and understood the opportunity.

Putting it all together

I don't think the average novice investor should jump head first into value investing. It's a tough old game and it requires knowledge, skill and patience and my advice is to learn by running some fun money on small caps, understand how a company works, properly diversify and generally build up your knowledge of the markets in your 20s and 30s.

Once you've got this basic level of confidence and knowledge, start to experiment with value investing. The challenge is that there aren't that many consistently successful value fund managers out there, so you'll probably have to do most of the work yourself. You'll make lots of mistakes and in particular you'll fall victim to endless value traps, where the market got it right and your unloved gem is actually totally useless.

But experience and mistakes will eventually make you a better investor, and over the years value investing will start to pay off, especially if you put aside a 10 per cent to 20 per cent portion of your risk capital into a value satellite portfolio. If this value investing stuff works and you practise over 20 to 30 years, I'm absolutely convinced it'll deliver at least 2 to 3 per cent annual outperformance over many decades.

Compound those numbers and by the time you retire you could produce a pot of risk capital that is at least double that of your peers.

24 What type of risk are you willing to take?

> 'To dare is to lose one's footing momentarily. To not dare is to lose oneself.' Søren Kierkegaard

> 'I dip my pen in the blackest ink, because I'm not afraid of falling into my inkpot.' Ralph Waldo Emerson

> 'Progress always involves risks. You can't steal second base and keep your foot on first.' Frederick B. Wilcox

> 'Why not go out on a limb? Isn't that where the fruit is?' Frank Scully

> 'Yes, risk-taking is inherently failure-prone. Otherwise, it would be called sure-thing-taking.' Tim McMahon

Deep versus shallow risk

We've already become well acquainted with the concept of risk in this book, noting that taking risks is possibly the only sure-fire way of building wealth over the long term. But risk is also, self-evidently, dangerous and the smart investor and cagey business person alike only ever takes considered, measured risks.

To truly understand the threat posed by risk we first need to give it a little more shape, and explain that risk can come in many different shapes and forms. For me the best distinction between different types of risk comes in a book called *Deep Risk* by the US investment writer (and medical physician) William Bernstein. Mr Bernstein is a brilliant observer of man's economic affairs and can always be relied upon to take the long-term view, based in his case on a detailed historical analysis.

Bernstein argues that investors in particular need to be alive to two forms of risk – shallow risk and deep risk.

Shallow risk is typically experienced by stock market investors in volatile years when shares can go up and down by as much as 30 to 50 per cent per annum. This ebb and flow in the stock market is as natural as night following day, and Bernstein is almost certainly right to suggest that for the investor with a truly long-term horizon (more than 25 to 30 years), shallow risk is worth taking. Investors panic about bad years where they lose, say, 40 per cent of their money, but history suggests that in most cases these terrible years are eventually accompanied by a few good years where most if not all those returns are made up again.

There are widely publicized exceptions to this rule, not least Japanese stock markets where investors are still waiting to recoup their money 20 years later, but most financial markets eventually recover, making good most if not all the losses experienced.

Bernstein also identifies another more deadly form of risk called **deep risk**. This form of risk involves total capital loss, from which there is likely to be no complete recovery – or any recovery at all!

There are many cases of this deep, complete, utter capital loss in the history of the 20th century and I have no doubt there'll be more than a few examples in the 21st century as well! Bernstein suggests that deep risk – involving complete destruction of your risk capital and sometimes even your cash deposits and housing wealth – is associated with the 'four horsemen of the economic apocalypse'.

The first and most deadly threat is **inflation**, where rates increase by more than double digits for a number of years. Bernstein suggests that investors need to be on constant guard because inflation has been a proven killer i.e. the corrosive effect of persistent inflation is that it eats into the 'real' value of your existing wealth.

Next up is a horseman of the financial apocalypse called **deflation**, which is the reverse of inflation i.e. consistently falling prices. The concept of falling prices sounds great fun on first inspection except that in reality it's usually accompanied by chronic economic depression followed by political cataclysm. **Government confiscation** or **expropriation** is the next great worry (especially for those with a predilection for gold) and could vary between Argentine-style pensions grabs through to Bolshevik revolution. This threat is possible but unlikely.

The ultimate threat is **civil war** or just **global war**, which is effectively impossible to predict and generally bad news for all concerned, not least the poor individuals that have to fight it!

For Bernstein, the most likely threat to our personal wealth comes in the form of inflation, where rates, such as the retail price index, hit double-digit percentages for at least a few years if not more!

This risk involves investors thinking long and hard about building some form of inflation protection into everything that they do. In this book we'll look at this concept of inflation protection in much more detail, especially in a later chapter where we'll look at an idea called the Permanent Portfolio, which looks to protect an investor against not only inflation but also deflation and confiscation.

But for now I want investors to recognize that inflation is the most likely deep risk and that they need to do something about it. I also want readers to realize that shallow risk is maybe worth taking if you have the right time horizon.

DON'T CONFUSE OBVIOUS SHORT-TERM VOLATILITY FOR LONG-TERM HIDDEN RISK

We've already discussed the idea of myopia in this book, which involves an excessive focus on short-term risk – statistically captured by the variability of a price over a period of time, measured against the average.

We obsess about what is in effect visible risk, evident from financial markets that trade in things like shares. We panic at sudden 5 or 10 per cent moves in the price of a share and then fuelled by our short-termism and myopia take the view that this volatility is not appropriate.

For the truly risk averse (who are unlikely ever to be truly wealthy) that might make sense, but for me these risks are obvious and unsurprising. You shouldn't be stupid and take lots and lots of these risks but losses/drawdowns go with the territory.

In my humble opinion, we all ignore much more hidden, deep risks, where societies and individuals fail to take certain calculated risks, effectively settling for the predictable. Young people who don't take risks are in effect handing the responsibility for wealth creation either to someone else, the government or future generations. Societies that don't take risks and demand immediate gratification followed by generous benefits and guaranteed pensions are also passing the buck.

Economics teaches us that this short-term focus eventually results in a political form of deep risk, for which read 'economic crisis', usually involving high debt levels, punitive taxation and some form of government confiscation possibly followed by inflation. Individuals looking to build up various pots of capital should regularly review the hidden forms of risk and consider what impact it may have on them.

YOUNG INVESTORS NEED TO TAKE SHALLOW RISK

We've already discussed the idea of different time horizons in an earlier chapter, suggesting that younger people need to take some considered risks. For me that involves a simple, basic truth – younger people and especially those under the age of 40 need to focus on investing in shares. In fact I'd argue that anyone under the age of 40 who has built up risk capital (maybe in a tax-free savings account or pension) should have 100 per cent of their assets in shares and risky stuff. More importantly, they should be willing to suffer losses of 20 per cent or more in a bad year. They should in fact take those bad years as a signal to invest **more** not less!

These young people can afford to take the shallow risk that Bernstein discusses and they should be brave and courageous about the ebb and flow of markets. Ideally, I'd suggest ignoring the constant news flow and only occasionally looking at your share/funds account once every few months. You may have a bad year or two, but you've got many more decades to make up those losses!

OLDER INVESTORS MUST PROTECT AGAINST DEEP RISK, ESPECIALLY INFLATION

Any investor over the age of 60 almost certainly needs to take a different approach to risk, focusing on the dangers of Bernstein's deep risk. Rampant inflation – the most likely risk – is not great for anyone, but most young people will have time to recover from its perils. They might even benefit in odd ways, as the economic order is re-arranged. But inflation absolutely destroys accumulated wealth for pensioners. It kills every one of your post-retirement plans stone cold dead. Crucially, as your ability to build up personal capital via work is severely constrained as you're now effectively out of the jobs game, you'll have no way of compensating for the loss of wealth generated by inflation.

Putting it all together

Within the rarefied world of investment analysis, risk has been put on a pedestal and turned inside out by quantitative analysis using statistics. Ideas like risk budgets and risk parity abound, having been constructed using the idea that risk can be measured by the periodic volatility up and down of a share or a bond (which are usually much less volatile) expressed as a percentage. This analysis is not without its strengths but for me the greatest risks are the hidden risks that destroy permanently your capital and your wealth.

These deep risks are sometimes about capital loss (through, say, government confiscation or the cumulative effect of inflation) but we should also be alive to those involving an opportunity cost i.e. your fear of something led you to avoid taking an action, which eventually makes you poorer.

Anyone who ignores the opportunity presented by shallow risk is making as big a mistake as the investor who is oblivious to deep risk and takes no effort to preserve their capital. Both involve opportunities foregone, with destructive long-term effects – an impoverished retirement in both cases!

25) Ride the tech tiger

> 'There will come a time when it isn't "They're spying on me through my phone" anymore. Eventually, it will be "My phone is spying on me".' Philip K. Dick

> 'The production of too many useful things results in too many useless people.' Karl Marx

> 'All of the biggest technological inventions created by man – the airplane, the automobile, the computer – says little about his intelligence, but speaks volumes about his laziness.' Mark Kennedy

> 'Never before in history has innovation offered promise of so much to so many in so short a time.' Bill Gates

> 'You can't just ask customers what they want and then try to give that to them. By the time you get it built, they'll want something new.' Steve Jobs

Technology and wealth: a tricky affair

If you want to understand the pace of technological change in the few decades since the Second World War, just sit down with your extended family at Christmas and ask what everyone used to do to relax during an average evening in winter.

My generation, Generation X born after 1965, probably had TV, a book and an electric fire in the lounge... oh and the pub down the road for the older teenagers. My parents' generation had radio (wireless), books and a coal fire as well as the national network of workingmen's clubs on every street corner. My kids have smartphones and online TV delivered via tablets, which they all watch in different rooms of a house, heated by net-savvy smart controls, with the Internet delivered by Wi-Fi and power cables. And all the pubs are closing down as we speak!

Technological change has I think impacted us all in very profound ways and yet there is some evidence that it isn't necessarily making us all much wealthier. No one would for one minute question the profound productivity changes unleashed by steam engines, the motor car, electricity and global air transport – to name just a few disruptive technologies. The Internet has undoubtedly created wealth in various hot spots and made us all more interconnected but a growing number of economists – including Tyler Cowen whose ideas are the subject of another chapter – would argue that more recent innovations have produced increasingly diminished society-wide benefits. In simple terms, we've picked most of the 'low-hanging fruit' of technological advancement and we're now largely pioneering technologies that are great to have but hardly 'must have'!

This criticism of technology doesn't go unchallenged, with many researchers arguing that we're underestimating the profound consequences of permanently 'online' societies, with accompanying global real-time information flows. Tech cynics might argue that technological change might be kicking in say just 0.5 per cent to 1 per cent a year in additional productivity improvements to our national economies on an annual basis but tech enthusiasts (and more than a few academics) reckon the real number is much more than 1.5 per cent per annum in GDP growth terms.

The much bigger point though is that technology and its impact on our wealth is problematic, as we've already noted in our chapter on the machine trap. I don't want to rehearse the pros and cons of technology in these pages. Instead I want to make a number of uncontroversial observations about innovation and its impact on the average reader.

The first uncontested claim is that once a profound technological revolution is unleashed upon the world, very few of the army of creators and innovators (as well as owners of those businesses) actually enjoy long-term benefits from the subsequent transformation. Of course, Bill Gates benefited from his software technology but economists have estimated that 99 per cent of the total economic benefits from technological innovation (largely through enhancing productivity) actually end up being enjoyed by the wider society!

Our next claim is that I would contend that it's extremely difficult to predict what the next disruptive technologies will be and who will be the dominant players in each new wave of change.

My last claim is that technology is – in our world at least – the chief driver of what has been called creative destruction, a wonderfully elegant term used to describe the great waves of industrial and economic change unleashed over time utilizing new productivity-enhancing innovations. The problem is that creative destruction has a strange way of humbling once mighty organizations and destroying entire career structures. If we're to focus most of our energy on creating wealth through our personal capital, we need to have in place some strategies for dealing with innovation and its impact on our career.

TECHNOLOGY AS A STOCK MARKET INVESTMENT

The most obvious way to accumulate wealth through harnessing technology is to invest in it through stocks and shares. Who doesn't know someone who's supposedly made a small killing by betting on the latest technology-based initial public offering (IPO), a process by which a company such as Facebook or Twitter is listed on the stock market.

Many of these IPOs become insanely popular and the markets end up valuing these relatively new businesses at simply unbelievable multiples, with the result that the share price frequently starts to slide soon after hitting the market.

My advice is to ignore these tech IPOs, and not to invest in individual technology-driven stocks, unless you have some special inside knowledge or skillset. It's largely a mug's game and you'll end up destroying your wealth. I'd always make use of a fund manager within the technology space, as they're better equipped to understand the key trends in the industry.

TECHNOLOGY AS A BUSINESS CHALLENGE

Creative destruction powered by wave upon wave of technological change is a marvel to behold and creates huge opportunities for everyone from the eBay seller sitting at home connected to the web through to the hot tech start-up in a garage.

Yet it's also incredibly difficult to generalize on what you should or shouldn't do as an entrepreneur. What I would say is that in my experience the greatest wealth seems to be generated by two generic opportunity sets – helping businesses integrate new ideas and technologies within existing processes as well as teaching and working with people/businesses to use new technology more efficiently.

Veritable legions of highly paid consultants have been unleashed upon the world to make sure that either staff know how to use a new technological product or that an existing sales/admin system works properly with some amazing new Internet-based service. Most of these consulting types are very different from the rocket scientist types who develop the technology – they're people-orientated professionals who understand how business and people within these structures work on a day-to-day basis.

TECHNOLOGY AS PART OF YOUR PERSONAL CAPITAL

It's also impossible to give any sensible advice about how technology can work around your career, as every single reader will be impacted in a unique way by technological innovation, but I would make one small, very practical observation which is that if nothing else you need to use technology to cultivate your personal brand. In simple terms, make sure your life on any sort of social networking tool is professional and appropriate. Practically that means building your digital presence through Twitter, blogging, Instagram, Quora and skill-specific centres like GitHub. I'd also suggest that blogging should offer you an outlet for your interests, thoughts and writing. Start now – even a little will make you far more desirable than someone who isn't active at all.

Putting it all together

It would be terrifically easy to conclude this chapter by giving you some utterly fatuous advice about embracing technology by going back to school/college and learning a new job that involves working with the next generation of smarter machines.

Unfortunately, my suspicion is that what you learn in college will probably be partly or completely obsolete by the time you actually get anywhere near technology as practised in the big, bad outside world.

In my experience the technology industry is moving so fast that products invented today will almost certainly be superseded by newer improved versions in almost no time at all.

The lesson is not to focus on learning about a specific technology as such. In particular I'd be worried that the very latest cutting-edge technologies will be heavily protected. That means that if you want to work at bleeding edge outfits, you'll probably have to have an incredibly niche set of skills or will probably end up learning the details on the job anyway!

Education courses are unlikely to have access to these new technologies.

Better in my mind to show future employers that you are:

- flexible and adaptable and have numerous work backgrounds/work identities
- are willing to constantly learn new skills to enhance your personal capital, and
- you have real experience in a very practical way of the challenges facing businesses in today's hectic, connected world.

26 Emerging markets?

> 'This world is clearly emerging before our eyes. The shifts ahead, the opportunities ahead are massive.' Carly Fiorina

> 'With a population of more than 600 million people, an emerging middle class that is driving strong consumption, and a robust and resilient economy, Southeast Asia presents a compelling growth opportunity for Starbucks.' Howard Schultz

> 'Asia is rich in people, rich in culture and rich in resources. It is also rich in trouble.' Hubert Humphrey

> 'Africa will thrive.' Bono

> 'Courage taught me no matter how bad a crisis gets, Mexico isn't going to disappear, and that if I have confidence in the country, any sound investment will eventually pay off.' Carlos Slim

Think long term and follow the people...

There's an old adage in investment, which is that if you are seeking opportunity you should go where the 'growth is', which simply means that if you're looking for capital gains, as an investor you should focus on where top-line sales and bottom-line profits are growing the fastest. This adage powers the whole idea of investing in what are called growth stocks (sexy technology businesses, for instance, that are growing their profits like crazy) but it's also hugely important for what I think is perhaps **the** most important investment trend of our age, namely emerging markets.

All about us a grand global transformation is underway, involving concurrent waves of urbanization, industrialization and consumerism throughout what was once called the Third World but is now regarded as the developing world, although a slightly less loaded term, namely 'emerging markets' has arisen to take its place. These emerging markets are countries – the likes of China, Brazil, India and beyond – that are growing at a phenomenal rate and could be tomorrow's economic superpowers. Investment bank Goldman Sachs even contends that the Chinese economy will be the biggest in the world within the next ten years!

I'm not going to barrage you with statistics but here are some big numbers to get you thinking. The emerging world currently plays host to:

- 82 per cent of the world's population
- 75 per cent of the land
- 63 per cent of total industrial resources, and
- just 36 per cent of total global GDP.

Given this huge macro-economic opportunity, is it any surprise that these emerging economies are growing fast? Over the period from 2002 to 2012 these developing nations produced an average growth rate of 6.5 per cent per annum, while developing Asia (places like China) churned out growth at 8.5 per cent per annum. By contrast, the average global growth rate was a tad under 4 per cent while the 'advanced economies' produced rates of just over 1.5 per cent on average.

Go where the growth is… go emerging markets!

And that proclamation has also been relevant for investors in things like shares. Since the index firm MSCI first introduced its EM index back in the late 1980s (EM stands for emerging markets), average investor returns from money in the index have averaged 20 per cent per annum (for the period from 1990 through to 2012). In 70 per cent of those 23 years, EM stock markets have produced a positive return and even over the past 10 years annualized returns have hit 7.5 per cent – not bad for a global market that's scared of taking risks. Over the last five years by contrast average annual returns have been more impressive at 13 per cent p.a.

But here's the rub about all these dizzying statistics.

Just because EM equities have produced amazing returns for the past 20 years doesn't mean that they'll continue to produce equally amazing numbers over the next 20 years. Optimists will beg to differ and observe that when we look at economic forecasts that growth differential is likely to be even more pronounced over the next decade!

Yet academics have discovered a rather amazing fact, namely that just because a nation is growing at a fast rate (as measured by things like the GDP growth rate), doesn't mean that investors in local markets will enjoy identical (positive) returns. In fact there's some evidence to suggest that rates of return from shares and GDP growth are **inversely** related i.e. faster-growing countries have poorly performing stock markets whereas boring, slow-growth countries (like, say, Belgium) have produced better investor returns. Many investors argue that boring Belgians are good whereas racy China is a potential growth trap!

I think there's a huge amount of truth in this academic criticism. In my humble opinion the bottom line is that it's a lazy assumption that just because a country like China is growing fast, that means its local stock market will grow at the same speed. Investors chasing growth prospects have to work harder to find the opportunity for creating wealth.

FIND THE RIGHT MARKETS

Many investors attracted to the growth potential of emerging markets simply push their money into a major EM index tracking fund, hoping to catch some of the returns from this global societal transformation. I think that's a potentially dangerous tactic for the reason I've just mentioned above.

I think you need to be very discriminating and focus on three simple ideas. The first is that some countries have more potential than others, thus you might need a country-by-country approach or you might even consider combining that with a sector-by-sector approach i.e. only invest in, say, emerging market consumer or utility firms. The next criterion is to look at the corporate governance in each country and see whether local businesses respect their outside shareholders properly. Do they pay a dividend for instance if profits boom or do they just keep ploughing money into yet more shiny new factories? Are there western directors on the board to represent 'our' interests and are the accountants respected? My last consideration is price and value i.e. is the local market or sector competitively priced relative to the risks and the flow of profits. In my experience some national markets such as India are nearly always highly priced (given the risks) whereas some other countries (say, South Korea) represent much better value for money.

FOCUS ON FRONTIER MARKETS

Investors looking for opportunity need to think long and hard about that national variation point from the previous paragraph. I think certain regions such as Asia, for instance, are far more attractive than, say, Latin America. But beyond this I also believe that there's an even more interesting gaggle of nations that are smaller than these emerging markets, which are called frontier markets. These countries – mostly in Asia, Africa and the Middle East – boast smaller stock markets, more illiquid stocks and, in my view, keener valuations. I think the prospects for these small, fringe markets are absolutely huge and investors haven't quite woken up to the opportunity yet. If I had one big bet for the next 30 years, it would be on a massive stock market boom in Africa.

THINK BONDS, FOREIGN EXCHANGE AND PROPERTY

One last observation on the relationship between top-line national growth (lots of it in the developing world) and bottom-line profits. Investors quickly make the link into shares and equities as the main way of capturing this transformation but in my experience local bonds (issued by governments and local businesses) might actually represent a bigger opportunity as does local property i.e. second homes for holidays. Typically, those countries deemed as risky (most emerging markets and certainly most frontier states) are forced to offer a big yield on their bonds if they hope to attract western investors. But as these countries become more advanced, those yields decline and the price of the bonds go up. Equally in property, early stage buyers have to contend with poor transport infrastructure and bad local governance, not to say lack of local mortgages, but as the state develops everything changes. Local mortgage markets emerge, and house prices shoot up. More tourists start to flood in, improving transport links. Cue increased local house prices, especially as more western investors start to show an interest.

As an investor who's long put money to work in these developing nations, my biggest gains have been from buying quality properties in countries that are regarded as 'primitive' (in my case, Turkey in the 1990s), local currency bonds from countries regarded as too risky (in my case, emerging markets bond funds) and frontier markets in Africa.

Putting it all together

Emerging market investments are, obviously, for the long term. You absolutely shouldn't invest in EM equities, bonds or property on a 1-to-5-year time frame. Ideally this is a 10-to-30-year proposition. For the more adventurous among you, I would be radical and recommend that you have at least 30 per cent of your portfolio exposed to emerging markets either directly (through local investments) or indirectly through, say, western businesses such as Unilever and Diageo, which have huge local interests. In fact I know of younger investors who have told me that they have all their risk capital focused on these growth economies, a bold plan which I can't help but think is the smart call for the patient among you! But if you are going to make this kind of big, focused bet do your research first! Pick your countries, your stocks and your kinds of investment (houses, bonds and equities) carefully.

27 The liquidity challenge

> 'What everybody is focused on right now is liquidity... People are passing up I think pretty solid opportunities that are relatively illiquid because of the uncertainty with the investor base.' Phil Falcone

> 'Ability to handle liquidity is a major advantage for long-term investors.' Jeremy Grantham

> 'What we know about the global financial crisis is that we don't know very much.' Paul Samuelson

> 'When there is a crisis, that's when some are interested in getting out and that's when we are interested in getting in.' Carlos Slim

> 'I buy on the assumption that they could close the market the next day and not reopen it for five years.' Warren Buffett

Why illiquidity can work to your advantage

You may remember the global financial crisis of 2008 and 2009. In truth, a large part of the blame for this truly terrifying financial and political event rested on a technical question based around liquidity.

In very simple terms, many large institutions (banks, hedge funds) nearly went bust because they held a planet-sized load of illiquid assets on their balance sheets. These illiquid funds and structures included mysterious-sounding mortgage debt structures and even more mysterious options-based structures that paid off if a debt lapsed into default. Lots of acronyms were bandied about but the essential fact was that at the precise moment these institutions needed to get their hands on some ready cash, they couldn't sell these notes, structures and funds i.e. they were illiquid and couldn't be readily converted into cash unless the seller was willing to take a massive haircut on the price ('marked-to-market' in the jargon).

Why my interest in these illiquid structures, and what on earth has it to do with readers looking to accumulate wealth? Well, many fortunes were indeed lost in 2008 and 2009 because the so-called professionals (and their clients) had bought all sorts of toxic, illiquid rubbish that collapsed in value. Fortunes cratered and many were made destitute. But the unwritten story of this crisis was that eventually vast fortunes were also made (by hedge fund managers such as John Paulson) from these illiquid investments. Investors with a long time horizon and a willingness to sit tight during market turbulence meant that smart, patient types – who'd done their research – were able to pick up what they thought were great assets for just a few tens of cents on the dollar. Eventually, when some semblance of normality returned, this 'junk' sky-rocketed in price.

Let me make this very clear. Many of the very greatest investments have been made by courageous brave patient investors who've bought the right asset – usually an illiquid one – when everyone else is capitulating and turning their shares or bonds into ready cash.

But there is an obvious risk or two... as you'd expect! If you don't do your research you may actually end up buying junk that absolutely no one wants, and thus you can't sell. So like everything you have to do your research. Also, a strategy of buying illiquid assets is **absolutely not** for the investor who a) worries and frets, and b) needs cash at regular intervals. If either of these apply to you, skip this chapter, but not before you read the next few paragraphs!

Illiquidity in the technical language of the trade gives you a premium in terms of returns if you are patient and careful. That premium – a profit – takes a while to realize and is not without risk but it incontrovertibly can and does produce spectacular gains.

I'd focus on four key types of illiquidity, with a view to either completely avoiding or alternatively using as an opportunity, depending on your attitude towards risk.

1. Assets that are inherently difficult to sell very quickly when everyone wants to head for the exit (think commercial property).
2. Funds where there's what's called restricted liquidity imposed by the fund managers. Would you want to be in a hedge fund or private equity LLP where everyone is trying to sell and the price is plummeting but no one can sell because they're all locked in (hedge funds and private equity)? Thought not!
3. Assets where there's no sensible secondary market i.e. a place where buyers and sellers come together to set a price after they've initially bought the investment. This could be shares, bonds or even financial products such as life endowments. I'd also include emotional assets such as art.
4. Last but by no means least, you need to be careful about assets that are normally liquid but can become very unfashionable. This could result in the 'normal' secondary market seizing up and the spread between the asking/selling price turns into a veritable black hole of epic proportions.

If I've made illiquidity sound a tad scary, good! It can be and it needs careful management. Yet I also think all the best investments I've ever made have been in illiquid stuff that at some point everyone (but me) hated.

DO THE HARD WORK: OF TIME HORIZONS, RISK BUDGETS AND RESEARCH

I think the adventurous investor looking to make a big difference to their wealth should draw up a mental plan based on three simple ideas. The first is that they should divide their risk capital into liquidity and risk-based budgets i.e. the main bucket should be lower risk, higher liquidity while a satellite bucket could be for illiquid, high-risk stuff. They should then accept a time horizon of between five and ten years for the illiquid assets and stick to it. Next up they do their research. To identify real opportunity in illiquid areas requires real focus on determination. In strategy 3, I explain where I spend much of my time hunting down opportunities. Your knowledge might suggest a different area. Maybe you really know property markets or perhaps you understand technology. Whatever your specialist skill set, focus, focus, focus.

BUBBLE-WATCH AND KEEP CASH IN RESERVE

My next strategy is connected to a later chapter that focuses on bubble-watching. For the purposes of this chapter we're simply going to observe that markets go through unrelenting phases of caution, greed, fear and then paranoia. The last phase (paranoia, which in turn is helped along by capitulation where every sane person gives up the ghost and sells) is what we're looking for.

According to economists, the illiquidity premia (the extra return you get from investing in difficult-to-sell stuff) massively increases in crisis situations. How do you know when we've hit this awful phase? Newspaper articles tell you we're in deep **** and the spread between the selling and buying price becomes cavernous. Having done your research already, you know the difference between a diamond in the rough and genuine junk! You should also have some cash in reserve, ready and waiting for you to pounce and buy your asset/s. Once purchased, think about going away and making lots of pots of tea and probably get on with the rest of your life for a few years. Eventually confidence returns, those spreads collapse and the underlying assets shoot up in price. Mission accomplished!

CLOSED END FUNDS AND INVESTMENT TRUSTS

Plenty of hedge funds and private equity outfits operate a version of my strategy, helped along by amazing research departments and lots of money (some of it cheap debt). But you can run this illiquidity trade using more accessible markets such as listed investment funds or trusts. In the US these are technically called Closed End Funds, while in the UK we call them investment trusts. Many of these funds invest in slightly more exotic stuff like foreign property or emerging markets shares. When panic erupts the price of the shares in these specialized funds collapses. Suddenly a big difference opens up between the share price (as established by the market makers) and the total value of all the fund's assets on a per share basis (called the net asset value per share). Say the total net assets per share are £1 but the share price trades at 50p – this is a huge discount to the 'book value' (the total assets of the fund) of 50 per cent. Sometimes this massive discount (not uncommon by the way) is entirely justified largely because the assets really are junk and there are literally **no buyers** of the shares. But sometimes these discounts become stupid given the quality of the assets. More than a few investors patiently look for quality funds on a big discount and then they buy, waiting for the difference between the book value and the share price to narrow.

> ### Putting it all together
>
> Don't invest in illiquid assets if you're in your 70s or you are using money that you may need to access in the next year or so. Use my four features of illiquidity to check your existing assets and make sure you're not vulnerable to these risks.
>
> But if you are adventurous and willing to take risks I'd say that the biggest gains you'll ever make will come from illiquid assets and so if you do commit to this form of investing, put a decent chunk of your assets to work (say 10 or even 20 per cent) and also make sure you have some cash reserves so that you can put money to work as markets ebb and flow. And understand bubbles as well as the ebb and flow of markets, a subject we'll touch on a bit later.

28 Delight in the humble dividend

> 'Do you know the only thing that gives me pleasure? It's to see my dividends coming in.' John D. Rockefeller

> 'I don't like stock buybacks. I think if a company has the money to buy their stock back, then they should take that and increase the dividends. Send it back to the stockholder. Let them invest their money again from the dividends.' T. Boone Pickens

> 'I use dividends rather than earnings because they more accurately reflect whether a company's board feels good about its business, balance sheet, ability to sustain working capital costs, and its future in general. Earnings tell you nothing about that, and can be manipulated.' Ian Nakamoto

> 'A cow for her milk. A hen for her eggs. And a stock, by heck, for her dividends.' John Burr Williams

> 'I can calculate the motions of the heavenly bodies but not the movements of the stock market.' Isaac Newton after he had been wiped out in a stock market crash

Why the dividend is so important

Long-term historical studies have shown that anything between 30 and 95 per cent of the total extra return from investing in a share or a stock market (via fund) can be traced back to the regular dividend cheque. These annual or twice yearly payments are made by a company to its shareholders out of the cash profits produced by the business.

In principle, we can trace a fairly straightforward linear relationship between the growth in an economy, increased profits and bulging dividends paid to shareholders. If we assume that the long-term trend growth of the US economy for instance over the past 100 years has been around 2.5 per cent per annum (over the period between 1947 and 2013 this GDP growth rate was actually closer to 3.2 per cent), then we can say with some certainty that corporate profits (called earnings) are likely to grow by between 0 and 2 per cent in excess of this GDP growth rate. Dividends are likely to grow at a rate of about 1 per cent above that growth rate in profits i.e. as profits grow, companies tend to have more money available to boost dividends.

Once we weave some magic into the numbers we can see that the long-term dividend growth rate on average for most US quoted companies has probably been between 3 and 6 per cent per annum.

If we now look back at the long-term historical records for total shareholder returns (capital gains and total dividends paid, lumped together as a total return) for investing in US shares we can see an average long-term return of between 6 and 8 per cent per annum, most of which is related to that dividend payout and its growth over time.

But dividends get even better.

First off, as we're about to discover dividends are easy to reinvest back into the shares of a company that pay them out. How often does the financial services industry offer up what amounts to a brilliant free lunch for the ordinary customer?

Next up, dividends also tend to grow in line with – if not in excess – of inflation. This should make some sense, as most big companies that pay a generous dividend are able to increase their prices to consumers at least **in line** with if not in excess of inflation rates.

Lastly, dividends tend to be fairly stable, which simply means that while a share price can shoot up and down on a daily basis, most dividend payouts tend to stay steady if not actually **increase** over time.

So, all in all, dividends seem like a fabulous idea for making you wealthy. Yet there is a fly in the ointment which is that every once in a while, especially in a recession, companies might struggle to pay those regular cash cheques to investors, in which case the dividend might have to be 'stopped'.

Investors hate this non-payment of dividends, which is why even those companies that are somehow forced to stop paying, tend to do their damnedest to restart again soon after the recession has finished, making good for their past misdeeds by promising a progressively increasing dividend cheque in the future!

FOCUS ON THE DIVIDEND YIELD… INTELLIGENTLY

The bottom line for most investors is that a focus on dividend-paying stocks makes a huge amount of sense, to such an extent that we should focus on these 'high-yielding' companies as a core part of our portfolio of equity assets (stocks and shares). I think this particularly makes sense for the largest part of your portfolio of risky assets that invests in the largest companies in the most developed markets around the world i.e. the US, the UK, the Eurozone and Switzerland.

Yet you also need to hunt down high-yielding businesses, intelligently. One challenge is very high dividend levels can sometimes indicate that a company is in trouble, with a poor balance sheet (loss of debts) whose share price has collapsed in value i.e. this collapse in value has pushed up the dividend yield. As the share price collapses, the dividend yield as a percentage keeps growing until the company is forced to admit that its balance sheet is so bad it can't afford to pay out any cash to shareholders. So, be careful about unrealistically high dividend payouts and always take some time to check out the balance sheet and investigate any signs that the company is heading into financial trouble!

REINVEST THE DIVIDEND

Here's a simple idea. Rather than take the regular income from dividends, why not use the cash to buy even more shares in the company? Dividend reinvestment is dead simple and can boost that long-term return from investing in equities – to the point that some studies suggest that over the past 100 years nearly 95 per cent of the total return from risky shares can be accounted for by dividends and their reinvestment.

Two simple mechanisms stand out for dividend reinvestment. The first is that most very big corporates in the US and the UK offer their shareholders the chance to reinvest the regular cash dividends in more shares in the company, usually at close to zero cost. These dividend reinvestment plans (called DRIPs) are quite simply the greatest financial freebie ever! Use them as much as possible. Stockbrokers may also offer a similar facility for shares owned via your account, but charges may be a tiny bit higher.

If you invest in a fund that is tracking a key market, consider taking the accumulation option – in exchange-traded funds that track an index like the S&P 500, this is also called the total return option. In both cases you are rolling over the dividends from the fund back into more shares, again at close to zero cost.

INTERNATIONAL DIVERSIFICATION FOR DIVIDENDS

In this book we constantly keep returning to the idea of diversification as a way of controlling risk within your risk capital, but it is hugely important when it comes to investing in dividend-paying companies and their stocks. I would suggest that you make sure you are internationally diversified both at the company level (companies from different stock markets around the world that pay a dividend) and in a fund i.e. make sure you are investing in a mix of internationally diversified dividend equity funds. More and more Asian companies, for instance, are now looking to pay a dividend to their shareholders and we can generally see a positive move around the world to reward investors with a regular income.

Putting it all together

The acute reader will have spotted by now a familiar force lurking in the shadows of my dividend argument – compounding. We've already explained how some parts of the financial system reward the long-term, patient investor who is willing to constantly recycle money into rewarding but risky ideas, and dividend reinvesting is one of them. The idea of dividend reinvestment is an explicit form of positive compounding but I think the discipline of focusing on higher yield stocks offers up access to another hugely powerful compounding mechanism – growing corporate profits. Over time, big companies are able to progressively grow their profits, in an almost relentless fashion, apart from the odd recession! As those cash profits stack up, the management at these big businesses sometimes choose to reward investors with another progressively increasing flow of money – the dividend! If it sounds a bit like a perpetual growth engine… well, it is. And it has worked for wealthy investors as long as they are in the game for at least the next 20 to 30 years.

A focus on dividend-paying large company stocks should form the central component of your core equity portfolio, which in turn will be the most important part of your wealth strategy via the accumulation of 'risk capital' for your retirement. Dividends matter!

29 Everyone's favourite – tax!

> 'When there's a single thief, it's robbery. When there are a thousand thieves, it's taxation.' Vanya Cohen

> 'Unquestionably there is progress. The average American now pays out twice as much in taxes as he formerly got in wages.' H. L. Mencken

> 'Certainty? In this world nothing is certain but death and taxes.' Benjamin Franklin

> 'I like to pay taxes. With them, I buy civilization.' Oliver Wendell Holmes, Jr

> 'Once you realize that trickle-down economics does not work, you will see the excessive tax cuts for the rich as what they are – a simple upward redistribution of income, rather than a way to make all of us richer, as we were told.' Ha-Joon Chang, author of 23 Things They Don't Tell You About Capitalism

Living with high tax levels

Taxation – its shape and application and what it tells us about the nature of government intervention in the workings of the private economy – excites huge ideological fervour, with increasingly acrimonious debates between the left and right. This book takes no particular side on these debates, although we are inclined to take a cynical but realistic view, namely that there's a lot of it about (tax) but there isn't a great deal you can do about it usefully except worry yourself sick about the whole affair.

What we can say with some certainty is that tax evasion is becoming increasingly difficult unless you happen to be super-wealthy and thus able to afford top-notch tax advice from specialist consultants. It is a possibly sad comment on this world that all but the super-rich and the very biggest companies can afford to hire the services of tax evasion experts. Most of the rest of us are probably resigned to paying up what we owe, with a small degree of latitude around the relationship between tax avoidance and tax planning.

Whereas tax evasion is a definite non-starter for all but the super-rich, tax avoidance is entirely legal. It is simply an active stance towards minimizing your tax, and in all the major developed economies it is allowed if not actually encouraged. Unfortunately, governments around the world are also now tightening up the rules that allow avoidance to such an extent that most of the 'loopholes' are vanishing before our eyes.

Tax planning by contrast is usually encouraged by governments with varying degrees of generosity. The main route for tax planning is to use tax allowances and tax-based savings structures to minimize income and capital gains. Within this overall distinction between tax planning and avoidance I'd also identify six simple facts of life, none of which are remotely controversial – nevertheless all are important:

- Try to maximize your exposure to capital gains based taxes while minimizing your liability to income tax. In most developed economies income taxes seem to be increasing steadily over time whereas capital gains based taxes are usually fairly stable in order to encourage long-term capital formation.
- Taxation on enterprise is usually at a lower rate, and is designed to encourage investment in new or young businesses.
- Freelance workers, or those who own a company, usually have greater flexibility to manage their tax planning and minimize taxes, if only by dispersing ownership of a company between family members and charging sensible costs to the business.
- In most cases, the most generous tax breaks offered by governments tend to come with fairly restrictive conditions that determine how you can use your wealth.

There is almost inevitably a trade-off between tax subsidy and restrictive rules governing those who benefit.
- Tax regimes around the world tend to offer preferential treatment to those who invest in residential property (usually tax free if it's your primary residence) or are willing to lock their money up in investments for a very long time (via increasing tax reliefs that accumulate over time).
- Inheritance-based taxes are usually fairly difficult to evade unless you are willing to spend a great deal of money on expert advice or make use of government tax schemes that encourage you to make risky investments.

Once one accepts these tax truths I think you can be fairly creative and active with your tax management.

I would maintain that you have both a duty to pay tax and a duty to make sure you don't pay **too much** tax. Neither is contradictory. Taxation supports the basics of our society and we'd **all** be collectively poorer if only a few people paid tax. In fact in most surveys, the best places to do business and accumulate wealth are usually those jurisdictions with the higher tax rates and more punitive fiscal regimes. Safe, legally minded societies that respect wealth creators tend to be societies that are well regulated, well governed and taxed at a higher rate.

Yet that duty to pay tax doesn't mean you should not plan tax carefully in order to minimize your annual bill.

Luckily, I have three simple strategies for keeping the taxman at a safe distance.

MAX OUT YOUR TAX-FREE SAVINGS PLANS SUCH AS AN INDIVIDUAL SAVINGS ALLOWANCE (ISA)

The good news is that both the UK and the US governments offer fairly generous tax-based savings schemes. Take advantage of these and use your annual contributions allowance to the absolute maximum. In the UK the very best scheme is centred on the ISA (individual savings allowance), which lets investors put aside a fixed amount every year – any gains made within this plan are entirely tax free for the rest of your life. There are a growing number of ISA millionaires in the UK and these lucky people now have a huge pot of money where they can frankly do what they want with the money. Follow their example! Max out those savings allowances and make use of your partner's allowance as well. You may even be able to pay money tax free into a children's savings account – again make full use of these schemes and look on them as a tax-efficient way of saving for school and university fees.

MAX OUT INCOME TAX ALLOWANCES

If the government gives you an income and capital gains tax allowance, use it! And if your partner has a tax allowance, use theirs as well. In fact do everything in your power to make sure that you stay below any higher tax rate bands by using up every last penny and pound of your annual income tax allowance. I'd also observe that those in business should try to shift as many of their gains as possible into capital gains tax-based structures, thus benefiting from lower tax rates in most countries.

DON'T FOCUS EVERYTHING ON THE PENSION POT

One of the most popular forms of tax-advantaged saving is through a pension scheme. Most developed world countries privilege this form of long-term saving. But those tax subsidies usually come at a cost. The first is that tax is usually applied on the way out i.e. you have to pay tax on any income or capital gains produced by your pension once you are retired. Also, the rules governing what you can do with your pension are usually fairly rigid, even punitive in some cases. In the UK, for instance, most pensioners have traditionally bought an annuity of some sort. This age-old financial structure obviously has the advantage of paying an income but eventually you'll end up losing all your invested capital when you die. Last but by no means least, pensions are an obviously easy target for governments looking to raise extra revenues or even confiscate private capital. These concerns make some investors rightly nervous of focusing entirely on a pension, especially when governments also offer other tax-free savings structures such as ISAs. My advice is to heed these concerns and run both a pension and other tax-advantaged savings schemes such as ISAs.

Don't rely exclusively on a pension. In fact, I think there's much to be said for actually putting less money in a pension and then prioritizing your contributions to tax-free structures such as ISAs.

Putting it all together

Many wealthy investors obsess about tax, going to quite extraordinary lengths to evade and avoid tax. I'm not about to tell you that these people are bad or evil nor that they don't have a point about excessive taxes levied on wealth creation. My simple observation is that this focus on tax avoidance (I'm being generous here and not mentioning the evasion word) usually ends up putting them in the firing line of a vengeful and observant taxman and gobbles up a huge amount of time and money (paid to tax experts). Maybe you'll think it's worth taking these risks as your wealth accumulates but I have my doubts.

My sense is that we should focus on creating as much wealth as possible and then worry about the challenges of tax later.

Most importantly, we shouldn't become obsessed by tax-based investment opportunities that are actually lousy ideas! In the UK many investors have pumped money into all manner of suspicious schemes involving venture capital, films and derelict property only to discover that the underlying investment is just plain awful. The hyped tax advantages may help soothe the pain, but a bad investment is still a bad investment even though it may be tax efficient!

30 On speculation

> 'Day trading is like grabbing coins in front of a steamroller. You will get rolled over.' Neil Weintraub

> 'Fear inhibits risk-taking, just when you should take risk.' Larry R. Williams

> 'Most of the time the market rises. Unless it is a real bear market, all attempts at market timing backfire and become very costly. But when you actually encounter a real bear market, recognizing it and taking corrective action is near life-saving.' Ken Fisher

> 'Nothing works all the time.' Old saying

> 'The Fox knows many things but the Hedgehog knows one great thing.' Archilochus

Do you have what it takes to speculate?

Outsiders to the world of money often look upon investors, speculators and traders as the same kind of person. Big mistake! In my opinion most wealthy people are in fact successful investors in that they are willing to take some risks in order to grow their capital over the long term, but only in a considered risk-aware manner. They are usually not speculators.

Speculators by contrast are much more active in their trading activity, tend to 'trade' more often than the long-term buy-and-hold investor and then tend to take greater risks by betting on information, strategies… 'stuff' that they know a great deal about.

These speculators might even gear up by taking on a loan to increase their potential reward.

Our last category: traders by contrast are addicted to the chase of money markets and investment. They constantly sit in front of their computers or 'CrackBerrys' looking for a small edge that makes them some money… today!

In almost every example I can recall, traders end up becoming nothing more than professional gamblers, slaves to a system that will eventually defeat them – that is unless they can somehow convince other investors and a prime broker that they should in fact become a hedge fund… in which case many then become insanely wealthy by pocketing excessive fees! And even then in truth most professional hedge-fund traders fail to make superior returns (especially after those big fees) and that failure is even more acute when you think what advantages they have, including access to world-class risk control and IT systems.

Ordinary investors who become traders by contrast nearly always lose. I know this for a fact because I've seen internal data from large UK-based spread betting companies that shows that at least 90 per cent of all their active day trading clients **lose** money consistently.

Clearly it's not in the interests of these very successful spread betting firms to openly publicize this data but it is nevertheless a dirty secret that everyone seems to know about in the world of finance. What's even worse is that of the 5 to 10 per cent who do prosper and consistently make money, most of those are actively monitored by the firms and constantly hedged against so that they can't make **too** much money!

Day trading is a mug's game and is best avoided.

Unless you are the lucky 1 in a 100 or even 1 in 1,000, it won't make you wealthy – quite the opposite in fact.

Speculation is a rather different, slightly more measured affair. I think good old Wikipedia sums up this ancient pursuit very succinctly as 'the practice of engaging in risky financial transactions in an attempt to profit from short- or medium-term fluctuations in the market value of a tradable good such as a financial instrument, rather than attempting to profit from the underlying financial attributes embodied in the instrument such as capital gains, interest or dividends'.

This, I think, hits the nail squarely on the head: it's higher risk than investing, involves shorter time frames and is generally an activity that uses financial instruments such as shares to produce a capital gain. Speculators might leverage their returns by borrowing money and they might even look to buy and sell their chosen investment in a period that might not be much more than a few days. If you do decide to engage in speculation, I'd make damned sure that you know what you are doing and practise for many years before risking a single penny or cent. I'd also use three simple strategies, as follows.

BE ALERT FOR TRENDS

Speculators are much more technical in their analysis of markets i.e. they might look in great detail at daily and intra-daily prices moves, using what's called technical analysis to spot 'trends'.

These trends can last for just a day or two or sometimes stretch out into many months but what you're looking for is a fleeting phenomenon called momentum i.e. where a market seems to be becoming increasingly optimistic/fearful over time with more and more traders looking to scramble on board as the market changes direction.

These momentum-based trends can be spotted fairly easily using this technical analysis.

DEVELOP YOUR OWN RISK/REWARD MANAGEMENT SYSTEM

Big, successful hedge funds jam-packed full of traders and speculators frequently boast absolutely brutal risk management systems. These might consist of a senior partner visiting a trader on a daily basis, scrutinizing every one of their trades and picking apart both their successes and losses. If that senior risk manager thinks that the trader/speculator is for one minute about to 'blow up' and lose the firm money, they'll withdraw their capital and possibly even fire them! In hedge fund land, risk management is taken very seriously and that starts by being brutally honest about the strengths and weaknesses of the hedgie.

That same discipline needs to be applied to the solo speculator operating on his or her own account. They need to make mistakes, preferably not with too much money, so that they can learn what works… and what doesn't! They've also got to be their most bitter critic, constantly examining their own track record.

Crucially, they've got to learn another lesson from their professional peers, which is that they should strive for mediocrity i.e. to make money not less than 51 per cent of the time but probably not much more often! By and large the most successful speculators would argue that two out of three in terms of hit rates is pretty amazing, whereas they'd frankly be happy for success just 51 per cent of the time – that 2 per cent margin over failure should make them money. Given this low margin of success, you'll frequently discover that successful speculators don't make a small number of big bets, rather they'd prefer to make a bigger number of smaller bets all based around a developing theme or trend. Last but by no means least, smart speculators learn from the past but they don't dwell too long on it. This means they are historically informed but accept that markets can change fundamentally and trends can vanish without warning.

DEVELOP A TRADING STRATEGY

Once a speculator has their risk control system in place, they need to be willing to be honest about their successes and failures. They also need to develop the technical tools to spot opportunities and trends. But the crucial last step is that they then need to develop a coherent strategy or investing focus. My advice would be to focus on just one or two markets at most, use historical analysis to spot opportunities and then talk to market players to see how these trends play out on a practical basis. In this strategy. timing is everything and I'd particularly argue that market crises tend to offer up the greatest opportunities, especially as investors begin to behave irrationally – driven by complete fear.

Putting it all together

I cannot emphasize enough that day trading is a wealth destroyer and that speculation can also be incredibly dangerous and risky. My sense is that the majority of readers should avoid speculation entirely. But I also think that smart investors, with detailed market knowledge, should think about every once in a while engaging in speculation if they're willing to take the risk. In my experience speculation, especially with the added bonus of leverage (trading with a loan account on margin), can work wonders, especially as markets start turning bearish. Increased volatility – as we've already mentioned – increases opportunity, and the chance to actually make money while everyone else is **losing** money might be too good to pass up! Crucially, this speculation in difficult markets might help preserve your risk capital and give you more cash in the bank to invest in markets once the inevitable rebound kicks in. But always, always, remember my last golden rule, embraced by speculators in particular, which is that you should always cut your losses short and let your profits grow and run!

31 The silent killer – inflation

> 'Inflation is as violent as a mugger, as frightening as an armed robber and as deadly as a hitman.' Ronald Reagan

> 'Whomsoever controls the volume of money in any country is absolute master of all industry and commerce and when you realize that the entire system is very easily controlled, one way or another, by a few powerful men and the top, you will not have to be told how periods of inflation and depression originate.' James A. Garfield

> 'Bankers know that history is inflationary and that money is the last thing a wise man will hoard.' Will Durant

> 'The first panacea for a mismanaged nation is inflation of the currency. The second is war. Both bring a temporary prosperity. Both bring a permanent ruin.' Ernest Hemingway

> 'Although most Americans apparently loathe inflation, Yale economists have argued that a little inflation may be necessary to grease the wheels of the labor market and enable efficiency-enhancing changes in relative pay to occur without requiring nominal wage cuts by workers.' Janet Yellen

The remorseless engine of inflation

Economics sometimes sounds a mysterious discipline, with lots of macroeconomic variables moving around in what sometimes seems like a chaotic fashion. For most of us though there are only three rates that make a real difference to our everyday life.

- The first is the growth rate of the economy, which will determine whether we all get richer or poorer.
- The second is the interest rate, which tells how much it costs to borrow a sum of money.
- The last rate is the subject of this chapter, the inflation rate.

This is very simply the general increase in the cost of a basket of goods and services measured by an index such as the Consumer Prices Index (the CPI) or the retail prices index (RPI). Inside this basket is a huge range of everyday items, nearly all of which have increased in price over time.

Luckily, we have a fairly comprehensive set of historical data points for inflation rates, both in the US and the UK. The long-term average US inflation rate over the past 100-plus years is 3.22 per cent, although this hides big decades of long variation – in the 1970s, for instance, the inflation rate averaged 7 per cent per annum, while in the first decade of the 21st century that rate fell to just 2.29 per cent.

Over much longer time frames we can see some even bigger variations, with the inflation rate between 1913 and 1919 averaging 9.8 per cent before slumping to -2 (negative) per cent p.a. (called deflation) between 1930 and 1939. And before you think that deflation (which is defined as consistently falling prices) is a complete exception, consider the fact that over the ten years prior to 2012, the average Japanese inflation rate was −0.07 per cent per annum.

Back in the UK, the average inflation rate tends to be a bit higher than in the US and Japan, with an average of 2.93 per cent per annum between 1989 and 2012.

This long list of numbers can sound very abstract – even irrelevant – until you realize that inflation simply measures the cost of living, which is generally increasing over time. Remember how compounding gets to work as the years shoot by, with small numbers (annual inflation rates of 2 to 3 per cent p.a.) eventually turning into really big numbers!

By and large inflation is a necessity of life and all you can reasonably hope to do is increase your income and the value of your investments at a rate that is in excess of this inflation rate (thus producing a real return). If you don't pull this off, you'll face a declining standard of living, and slow but steady impoverishment.

I'm inclined to think that inflation is probably the price of political and economic progress and that, like anything in life, it can sometimes get out of control and cause immense pain and suffering. But inflation can also impact people in very different ways. In simple, bold terms sensible levels of inflation (between 0 and 5 per cent p.a.) is probably **good** news for borrowers (if you think inflation will stay high, try to borrow as much as you can, as long as interest rates don't shoot up too much), **good** news for investors in equities (stocks and shares) and also **good** news for younger investors. By contrast, inflation is generally **bad** news for older investors, lenders, those dependent on a fixed income and investors in bonds (ironically, these are all likely to be the same people!).

UNDERSTAND THE CHALLENGE

The first and most important step for any investor is to attempt to understand the challenge posed by inflation and then to put some 'hard' numbers around this perennial economic phenomenon. For most of us, inflation is ever present and somehow wishing it'll go away is like thinking day won't follow night (the big exception being Japan where deflation is a big problem). As long as inflation rates don't shoot up past 5 per cent p.a. and then into the double-digit teens, our societies will probably continue to prosper and bumble along.

But you need to incorporate those likely long-term inflation rates into whatever financial budget or model you build. If, for instance, you've drawn up a spreadsheet that tells you what you need to save in order to build a pensions pot, make sure that you incorporate likely inflation rates into the value of your savings. In effect, inflation rates operate in a negative compounding way, subtracting a little bit every year from the current real (after) inflation value of your capital.

WATCH THE BREAK-EVEN RATE!

My strategy of always using the **real** return from any asset, investment or savings account is of course dependent on working out what the actual 'inflation rate' really is at any point in time! I'd suggest hunting down something called the Break-even Rate as a simple starting point. This market measure can be found on the Internet and tells you the level of inflation the financial markets anticipated by bond investors over the medium term of the next few years. This rate will vary as a result of a whole lorry-load of factors but it's a useful yardstick, and as I look online at the moment it's currently at 2.8 per cent in the UK and 1.9 per cent in the US.

MAKE SURE YOUR INCOME FROM PERSONAL CAPITAL IS INFLATION PROOFED

In later chapters we'll look at how investors can protect themselves against inflation's pernicious impact on savings and capital. But for now I'd simply repeat my earlier observation that financial assets such as equities (stocks and shares) are a decent long-term hedge against inflation. Yet the reality is that most of your wealth will in fact be created by building up your personal capital through a prosperous career or starting up a business. And here's the catch – not all careers and businesses offer a sensible hedge against inflation, especially if the market is over-supplied with too many qualified people and demand is not sufficient to soak up all that capacity. In these markets both businesses and workers/professionals might face stagnating real incomes or profits i.e. incomes that don't rise in line with inflation.

The core driver here is, of course, the market dynamics of your chosen career or business – whether supply and demand are in balance. Inflation though has a funny way of making those imbalances much more pernicious over time, as many middle-class Americans and Brits have discovered in recent years. This issue of falling real incomes isn't easily corrected but all I would say is that if you think you are stuck in this economic rut (declining real incomes, lots of competitors for your job as well as employers who can't afford to increase salaries because their own margins are too tight), think long and hard about maybe doing something different. In particular, if you can find a job where someone (usually the government) is willing to peg both salary increases and pension fund contributions to inflation, grab it with both hands!

Putting it all together

Inflation need not be a cataclysmic challenge for everyone, especially for those in their 20s and 30s. Central bankers would like those levels to be between 0 and 2 per cent per annum but my suspicion is that we could probably survive in a range between 1 and 5 per cent p.a. Yet once we start moving through 4 and then 5 per cent, with a likely end destination of, say, 7 to 8 per cent per annum, we're all collectively in trouble. Central bankers have a nasty tendency of slamming on the brakes at these levels as they fear that continuously high levels of inflation will eventually destroy economic signals and impoverish those on fixed incomes such as the retired. So both the absolute level of inflation and its quantum of change matters for all of us, and I think we should all keep a beady eye both on **actual** numbers but also **expectations** of change.

My message is simple – don't ignore inflation, understand it and build it into your plans and make sure you have invested in both personal and risk capital that can sustain the impact of inflation over the long term. That means investing in what are called 'real assets' (investments such as housing that increase in line with inflation) and in developing a career or business that can improve over time as inflation rates increase.

32 Future-proofing your investments

> 'The important thing is to concentrate upon what you can do – by yourself, upon your own initiative.' Harry Browne

> 'A great burden was lifted from my shoulders the day I realized that no one owes me anything.' Harry Browne

> 'Gold is a way of going long on fear, and it has been a pretty good way of going long on fear from time to time. But you really have to hope people become more afraid in a year or two years than they are now. And if they become more afraid you make money, if they become less afraid you lose money, but the gold itself doesn't produce anything.' Warren Buffett

> 'Gold gets dug out of the ground in Africa, or someplace. Then we melt it down, dig another hole, bury it again and pay people to stand around guarding it. It has no utility. Anyone watching from Mars would be scratching their head.' Warren Buffett

> 'Gold is the corpse of value...' Neal Stephenson

The lazy portfolio for the long term

Back in the 1970s, stock market and political commentator Harry Browne shocked many of his followers with a stunning idea, that of the permanent portfolio. Browne was a trailblazing economic libertarian who had advocated the importance of gold as the ultimate reserve currency of choice. In his world, governments were not to be entirely trusted especially when it came to both monetary intervention and repressive taxation policies.

Yet Browne had also begun to realize that the idea of pushing all your hard-earned capital into just one, shiny, asset class might not make the best sense, especially for those older investors looking to preserve their wealth. His innovative thinking – relegating gold to just one, important asset class – sparked a thought process that eventually resulted in a concept called the Permanent Portfolio, which in turn consisted of a diversified portfolio of investments that could preserve capital over the very long term.

Browne had hit upon a simple but powerful insight with a number of layers and actionable ideas. He recognized that investors needed protecting against numerous forms of risk (as we've already discussed in earlier chapters) including inflation, government confiscation and deflation. None of us quite know how these risks to wealth will impact our portfolio, so we need to protect capital at all costs, preferably using a simple-to-use methodology that can be used by any investor, young or old. The resulting Permanent Portfolio consisted of four simple investments:

1. 25 per cent of total assets in an index-tracking equity fund that follows the changing fortunes of the S&P 500 index. This investment would allow the investor to benefit from an economic upturn, at low cost (via an index-tracking fund) in a simple market 'following' style.
2. 25 per cent of total assets in physical gold. This would protect against future inflation trends and government confiscation.
3. 25 per cent in cash. Easy-to-access hard money has the great benefit of providing investors with some interest rate return as well as the ability to deploy capital when other assets become 'cheap' in value, an especially important goal as an economy starts to slow down.
4. 25 per cent in long-dated (10- or 20-year) US Government Treasury bonds. This last idea would give investors an income (as would that cash and those equities, via dividends) as well as some protection in case the US economy slumped into a recession, with shares collapsing in value and long bonds increasing in price.

What's happened in performance terms with this Permanent Portfolio strategy? A standard Permanent Portfolio strategy implemented using funds would have earned the investor 9.5 per cent annually from 1972 to 2011, which equates to almost 5 per cent a year after inflation, all achieved using relatively low levels of volatility.

In practical terms the portfolio does need some low-level maintenance, with investors looking to annually rebalance based around the idea that if an asset reaches 35 per cent of your portfolio on the upside and 15 per cent on the downside, you then buy or sell enough to get back to an even keel, which consists of each asset comprising 25 per cent of the total portfolio. Last but by no means least, any dividends should go directly into the cash account and not be reinvested.

On balance, I'd suggest that this permanent portfolio is an ideal strategy for the cautious, older investor who is actively worried about broad, macro-economic risks such as inflation or a recession – although I'd add some crucial tweaks.

INTERNATIONALLY DIVERSIFY

Browne developed his Permanent Portfolio for a US audience via his book *Fail-Safe Investing*. The book is a great read (though obviously heavily influenced by Browne's own libertarian agenda) and has stood the test of time. But it is an **American** book for a domestic audience that largely used local investment funds and structures. I would suggest international diversification for **all** readers including those in the US. It seems to me that replacing Browne's suggested 25 per cent allocation to US equities with an index-tracking exchange-traded fund (an ETF) that follows the MSCI World index makes sense. This latter index still comprises mostly US-listed companies but also has a big chunk of UK, Swiss, Japanese and continental Eurozone mega cap stocks. MSCI World ETFs are two a penny and relatively cheap to run, so an ETF represents great value. By contrast, I'd hesitate to replace the exposure to US 20-year government bonds with an international version. My sense is that these Treasury Bonds still represent the ultimate safe haven asset, while a global index might leave the investor more open to extra levels of risk from currency moves and local default scares.

LESS GOLD, MORE GOLD EQUITIES

My next important tweak is based on the work of an investment writer already mentioned in this book, called William Bernstein. In our chapter on risk, we outlined this American writer's views of **deep risk** and why investors need to have a diversified mix of assets to protect you against the four horsemen of the financial apocalypse – inflation, deflation, war and government confiscation. Bernstein has studied returns from a Permanent Portfolio and found that investors do take some big risks by implementing a 25 per cent allocation to gold.

Gold is a risky asset that can increase or decrease in price sharply. Crucially, gold is not quite as powerful as we first thought in most examples of rampant inflation – in fact, Bernstein discovers that gold works rather better in deflationary economies, where prices are falling, an economic environment that also benefits government bonds.

Lastly, Bernstein discovers that investors can also benefit from the ebb and flow of inflation/deflation by investing in precious metal equities i.e. gold-mining stocks. These investments in companies that mine gold do very well as inflation shoots up but rather less well in deflationary economies, where a physical holding in gold makes much more sense.

Using this insight I'd suggest the investor reduces their gold exposure to 10 per cent, split equally between actual physical gold and an index-tracking fund that invests in gold-mining shares. I would **increase** my exposure to the other three assets to 30 per cent each.

DO IT YOURSELF USING ETFS AND AVOID USING A MANAGER

There's a small but growing army of fund managers who offer actively managed permanent portfolios for the investor. I'd avoid these structures if only because they add a layer of costs to an investment strategy that can actually be implemented at low cost by the reader. Also, some of these funds take an even more idiosyncratic approach to the portfolio allocations than my own revision above.

In my view, you should make your life easy and follow the structure above using low-cost exchange-traded funds – in both the US and the UK there are literally dozens of different MSCI World ETFs, as well as gold bullion tracker ETFs, and US long dated Treasury bond index funds. The choice should be huge and nearly all managed at low cost. My only small revision might be to hold the cash element in two parts, one as pure cash on deposit, the other in money market accounts that might offer a slightly higher level of interest. Crucially, make sure you don't lock up this cash for too long, with one year the absolute maximum.

> **Putting it all together**
>
> Would I use a permanent portfolio for my own investments? No, not because I think the idea of diversifying against different outcomes is a bad one, but rather because I think an investor can do better. Superior returns are possible for the more active investor and in the next few chapters we'll examine your options. I'd also be much more cautious about Browne's suggested exposure to gold, which is why, in Strategy 2, I have made some very major changes, reducing the gold share to just 10 per cent. Browne believed in the redemptive power of the shiny metal but many other observers (including this one) are much less convinced. I tend to share Warren Buffett's view of gold, articulated at the beginning of this chapter. Crucially, betting on gold over the long term hasn't necessarily been the best idea, with sub-optimal returns from gold over much of the last century. My suggested 10 per cent exposure to gold both directly and indirectly via gold-mining companies feels about right for me. Lastly, make sure that you do operate an annual rebalancing exercise, with any asset class pushing past 35 per cent of total holdings sold down to provide funds to reinvest in the underperforming peers.

33 The property game

> 'I made a tremendous amount of money on real estate. I'll take real estate rather than go to Wall Street and get 2.8 per cent. Forget about it.' Donald Trump

> 'Ninety per cent of all millionaires become so through owning real estate.' Andrew Carnegie

> 'The major fortunes in America have been made in land.' John D. Rockefeller

> 'Landlords grow rich in their sleep.' John Stuart Mill

> 'Buying real estate is not only the best way, the quickest way, the safest way, but the only way to become wealthy.' Marshall Field

Residential property as an investment

Over the post-Second World War period, investments of all shapes and sizes have produced wildly different returns. The top performing risky asset of choice has to be equities – stocks and shares – which have produced some stunning long-term profits. Not too far behind we find property, either in terms of our own homes or as an investment. These 'buy to let' properties as they're called in the UK have also produced returns consistently above inflation but in reality investors have benefited from another big plus – they've used gearing to produce bumper profits. Very few investors in shares, for instance, would think about using a loan to help leverage up their returns over a decade or two but for property investors that's absolutely mainstream. Many property investors use loans that amount to anything between 75 per cent and 25 per cent of the total value of the property. Once that leverage is factored back into the returns numbers, it's obvious that property (commercial and residential) has produced massive gains in the post-war period.

And these returns shouldn't be a great surprise. Housing has always been a good inflationary bet, if only because it's one of the great necessities of life. Housing has also benefited (in the UK at least) from tight planning restrictions, which control the supply of new products. Investors have also been able to ride the tiger of extensive market deregulation (rent controls have been repealed in many cities) as well as financial market innovation. There are now literally dozens of specialist residential property lenders in both the UK and US market. Crucially, as this competition has intensified mortgage rates have fallen back (helped along of course by lower interest rates), which has made the potential for returns even more eye watering.

So housing remains one of the great long-term bets for investors. But there are some obvious 'challenges'. The first concerns a tension we're very familiar with – diversification versus focus. Logic suggests that the best protection against unforeseen events in local housing markets is a portfolio of different properties in an area the investor knows well. But I think it's fair to say that property – especially the type that can be easily rented out – is not that cheap anymore, so a portfolio of three to four units (professionals suggest that as many as ten might make the sensible minimum) will cost you a very large amount of money! That might make your overall investment portfolio dangerously skewed towards property overall i.e. you'd have your own home plus all these investment properties. That's great if you think house prices will keep going up, but it's a risk that most of us would be (and should be) unwilling to take.

Many investors might choose to focus instead on just one or two properties, and then spend a great deal of time managing those flats or houses. But again we face a number of risks. Management and letting costs might be quite high and the investor faces the very real prospect that they might suffer from weeks or even months where the property remains empty, producing no income – even though the mortgage still has to be paid! And there's the universal fact that good property needs to be both maintained and managed, which involves the landlord in all sorts of costs.

So, it should be immediately obvious that residential property as an investment is absolutely not without its risks. How should the careful investor manage this trade-off in risk/return, as well as focus and diversification?

THINK ABOUT YOUR TARGET TENANT

Before you even start thinking about buying a property, think about what your tenant will want. Who are they and what do they want? If they are students, your property needs to be easy to clean and comfortable but not luxurious. Alternatively, if they are young professionals it should be modern and stylish but not overbearing. Families, by contrast, probably have plenty of their own belongings and need a blank canvas. Critically, you have to focus on a property that is 'lettable'. Two-bedroom houses and flats are usually fairly popular in most markets and tend to appeal to the widest range of potential tenants, especially those who are finding it tough to get on to the property ladder. But these properties also tend to be the most expensive, if only because there are plenty of other investors chasing after them. Personally, I'd also avoid large family homes, which tend to appeal to fewer potential tenants – unless that is you intend to turn them into smaller units, in which case you'd better be good at doing your own DIY building!

GO FOR RENTAL YIELD AND COVER COSTS

Many investors get terrifically excited about the potential for capital gains from property, yet personally I'd be a little more circumspect, especially given the post-war property booms in both the US and the UK. My advice is to invest for income not short-term capital growth over the next one to ten years. That means that rent should be the key return for the property investor. To compare different properties' values, use their yield, which is the annual rent received as a percentage of the purchase price. For example, a property producing £10,000 worth of rent that costs £200,000 has a 5 per cent yield.

As a very rough-and-ready measure in the UK the 'average yield' for buy-to-let is around 5 to 6 per cent while high yielding properties such as homes in multiple occupation are 12 to 15 per cent, but you'll probably have to spend a small fortune maintaining these homes. If you can get a rental return substantially over the mortgage payments, then once you have built up a good emergency fund, you can start saving or investing any extra cash. For me the key though is managing costs. If I were starting out I'd try to buy a property that is not very old – this will mean less maintenance down the line. Do not get carried away about any purchase – it's an investment proposition not your home.

CHOOSE A PROMISING AREA

I think the best way of targeting some capital gain from a home is to target the right area, and especially those cities and towns that are 'up and coming'. Remember that promising does not necessarily mean most expensive or cheapest. Look for a wide range of factors – where in your town has a special appeal? If you are in a commuter belt, where has good transport? Where are the good schools for young families? Where do the students want to live? Personally, I'd try to avoid run-down areas – it's sad to say but poor-quality tenants will cost you money.

Putting it all together

Investing in residential property involves lots of practical considerations involving time and focus. Will you, for instance, rent your property out yourself (cheap in money terms, expensive in terms of your time) or get an agent to do so? Remember that agents will charge you a management fee, but will deal with any problems and have a good network of plumbers, electricians and other workers if things go wrong. I'd also remind you that many of the best investments are based on buying something you know in detail. Remember that it is difficult buying in an area you don't know well or is a distance from where you live.

Yet the most important question for me is one of gearing and interest rates. Many investors are tempted to buy a few properties to manage risk, but are then forced to take on huge loans. This immediately opens them up to massive interest rate risk. So a strategy to manage one risk – having multiple properties to dampen down loss of income from unlet properties – only increases another risk, which is vulnerability to interest rate rises.

If this frightens the heck out of you, you might be better off looking at a commercial property fund or real estate investment trust (REIT). These are professionally run funds that invest in offices, shops and factories and are frequently listed on stock exchanges. This means you can buy shares in them very easily and you don't have to take the loan risk, as any gearing in the fund will be wrapped up in the fund. I think REITs are the safer bet for the mainstream investor who has neither the time nor the knowledge to manage their own portfolio of homes.

34 The Armageddon fallacy

> 'Don't wake me for the end of the world unless it has very good special effects.' Roger Zelazny, *Prince of Chaos*

> 'They say the captain goes down with the ship, so when the world ends, will God go down with it?' Fall Out Boy

> 'The world is always ending for someone.' Neil Gaiman

> 'This is the way the world ends
> This is the way the world ends
> This is the way the world ends
> Not with a bang but a whimper.' T. S. Eliot in 'The Hollow Men'

> 'Don't panic' Douglas Adams, *The Hitchhiker's Guide to the Galaxy*

Economies are more resilient than credited

I spend a great deal of time talking to successful investors, wealthy strategists and weary entrepreneurs. By and large they're a charming bunch but I'd have to observe that there's also a regrettable male bias, with another skew towards the average age being well over 40, if not 50. None of this should be remotely surprising given key demographic and economic trends but it does tend to produce some subtle biases that I think go unacknowledged.

In particular, many older entrepreneurs and investors fall victim to what I like to call the 'irritable older male investor syndrome' or IOMIS usually expressed as annoying grumpiness with everything and especially all things financial.

Yet I would argue that my grumpy old investor syndrome has a much darker side to it that should alarm any reader looking to become wealthier and stay wealthy. Over the past decade a rather deadly strain of misanthropy and political doomsterism has infected many wealthy investors and business people with some very predictable results – they've avoided taking too many 'obvious' risks and emphasized capital preservation above everything else.

There are many strands to this predominantly older male issue, including a fear that the financial heavens are about to fall in, that Western civilization is doomed and that investing in anything involving complex financial markets hooked on debt will ultimately end in tears.

One strand of this argument (a very coherent one, I concede) is that following the great global financial crisis of 2008 we're now stuck in what's called a deleveraging groove, where everyone is desperately trying to reduce their debts by cutting back, producing chronically slow global growth in aggregate. The author and commentator A. Gary Shilling is perhaps the most articulate voice of these new deflationists, as they're called, who think that the West is stuck in a low growth rut with prices stubbornly refusing to increase.

Another strain of doomsterism and financial crotchety-ism emerges from those commentators and economists who are influenced by the Austrian school of economics pioneered by Friedrich Hayek and Ludwig von Mises. This well-connected strain of thought, very powerful in US libertarian circles and articulated by Ron Paul, emerged from monetarist thinking and has since mutated into a powerful criticism of Western economies. Perhaps the most innovative take on this thinking comes from Singapore-based investor Richard Duncan in his book *The New Depression*. Here's Richard's slightly scary vision of a world that is desperately trying to kick its addiction to easy, cheap debt before it plunges into an economic abyss.

'Visualize a sinking ship with captain and crew frantically bailing out water to keep the ship above the waves. Now instead of a great wooden vessel imagine a credit inflated rubber raft from which credit is leaking through numerous holes. Policymakers are desperately pumping more credit into the raft to stop it from going down. That raft is the global economy. Humanity lives on top of it. There are no lifeboats. If the raft sinks, people are going to die.'

Now I'm not going to say that either Duncan or Shilling are wrong – they're both eminently respectable commentators, who've got a great many calls right in the past. In particular I'd absolutely recommend *The New Depression* as a powerful critique of our credit-fuelled world.

Yet I would make three simple, optimistic, observations. The first is that forecasting is generally a mug's game, self-evidently! The second is that Western capitalism has been about to collapse because of its internal contradictions since the time of a certain Karl Marx and yet it somehow manages to stagger on and produce yet more opulence and genuine economic and social transformation on a simply mammoth global scale.

Lastly, I would highlight the particular weakness of the prevalent libertarian-influenced critique of modern capitalisms, which is that it's an unholy mix of sensible critiques combined with a natural risk aversion and age-based conservatism. Crucially, it's also hugely counterproductive and is likely to make you a great deal poorer over the long term.

As we observed in our earlier chapter looking at deep risk, what investors really need to worry about are any future inflationary surges. Alternatively, they should also be worried about the opportunity cost of not taking risk in order to grow their wealth. Every other fear, including the end of the financial world, is just conjecture and thus impossible to know.

OWNING GOLD

In an earlier chapter examining the idea of a permanent portfolio we encountered the allure/challenge of gold. Gold has its virtues (not many of them I'd suggest!), not least that investors **believe** that it protects them against the most likely systemic risk to their wealth, which is Inflation. Yet gold does not in fact protect your wealth against most inflationary episodes. It is by contrast useful in deflationary circumstances but history suggests that deflationary economies are uncommon and **not** a huge potential threat, although A. Gary Shilling might disagree.

Of course, gold could be hugely undervalued – the shiny precious metal as an alternative store of wealth in a world dominated by paper money and excessive credit creation. If that is the case a price of US$9,000 an ounce is theoretically possible. Yet I'd argue that that contention is a statement of simple faith and not in any way 'proven' by any fact that I've ever had sight of.

Nevertheless, even I as a gold bear would recognize that gold has its uses, which is why it might make sense to have something between 5 and 20 per cent of your wealth in older years in the shiny stuff. Just don't fool yourself into believing that it can't go down in price sharply (it has and will do so again, at some point) and that gold markets aren't volatile. Also gold is an alternative store of value but it is not a replacement for cash.

STASHING THAT CASH

Cash has enormous attractions for an older investor and I think it's fair to say that nearly every type of investor over the age of 40 should consider holding some of their wealth in cash. Perhaps the best argument for holding cash is as a way of funding future purchases of cheap assets, such as shares after markets inevitably move between bubbles and busts, i.e. cash has great future optionality value.

But cash is also a poor insurance policy against the most likely systemic threat to your wealth, which is increasing prices – aka inflation. To hold much more than 20 per cent of your portfolio in cash – unless required to do so for planning reasons – is probably a very stupid idea and likely to reduce the real value of your wealth in the long run.

CUTTING RISK THROUGH T BONDS

In an earlier chapter we outlined why bonds, especially the longer-dated ones issued by the US government, have been a great investment in the past few decades. Yet we also outlined why these supposedly 'risk-free' assets represent 'poor value' at best and are quite possibly very 'over valued' at worst. In the future this might change as bond prices move around (they might become much cheaper in which case they could become very attractive again) but investors worried about the imminent economic end of the world should consider the risk of owning assets in the biggest sovereign debtor in global history. I have no doubt that the US government is **the** safe haven state of choice but if you really believe the financial world is doomed, why own assets in the one organization that might just turn around and repudiate its debts… because it can do given its superpower status?

Putting it all together

This chapter serves as a warning to older investors and readers. We all become more cautious as we grow older and the need to preserve our capital quite naturally intensifies, but I believe that we should work incredibly hard to avoid two very dangerous risks. The first is that we believe the world around us is 'lost', 'out of control' and 'doomed'. This dystopian view of the world inevitably means that you end up being 'lapped' by the real world, which still has a tendency to rebound from its crises and prosper.

The other great risk you run is that you incur massive opportunity costs as you continually avoid making any bets on risk capital opportunities. It doesn't need to be this way! If you're worried about inflation, for instance – a sensible concern I'd argue – invest in real assets such as index-linked securities or hard assets such as land or property. Equally, you might look to invest in even riskier stuff like equities, which have proven inflation-fighting abilities.

35 The glittering illusion

> 'Be not afraid of growing slowly, be afraid only of standing still.'
> Chinese proverb

> 'Most people are beaten up by the market instead of beating the market.' Mark T. Hebner

> 'All change is not growth, as all movement is not forward.'
> Ellen Glasgow

> 'Success is going from failure to failure without a loss of enthusiasm.' Winston Churchill

> 'Stockbrokers exist to sell dreams.' City adage

The growth illusion

Collectively we're suckers for a good story.

In earlier chapters we've already encountered some of the legion of behavioural challenges that stand in the way of making us wealthier. One of the most pernicious, especially for older investors, is this narrative hook bias. In simple terms we all like a good story, especially if it involves something that is irresistibly growing and shows great promise i.e. sexy sells, dowdy sits on the shelf.

Older investors are especially vulnerable as they begin to realize that they might not have that many really successful investments left to find for their portfolio. One can almost hear the excited 50-something declare that: 'If only I could find one last tenbagger for my portfolio before I retire… it'll pay for a cruise or two.'

A UK-based investment strategist and behavioural expert James Montier very succinctly describes what happens next when this narrative bias – we like positive stories – kicks in. In the rational view of the world we're supposed to gather evidence, weigh and evaluate the facts and then decide on the best opportunity. In the story-based view of the world we still start by gathering evidence (from stories that are other people's recycled opinions), we then explain the difference between the story and the evidence ('ah, but next time that great business hits its targets and just wait to see what will happen as everyone jumps in!') and then we match the story to the possible decisions i.e. the story is allowed to frame our decision-making, with the imperatives of growth and opportunity towering over more rational reactions.

The reality as revealed in academic study after academic study is rather more sordid.

We can, for instance, easily divide the universe of stocks and shares into a number of distinctive camps, including a basic divide between what's called growth stocks and value stocks – although as an aside this exact-same analysis can be applied to virtually any 'asset' including property!

Growth stocks are usually expensive, which means that relative to say their profits and their dividends, we're asked to pay a high price for buying the shares. But that high price is 'deemed' to be worth it because the companies behind these stocks are growing those profits at a fast rate i.e. they're high growth. Value stocks, as we've already discovered in an earlier chapter, are usually fairly dowdy, as well as being unloved with low share prices relative to these metrics. So, how do these two types of stocks perform over the long term?

Investment writer William Bernstein looked at this distinction a decade ago and used long-term annualized data that looked at US stock markets between July 1963 and April 2002. He found that, on average, the 500 stocks in the S&P 500 Index returned 11 per cent p.a., while large-growth stocks (these are large capitalization stocks) also turned in 11 per cent. Small-growth stocks turned in 9.68 per cent.

As for large cap value stocks, Bernstein discovered that these produced an average return of 13.7 per cent while small cap value stocks trounced everyone else with a return of 17.5 per cent.

But there's one last point to make about these stats. Bernstein also looked at risk, measured by the average downturn in the share price relative to the average return and he found that in terms of risk there wasn't a huge difference between the different styles of share except that small cap growth stocks were inordinately riskier (for much lower returns).

The evidence I would contend is overwhelming.

We allow our collective enthusiasm for sexy stuff to overpower our rational side, producing poor long-term returns. But the good news is that we don't have to keep making these big investment mistakes if we follow three simple rules.

UNDER-PROMISE AND THEN OVER-DELIVER

The best investments are nearly always those with the lowest expectations, but which then go on to deliver the highest outcome. My own strategy is to look at any investable asset class (shares, bonds, housing) and then look down the list of the past 12 months, returns for individual sectors or companies. I'm searching for decent quality businesses or opportunities that have simply become unpopular because they've disappointed 'Mr Market' in recent years. A simple example might be to look down the daily list of stocks hitting their 52-week lows i.e. their share price has hit the lowest point for the last year. Most of those stocks thoroughly deserve their drubbing but every once in a while you'll find a decent opportunity. After researching it you discover that it's disappointed the market yet in reality it is actually a sound business. Finally you look to see if there's a catalyst for change like new management. Once reassured you buy, hoping for the company to over-deliver in the future!

THE CHINA TRAP

If you want to see the growth trip writ large, consider the case of China. The great Asian superpower's economy may have slowed down in recent years, but it's still growing at a phenomenal rate compared to Western economies. This high growth encourages many to assume that investing in local shares for instance is a great idea, because if the economy is growing fast, surely these companies must also be growing fast? Top-line growth seems to feed expectations for bottom-line investor returns.

Unfortunately, the exact opposite is true. In investing terms, it's usually a smarter idea to invest in the most boring countries like Belgium (apologies to all Belgian readers) largely because they're growing at a slower, more sustainable rate. The motor behind this is investor enthusiasm and the flow of capital. In China, capital floods into the business sector in search of that elusive growth. Too much money gets invested in the small number of decent business opportunities while the rest is simply wasted on unprofitable factories that are multiplying like crazy without regard to profit or the future. That capital intensifies the competition between businesses, which lowers profits and encourages yet more investment. Eventually, investors wake up and smell the coffee – margins aren't increasing and they're not making money. They exit the market as the bubble bursts and everyone grows very disappointed.

In boring places like Belgium, by contrast, national growth rates may be a great deal more subdued but that encourages businesses to be careful with their cash while investors are also more cautious. Businesses react by emphasizing profit margins and keeping the investors happy with generous dividends.

The moral of the story? Boring is best!

THE PRICE YOU PAY ALWAYS MATTERS

My last strategy is incredibly simple and based on a home-grown truth, which is the price you pay for anything matters. As I write, the price of elegant properties in prime central London are increasing at a frenzied rate (although by the time you've read this book the mania might, hopefully, have abated).

Prices for the best streets in, say, Kensington or Chelsea (the very poshest parts of Central London) are hitting obscene levels powered by the super-wealthy and a form of property snobbery. Price doesn't seem to matter in this scramble and more than a few market participants have been heard to say that value doesn't really have any meaning anymore. Rubbish, that's the greater fool theory. All markets are liable to bubbles and the price you pay matters – if it doesn't, you won't stay wealthy for very long.

> ### Putting it all together
>
> In my discussion of growth I've introduced a distinction between 'growth' and 'value' opportunities. This may seem a little complex for most readers but in reality they do end up having no other choice than to take a view on this divide. Many investors in, say, the stock market say they're not one nor the other but in reality they tend to shun stocks and businesses that aren't flavour of the moment and embrace those with huge potential that are creating great gushers of excitement. This is a simple and very dangerous form of growth investing i.e. buying all that looks sexy.
>
> In my view, growth is actually in many cases a dangerous illusion, although there are indisputably some great growth businesses out there. I wish I'd invested in Google in the early days, for instance, but I'm actually much happier to have waited many years and then bought the shares at a much lower price as everyone seemed to grow rather more jaundiced about the company and its prospects. A suspicion of growth doesn't mean you should avoid great growth businesses just that you should buy into them much later on when everyone else has grown bored and moved on.

36 Getting emotional about investments

> 'I'm just a temporary custodian of these works.' Michael Audain

> 'One of the almost peculiar characteristics of 20th-century collecting is that some people succeeded in giving the appearance of being smart simply by purchasing dumb art.'
> Joseph P. Blodgett

> 'Wine is one of the most civilized things in the world and one of the most natural things of the world that has been brought to the greatest perfection, and it offers a greater range for enjoyment and appreciation than, possibly, any other purely sensory thing.' Ernest Hemingway

> 'I'm an anorak. I've always been an obsessive collector of things. Richard Briers collects stamps. I collect cars and guns, which are much more expensive, and much more difficult to store.' Michael Gambon

> '[The most special stamp I've ever acquired is] what they call the "1-cent Z-Grill"... It's the only one in the world... an 1869 United States stamp I needed to complete my collection... It was very valuable, so I negotiated with the owner to exchange it for another stamp. But in effect it was a US$3 million purchase. I wasn't sure if it was a good price – it probably wasn't. But it let me form the only complete collection of United States stamps – that's pretty cool...'
> Bill Gross, quoted in Forbes magazine

Passionate investing

To understand the allure of emotional assets, let me start with a short tale.

In the aftermath of the Global Financial Crisis of 2008/2009 wealthy types started going to ground. The newspapers may have been full of stories about investment banks going bust and traders being thrown out on the street, but those of us who followed investment markets knew otherwise.

OK, the financial masters of the universe weren't having a great year, but let's be honest they all still made vast amounts of money.

Missing one or maybe two years' worth of million dollar bonuses is obviously miserable (!) but many of the financial elite were still making huge dollops of cash and within two or three years even those million dollar bonuses started coming back again.

But during the most depressing years of the crisis, heads went down and the financial plutocrats generally kept a low profile. Yet something strange was going on in the background involving stuff like art and vintage Ferraris.

A good friend of mine is a leading art dealer who also likes very expensive bottles of wine (who doesn't!). Business was tough in 2009 as no one wanted to be seen to be too ostentatious while tens of millions lost their jobs worldwide, but by 2010 business had picked up again. In fact, business picked up so quickly that he freely admitted – off the record – that the super-wealthy had never really stopped buying art, wine and amazing vintage cars. As profits shot back up at the banks and hedge funds, the tap opened wide. Spending on what some call 'emotional assets' – stamps, coins, wine, old cars and art to you and me – went crazy!

By 2011 my good friend admitted that business had never been so good. 'The super-rich are always worried about storing their wealth in just money, shares and bonds,' he told me. 'They also want a large part of their capital in mobile assets that they can put on their wall and then take down again if they have to run out of the country. Portable, precious, personal, emotional assets have an enormous attraction to the rich, helped along by their seeming ability to keep up with inflation.'

What about the 'returns' from investing in these emotional assets? What do the hard numbers tell us? UK-based private bank Coutts has been especially keen to trumpet its knowledge of those emotional assets – it's even tried to change the terminology used, by calling them 'passion-based investments'. In 2014 it announced that its index covering these passion-based investments was showing some seriously impressive medium-term numbers.

In January of that year the bank announced that its broad Objects of Desire Passion index had produced returns of 77 per cent in sterling terms since 2005, outperforming even shares. According to Coutts: 'of all the alternative investments… classic cars have returned the most since 2005, rising by 257 per cent, outpacing all other investments by more than 80 percentage points over the seven-and-a-half-year time frame. Classic watches have also proved they can stand the test of time, rising by 176 per cent from 2005 to 30 June 2013. Jewels returned 146 per cent in comparison, while the standout performer in the fine art space is the traditional Chinese works of arts sector, which rose by 163 per cent between 2005 and 30 June 2013'.

It's obvious to all and sundry that in the past few years these emotional assets have started 'mainstreaming' as it's called i.e. becoming a mainstream way of storing wealth. Should you take the plunge?

ONLY EVER INVEST IN WHAT YOU KNOW

I suspect the clue is in the title isn't it? These collectables are, after all, emotional, passion-based investments, which implies that you have both some knowledge of the assets and a view about their attractiveness. Stick to that biscuit tin description. Invest only in what you know about, care about and are obsessed about. You need to research these assets in exactly the same way you'd research a location for a new home or a value investor might investigate a potential diamond-in-the-rough stock. That means being patient, knowing what works for you and understanding when a 'bargain' is in fact a stupid investment.

INVEST IN QUALITY ASSETS WITH A LIQUID MARKET

Emotional assets can be difficult assets to sell in a panic – as we've already noted – yet even in good times markets for these 'investments' can dry up as sentiment turns fickle. If you are going to look on your passions as an investment I'd recommend sticking with high-quality examples, loved by the wealthy, operating in a global marketplace. In simple terms that means the very best examples of a particular niche. The very best Bordeaux wine, for instance, or the very best artists of the decade or even first-class quality stamps that are extremely rare and constantly in demand like the good old penny black. The knowledgeable investor might consider perhaps looking one level below this quality mark, to emotional assets that are about to become big as fashion evolves. But overall my advice is not to cut corners. Buy what's popular and just accept that it is going to cost you a small fortune to stay in the game. And if you don't have enough cash? Ignore emotional assets and stick with the sensible stuff like shares and bonds.

LOOK EAST

My last strategy is simple – pick an emotional asset class that wealthy Asian investors will cherish and chase up in price. Many Chinese plutocrats from business, for instance, have already been spotted buying insanely expensive bottles of Bordeaux wine, while a few have even snapped up elite vineyards in France. This is only the beginning of a very long term process whereby wealthy Asian investors look to park some of their precious capital offshore in emotional assets that a) have resonance with their own culture, and b) can be proudly displayed as living proof of their owners' success. Wine and some works of art have been the first to feel the impact but my sense is that the smart investor should look for the next big thing. Maybe Chinese stamps or banknotes? Asian coins or even vintage Japanese cars?

Putting it all together

So, are you tempted by these emotional, passion-based investments? Before you take the plunge indulge me in a quick reality check on these emotional assets. There's no guarantee they'll go up in price and there's always the risk that your favourite asset will go firmly out of fashion with a disastrous impact on prices. Emotional assets can shoot up in price and then come crashing down again, as bubbles and booms wax and wane. And be aware that when fear is rampant and every sane investor is heading for the hills, these emotional assets can be incredibly difficult to sell as liquidity simply dries up!

Given these concerns, even I accept that if you have a real passion for some work of art or a type of stamp there's nothing to stop you from taking up a hobby and then turning it into something a little more substantial by investing the odd per cent or two of your total assets in your passion. So, certainly, tie up say 2 per cent of your total assets in what you love by buying the best quality collectables you can afford but don't mistake it for an investment. I do have emotional assets myself (coins!) but I'm dubious about their 'investment' value. Personally I just think they'll be wonderful things to hand over to the kids, who'll probably flog them in exactly the same way I sold off some of my dad's precious stamps – quickly, cheaply and with no regard to value.

37 True to your bond

> 'Blessed are the young for they shall inherit the national debt.'
> Herbert Hoover

> 'If financial assets no longer work for you at a rate far and above the rate of true wealth creation, then you must work longer for your money.' Bill Gross

> 'What I put in the stock market, I don't have to touch in my lifetime. I want to live off my bonds. I want to be that safe.'
> Monica Seles

> 'Every portfolio benefits from bonds; they provide a cushion when the stock market hits a rough patch.' Suze Orman

> 'Both from the standpoint of stocks and bonds, an investor wants to go where the growth is.' Bill Gross

Investing in fixed income securities aka bonds

So far in this book we've spent a fair amount of time discussing the merits (and vices) of risky investments such as stocks and shares, only mentioning the 'less risky' stuff like bonds in passing.

In truth, none of us should ignore the world of fixed income securities otherwise known as bonds. In simple size terms, the global bond markets tower over the stock markets, with countless tens of trillions invested in every conceivable category of bond ranging from corporate bonds issued by emerging markets' businesses through to rock-solid US government bonds, also known as Treasury Bonds (T Bonds). The variety and scale of this market is absolutely staggering and I'd argue that once an investor heads past 40 years old, they should slowly but surely start to increase their bond exposure.

On paper there's a lot going for bonds. They are indisputably less risky than stocks and shares. Stock markets can and regularly do fall by more than 20 per cent in any particular year, whereas there are virtually no examples of bond markets falling at such a rate.

That lower level of overall risk is largely a product of the fact that bonds are a relatively simple financial instrument, a form of IOU masquerading as a financial security! Imagine if you lent say £10,000 to the government or a company and they make a payment comprising interest that works out at 5 per cent per annum. That means that as the investor who makes the loan you receive a yield (or coupon) that's equivalent to £500 per annum. The crucial twist is the structure of the loan – that IOU. That IOU is structured as a note or bond. Crucially, you should receive back the principal initial investment when the bond matures at the end of the period agreed between the lender and the borrower. There is, of course, an obvious risk that your borrower defaults, in which case you might get back nothing. But the reality is that defaults are usually much less important than the positive profits to be made from bonds. If you go online and visit the web page of New York University academic Aswarth Damodaran – at http://pages.stern.nyu.edu/~adamodar/New_Home_Page/datafile/histretSP.html – you'll see a long line of data that tells you the long-term returns since 1928 of various assets including US stocks, US Treasury Bonds and shorter-dated US Treasury Bills (these bonds boast a maturity in less than one year). Over the entire period between 1928 through to 2011 stocks overall gave an annual average return of 11.2 per cent while T Bills produced 3.66 per cent p.a. and T Bonds 5.41 per cent p.a.

But if we switch to shorter, more recent periods, the numbers begin to change markedly – over the period 1962 through to 2011, for instance, stocks returned 10.6 per cent p.a., T Bills 5.22 per cent and T Bonds an impressive 7.2 per cent. The most damning numbers come from the beginning of this century (2002 to 2011 to be precise), which show that stocks gave us just under 5 per cent p.a. whereas T Bonds produced 6.85 per cent i.e. supposedly riskless bonds outperformed risky equities.

As we've already discussed in this book, stocks and shares will nearly always outperform over the very long term but bonds can seem mightily attractive over much-shorter periods like the last decade. Bonds are also less volatile in terms of daily pricing, and produce a much more stable return (that regular yield or income is the game changer here), with a much lower chance of big losses. Add in the ability to use that predictable income to manage your future cash flows, and I think you can see why bonds have been such a star asset class in recent years!

INCREASE BOND EXPOSURE WITHIN YOUR PORTFOLIO

Many economists argue that a mix of bonds and stocks makes sense **for all investors**, regardless of their age. A typical portfolio might consist of 40 per cent in bonds and 60 per cent in equities, with the bonds producing a nice steady income-based return of say 3 to 5 per cent p.a. while the shares produce a small dividend yield and capital gains over the long term.

Yet I beg to differ with this approach. I stick with my earlier argument that all 20- and 30-somethings should have 100 per cent exposure to equities, with no bond holdings whatsoever. I'm convinced this risky approach is the only way to accumulate serious risk capital and I'd argue that the historical stats support my approach. But as our readers get older I think they do need to progressively increase their bond exposure within their diversified portfolios. As soon as you hit 40, I'd argue that you should increase your bond holdings by 2 per cent of the total portfolio every year i.e. at age 40 you'd have 2 per cent total bond exposure, then 4 per cent at 41 and 6 per cent at age 42 and so on. By the time most readers of this book hit retirement at 70, you'd be up at 60 per cent exposure to bonds, which is I think an appropriate maximum level.

CORPORATE BONDS FOR EXTRA YIELD

As you increase your bonds exposure through your middle years I would strongly argue that you shouldn't play safe and stick your risk capital in the least risky bonds on the market – US and UK government bonds. The chances of big capital losses on this government paper are **very, very** low but that probably also implies that the chances of decent returns are also equally small. The good news is that there are plenty of alternatives, including corporate bonds issued by all manner of businesses ranging from rock-solid outfits like McDonald's through to risky (junk) bonds issued by mid-sized companies. I'd argue that you diversify like crazy in your budding post 40 per cent bonds portfolio, buying government and corporate bonds, low- and high-risk securities, domestic currency bonds and foreign currency bonds. My own preference is for any bond holdings within a portfolio to be split 50/50 between government and corporate (which will include high-yielding junk bonds), with an equivalent 50/50 split between $/£ bonds and global bonds.

GO UNCONVENTIONAL

My last strategy is to think unconventionally about bonds, and research those securities that boast either an index-linked element (inflation-proof returns) or a floating rate where the income increases if interest rates start to rise. Conventional fixed-income bonds perform terribly in economies experiencing relatively high levels of inflation (and increasing interest rates) and as we discuss in later chapters, I think there's a decent chance we could indeed experience these higher inflation rates in the not too distant future. You need to protect yourself against this terrible eventuality (with a resulting bonds rout of epic proportions), which is why you might need to buy some bonds that actually **increase** in value as inflation and interest rates start to rise.

Putting it all together

Bonds are a great investment option for the cautious investor. They provide that steady income, the certainty of repayment in the future (in the vast majority of cases) and some small chance of a capital gain if you play your cards right i.e. you buy a bond when it's cheap and then ride an increase in its value through to maturity. In sum, they are a perfect financial planning tool.

But bonds are not **risk free**. Bonds can go up and down in value, very much in line with inflation and interest rates. The last few decades have been wonderfully kind to bond investors, who have in turn made huge profits. My suspicion is that this clement financial environment might markedly change at some point in the coming decade, especially as interest rates start to rise. Alternatively, in a benign economic environment the Western economies could continue to expand at sub-trend growth rates, helped along by falling demographic growth rates (in part from tougher immigration rules), which might combine to keep us locked in a low-inflation, low-growth environment. That could be better news for bonds – averting a bonds rout – but I also think it unlikely even in this scenario that that you'll see much more increase in the price of most low-risk bonds. My core advice is to be cautious and gently increase your bond exposure, keeping a beady eye on those inflation and interest rates.

38 Playing catch up?

> 'Spring passes and one remembers one's innocence.
> Summer passes and one remembers one's exuberance.
> Autumn passes and one remembers one's reverence.
> Winter passes and one remembers one's perseverance.'
> Yoko Ono

> 'I'm kind of comfortable with getting older because it's better than the other option, which is being dead. So I'll take getting older.' George Clooney

> 'When you're young, you always feel that life hasn't yet begun – that 'life' is always scheduled to begin next week, next month, next year, after the holidays – whenever. But then suddenly you're old and the scheduled life didn't arrive. You find yourself asking, 'Well then, exactly what was it I was having – that interlude – the scrambly madness – all that time I had before?'' Douglas Coupland

> 'One of the pluses of getting older is you set some limits.' Nicolas Cage

> 'And meanwhile time goes about its immemorial work of making everyone look and feel like shit.' Martin Amis

How to catch up with your wealth plans later in life

Here's an investment truism.

'The rule of thumb is that you should save anywhere from 10 to 15 per cent of your income towards retirement.'

It's oft stated (in this case in an interview with an expert from US group Fidelity Investments) but these 20 words nicely sum up the accepted wisdom about building up your pot of risk capital. You need to save a large proportion of your income to fund your later years.

These same experts at Fidelity recently expanded on this truism to issue a bunch of very powerful savings guidelines. They suggested that:

- At age 35, you should have saved an amount equal to your annual salary.
- At age 45, you should have saved three times your annual salary.
- At 55, you should have five times your salary.
- When you retire at age 67, you should have eight times your annual pay, although more than a few financial experts reckon this number should be above 10 times your annual pay!

Sound simple enough doesn't it!

The problem is that what's a truth is very rarely a reality.

Humans, as we've already discovered many times in this book, have a way of ignoring rationality and truths and replacing them with behavioural tics and grim necessity. Our Fidelity guidelines, for instance, assume that you begin saving when you are 25 for your pension, when in fact most evidence suggests that the real number (after putting aside enough money for a property) is 35. These numbers also assume that whatever money you build up in your pension plan (in the US a 401(k) plan) is matched by your employer (not as common as we'd like), that your income grows faster than inflation (rarely the case in recent decades) and that shares increase in value by about 5.5 per cent per annum (a safer assumption, though shares can of course be hugely volatile).

Yet the big 'elephant in the room' is that many of us don't put aside enough money in the first place! Fidelity is honest enough to admit that this is possibly the case. Back in 2013, for instance, another piece of research by the large US firm revealed that the average balance in a 401(k) pensions plan was just US$80,600, although these numbers also suggested that for those savers who were continuously employed in a workplace plan for the past decade, the average balance rose to US$211,800. Sadly, the average 65-year-old couple retiring in 2013 would need US$220,000 to spend on health care costs alone. Under-contribution towards pensions and risk capital pots is endemic in both the US and the UK. Recent research by economists suggests that most workers are only putting away 6 to 7 per cent of their annual income into a 401(k) or workplace retirement plan, not the suggested 10 to 15 per cent.

But it gets much, much worse.

Another report, this time by financial services website HelloWallet, revealed that most Americans with 401(k) plans were accumulating debt faster than they're saving for retirement! The researchers in this particular report suggested that the amount that retirement plan participants spent to pay-down debts had risen nearly 70 per cent over the past 20 years to 2013. The problem? According to the report 'many workers argue that they are unable to contribute as much as they would like to their 401(k) plan because they have more expenses and less income than they had in the past. The problem is most pronounced for those closest to retirement. Half of retirement plan savers 50 to 65 are accruing debt faster than they're building up their savings. The HelloWallet report reveals that many older investors are spending an average of 22 per cent of their income paying down debt. Astonishingly, the average sum saved for retirement for this 'at risk' group was just two years of retirement income.

Given that the vast majority of readers face **at least 17** years in retirement at age 65, what should we do if we find we're falling behind on our plans for building up our pensions or risk capital?

PUT MORE MONEY INTO YOUR PENSION NOW!

The simplest strategy when faced by a 'later in life' financial crisis is to just put as much money as possible into your long-term savings plans. Putting an additional 1 per cent of pay into your 401(k) or employer-sponsored retirement account every year can make a big difference. Remember that you can put up to US$17,500 in a 401(k) during one year and an additional

US$5,500 if you're 50 or older. Stash the maximum amount into your individual retirement account (IRA), too – up to US$5,500 in 2013 or US$6,500 for those aged 50 and over. Work out how to free up some spare cash (see next strategy) and max out your contributions as quickly as possible.

DOWNSIZE AND REDUCE EXPENSES TO MANAGE CASH FLOW

Maximizing your contributions to a pension plan implies you can actually find a way to free up cash from your budget. In order to do that your first and most important step is to determine your net worth – a familiar message in this book! Start by asking how much do you owe versus how much you own? Then establish that budget (if you haven't already) and then stick to it! Finally take a long, hard look at your lifestyle. You may need to reduce many expenses now to ultimately reach your retirement goal. It might even be worth thinking about moving to a cheaper area in order to cut costs.

RETIRE LATER

If all else fails, think about retiring later. This of course assumes that you've thought long and hard about a 'third age career' i.e. a career or job that you can happily and remuneratively pursue in your 50s and 60s. These aren't two a penny within our existing labour markets but they might allow you to forestall the retirement D-Day and thus let you build up a bigger pot. If you can move your retirement age on by five years you could a) give your pension pot a big boost by reducing the number of years you need to save up for, and b) give yourself five extra years to make contributions.

Putting it all together

I don't think there's any single magic bullet that will prevent you from living dangerously (financially at least) as you approach retirement with an insufficient pensions pot. A combination of measures – which might even include working

after your retirement – will probably do the trick. I also think we underestimate another huge factor – excessive fees charged on pension savings plans. A recent research report by a Yale University academic estimated that getting on for half the deficit in many investors' long-term savings plans could be explained by charges that were simply unacceptable. Luckily, you can address this last challenge by switching to cheaper investment funds (such as index-tracking funds) and doing a little more of your own DIY investment management.

But lurking in the background of this chapter is another much more concerning issue, constantly increasing longevity. Many younger readers of this book will have no other choice than to retire at 70 by the time they get to their later years. Yet even this much later pensions age might thrust them into a financial crisis as they discover that human longevity statistics have been consistently underestimating progress in recent decades. Many experts reckon that within 30 years the average expectancy of a 65-year-old male will have increased from the current 17 years to as much as 25 years by the middle of the century. If that's the case, simply increasing the retirement age by five years isn't enough. We might need in fact to increase it to as much as 75 years and also ask pensioners to put aside **extra** additional funds to help compensate them for substantially increased personal health care costs (which can easily amount to more than US$100,000 in total). So, even when you thought you were safe, along comes the wonders of modern medical technology to remind us of why we all need to radically increase the returns we make from our investments.

39 Invest where you have an edge

> 'Behind every stock is a company. Find out what it's doing.'
> Peter Lynch

> 'Owning stocks is like having children – don't get involved with more than you can handle.' Peter Lynch

> 'The worst thing you can do is invest in companies you know nothing about. Unfortunately, buying stocks on ignorance is still a popular American pastime.' Peter Lynch

> 'Never invest in any idea you can't illustrate with a crayon.'
> Peter Lynch

> 'Know what you own, and know why you own it.' Peter Lynch

Familiar is better

In this short chapter – the first in our section looking at practical, everyday ideas to help make you wealthier – I want to draw on the wisdom of the chap relentlessly mentioned in our quotes section, Peter Lynch. I think it's fair to say that after perhaps Warren Buffett and, arguably, Benjamin Graham, Lynch is regarded as one of the greatest money-makers and investors in history. He managed the fabulously successful mutual fund Fidelity Magellan between 1977 and 1990, during which time its average annual return was 29.2 per cent.

But it's not really this investment record that has lived on – impressive though it is – more his common-sense approach to investing, which he was keen to share with anyone willing to listen to his interviews or read his excellent books. Lynch argued strongly that we can all make money from investing by simply being logical, intelligent and disciplined. Crucially he argued – rightly, I believe – that the ordinary person in the street has more advantages than the very biggest institutions. In Lynch's world view, we collectively as individuals have the edge and all we need to do is harness our common-sense skills to take advantage of that opportunity.

At its core, Lynch's philosophy was very similar to that of Warren Buffett and many other successful investors and business people. He believed that capital was precious and should not be squandered. That required patient research and due diligence, largely based around minimizing your risk by investing in solid businesses that were undervalued by everyone else, especially the big institutions. Crucially, he believed, you should only ever invest in businesses you understood, probably knew very well anyway, and could test on a regular basis. Lynch constantly implored us all to kick the tyres of every business we invested our capital in.

That familiarity instantly, he argued, gives us an edge! We can invest in stuff we intimately know and feel confident about. But there's more to our edge than just buying the familiar. Lynch argued that the big institutions with their huge pools of capital are held back by constraints that shouldn't concern the rest of us.

What's our edge?

In simple terms, Lynch argued that you can do the detailed up-close analysis that takes time looking into a company. In a big company that'll require a highly paid professional to spend thousands of pounds of their time snooping around business offices when they'd rather be sitting in boring meetings looking at PowerPoints and winning the promotion game! I also think you'll probably have a greater tolerance of risk, which means that if you've a long enough time horizon (say, ten years or more), you can afford to take losses of 20 per cent or more investing in something you really, truly believe in. For the average institution, any loss much beyond 10 per cent is usually fairly terminal for a manager's career. You can also use the product of the companies you invest in on a regular basis, allowing you to add a proper personal dimension to every decision about investing. Last but by no means least, you can invest in illiquid stuff over long periods of time because you don't have to answer to nosey regulators who worry that stuff that isn't easy to sell could crash and burn.

RESEARCH AN OPPORTUNITY IN THE SAME WAY YOU'D RESEARCH A NEW HOME

How do we harness these advantages to give us an edge? My first strategy is the simplest and is a call to look on any investment in the same way you'd (hopefully) look at buying a home you're going to live in.

What are your key steps in house buying? You start online and relentlessly look at all the opportunities, constantly on the lookout for the exact right property that ticks all the right boxes.

Then you talk to the estate agent, and visit the property.

But even after you've visited the property, you probably go back again and again… constantly looking for a fault. You also probably walk around the neighbourhood and see if the 'locale' ticks the relevant boxes – safe, good shops, easy access to work? Then once your mind is made up you make an offer, but you probably never ever buy anything unless you think the price is right.

Why not do exactly the same for buying any other investment? Relentlessly research online and search through equivalent opportunities, running a form of SWOT (strengths, weaknesses, opportunities, threats) analysis for each idea. Then go and visit the company on its website, understand what it does. Next up visit the company's front line, say, its shops or its offices. Maybe you'll be able to buy some of the products and understand what makes the company different – and what gives it its competitive moat of advantage.

MYSTERY SHOP!

My next strategy draws on an idea used by a very successful small fund manager I know very well. He's managed money for more than a decade on a very contrarian basis with fairly minimal resources – he has about five people working for him in total. His central idea (which has made his investors huge profits) is to follow through on strategy one and then draw up a hit list of familiar businesses that he can ask all his friends and neighbours to research via mystery shopping. He asks them to try out the products and service and see what they think. He even provides them with some simple checklists such as whether the business makes its customers wait too long to get served (assuming they're in a retail environment) or whether the customer service response times are a bit tardy. As this mystery shopping doesn't actually require too much hard work, he won't pay them for their time but he will pay for buying the product or service they're shopping for. This mystery shopping exercise is designed to harness the power of your friends and colleagues in a fun way to back up – or disprove – your central investment thesis.

HARNESS THE POWER OF THE CROWD

My last strategy is also used by my friendly investment fund manager, which is to harness the cutting edge of the web. In the past few years we've seen a huge explosion in the number of online review websites where you can very quickly get a sense for how the business is being 'reviewed' by its customers. There will inevitably be the odd bitter twisted critic or two but very quickly you'll be able to get a snapshot of whether the business is well regarded… or not! Crucially, I don't want you to focus too much on the price being asked for the product. Many people will complain about this regardless, whereas a focus on service, ease of purchase, policies as regards returns and so on is a much more useful guide.

Putting it all together

Armed with all this information I think you can then begin to make the right decision about your opportunity. What we're really looking for here is an investment opportunity – be it a share or a potential property investment – where you think you're buying a quality 'asset' at a decent price that will slowly accumulate in value over the next five to ten years.

The key here is to buy something that is underappreciated but valuable, with that good 'value' offering you some margin of safety in terms of risk.

Crucially though, once you've made your decision – in a hopefully rational and informed manner – you need to be as rational in the 'housekeeping' (or management) of these ideas and opportunities as possible. Lynch constantly reminds us to be considered but not emotional about our investments. We need to keep a beady eye on the business and see if everything is going to plan and that it is still 'underappreciated' by the market. If it isn't, sell it and move on to the next opportunity, of which there are many for the private investor. Remember you have the edge and there's always new opportunities out there, you just need to make sure you've invested in the right opportunities… at the right price.

40 Timing your investments

> '"Market timing" is unappealing to long-term investors. As in hunting deer or fishing for rainbow trout, investors have learned the importance of "being there" and using patient persistence – so they are there when opportunity knocks.' Charles Ellis, US engineer

> 'What to do when the market goes down? Read the opinions of the investment gurus who are quoted in the WSJ. And, as you read, laugh. We all know that the pundits can't predict short-term market movements. Yet there they are, desperately trying to sound intelligent when they really haven't got a clue.' Jonathan Clements

> 'Do you know what investing for the long run but listening to market news everyday is like? It's like a man walking up a big hill with a yo-yo and keeping his eyes fixed on the yo-yo instead of the hill.' Alan Abelson

> 'Only liars manage to always be out during bad times and in during good times.' Bernard Baruch

> 'Market timing is impossible to perfect.' Mark Rieppe

Can you reduce risk by moving in and out of the market?

The consensus seems to be to buy and hold over the long term. Does that mean I should never attempt to time the market? The standard long-term advice from most equity enthusiasts is to run a buy-and-hold strategy, i.e. stick with shares through thick and thin and do not try to change your buying and selling behaviour based on market conditions. A host of both academic and broker research suggests that trying to work out the best time to 'buy the market' is difficult at best and disastrous at worst.

For buy-and-hold enthusiasts the idea that private investors sitting at home watching their computer screens can somehow judge the direction of sophisticated global markets is frankly delusional.

Researchers at the Schwab Center for Investment Research in the US have put some hard numbers on the cost of this curious behavioural vice of obsessing about the ups and downs of stock markets.

These researchers looked at three buy-and-hold investors who each received US$2,000 annually for 20 years to invest in the markets, a grand total of US$40,000. Two decades later here were the results:

- **The Perfect Timer** – US$387,120. Strategy? The money is put into the market at the monthly low point every year.
- **Treasury Bill (government gilt) Investor** – US$76,558. Strategy? Terrified of shares, the investor puts their money only into Treasury bills.
- **Autopilot Investor** – US$362,185. Strategy? This investor automatically invests the money on the day received and then leaves it alone.

Market timing RIP? Probably, but don't kill the idea of moving into and out of a market just yet. There is a fly in the ointment of this conventional wisdom. I want you to go to Yahoo's finance section, where you can download the full data set of price returns for the Dow Jones Industrial Average since inception at the end of the 1890s. Take these data and then chart them, and you will see long periods of dreadful price returns. The trend overall is clear – up – but there is a huge amount of variation on the way. For example, if you invested in the beginning of April 1929, the Dow was at 333.79, but it did not hit that level again until April 1954. The dismal tale? Markets and investments can go wrong for entire decades if you are unlucky!

In fact, if we're not careful we can become victims of our own 'lifecycle' of investing. In reality we have to pick a 20-to-30-year buy-and-hold investment window. When we are young, we do not really save much (or at least I didn't), so when we start saving in earnest, it is probably around our late 20s or early 30s. We therefore accept that we have 20–25 years in which we need to spice up our returns by investing in risky assets before we hit our 50s, at which point we start to 'derisk' a tad, which means winding back into safer assets such as bonds. However, if we pick the wrong 20–25-year period in stock markets we could be in trouble! Maybe we need some form of signal that tells us when to move from one investment idea to the next?

WATCH THOSE SIGNALS

In an earlier chapter we looked at how economic signals can be hugely useful – maybe the trick is to use these in working out what to invest in… and what not to invest in!

Professors M. Hashem Pesaran and Allan Timmermann looked at simple systems to market time in a paper for *The Economic Journal*. Using data sets from 1970 to 1993 their work suggested that without the benefit of hindsight, an investor could have correctly predicted the direction of the UK stock market roughly 60 per cent of the time on a monthly basis. These academics reckoned that using publicly available information, such as interest rates, money growth, oil prices and growth in industrial production, investors could tell when to start selling assets as markets become worried about increasing levels of risk.

To run this system, go back to my previous chapter on signals and then incorporate ideas about bubbles and start watching the markets carefully.

AVOID VOLATILE MARKETS

Another tactic could simply be to get out of a market and preserve your capital when investors start to panic. Technical analysts at Birinyi Associates looked at market data and showed that investors who were out of the market during the five worst days each year do astronomically better than those who hold their stocks throughout each year. For example, in 2000, the S&P 500 Stock Index dropped 10 per cent (not including dividends), but an investor who invested in the S&P on every day but the five worst days of 2000 made a profit of 9 per cent. In 1998, being out of the market during the five worst days would have given you a return of 56 per cent instead of 27 per cent. Overall, a dollar invested in the S&P stocks in 1966 became US$12 for the buy-and-hold investor (again, without dividends) but an incredible US$987 for the investor who missed the five worst days each year.

SPECULATORS COULD USE KEY INDICATORS

US wealth manager Mebane Faber has also suggested a clever idea that is worth getting your head around even though it is a bit technical. Faber went looking for a system that is simple to administer and clearly tells you when to buy and when to sell.

His solution is something called the 200-day simple moving average for an index like the S&P 500, one of the most basic technical analysis indicators. It is worked out by adding up all the closing prices (for an index or a share) for the past 200 market days and dividing by 200.

According to Faber, the rule is to buy when the asset price or market shows a monthly price above the 200-day moving average and sell when it moves below. It is not really more complicated than that, although one implication is obvious: you will be spending a fair amount of time holding large parts of your portfolio in cash.

Putting it all together

The bottom line? On balance I wouldn't recommend market timing in any shape or form for the vast majority of readers with two notable exceptions – those of a speculative nature and older investors fast approaching retirement. It's obvious why speculative types might be interested in market timing largely because they are much more short term in attitude and outlook. But I also think older investors might think about this approach because they absolutely cannot afford to take risks with their capital. If they want to start accessing their savings pot for an income but they haven't 'derisked' their investments they might look to control risk by using one of the strategies above, largely in order to avoid any massive market downturns just before they retire!

41 Buying and selling discipline

> 'One of the great lessons I've learned in athletics is that you've got to discipline your life. No matter how good you may be, you've got to be willing to cut out of your life those things that keep you from going to the top.' Bob Richards

> 'The price of excellence is discipline. The cost of mediocrity is disappointment.' William A. Ward

> 'The market does not know if you are long or short and could not care less. You are the only one emotionally involved with your position. The market is just reacting to supply and demand and if you are cheering it one way, there is always somebody else cheering it just as hard that it will go the other way.' Marty Schwartz, aka Pit Bull

> 'The most important rule of trading is to play good defence, not great offense. Every day I assume every position I have is wrong. I know where my stop risk points are going to be. I do that so I can define my maximum possible draw down.' Paul Tudor Jones

> 'Taking small losses is part of the game. Taking large losses can take you out of the game.' Doug Kass

When to buy and when to sell?

You don't have to be a 'trader' as such to care about how to trade. Buying at the right price, as well as selling at the right price, requires discipline and patience, as is the ability to know when to take a profit and when to cut a loss. Too many investors and business people I've run into blow their self-evident advantages by trading in the wrong manner. They might, for instance, spot a good opportunity and then decide that because they're worried about the chance that the market might turn against them in some unforeseen way, cut their profits and sell quickly, taking profits. Sometimes this makes sense, sometimes it doesn't. The key is to understand what kind of investment you're making and then shape your behaviour around that discipline.

At its core we need to remind ourselves again of the familiar distinction between a focused opportunity as opposed to the more diversified opportunities that sit in your portfolio. With some investments we've really done our research and we're willing to take extra risks because we think 'it's worth it' i.e. we've managed risk through knowledge. With other opportunities by contrast we don't have that in-depth knowledge of the particular opportunity, nor the inclination to spend the time to acquire it. In this scenario we're looking to manage risk by diversifying between ideas and balancing losers with winners.

This focused/diversified tension should inform how we trade an asset or investment. With an opportunity we know a great deal about we should be worried about selling out too early, especially if we really 'believe' in the idea. Equally, by tying up your capital in that asset we don't want to make a mistake by picking the wrong opportunity, so we should be willing to cut losses quickly.

The key bias we're looking out for in this situation is called loss aversion. In simple terms, it means that we stick with our losing positions — because we're emotionally invested in them — and then sell our successful positions far too early. This approach really doesn't make much sense for those investments we really believe in. In fact it's positively stupid and will make us much poorer over the long term.

Yet it's also true that in the more diversified parts of our portfolio we should maybe take a rather different approach and look at taking profits at a sensible moment. With these more disparate ideas, where we don't have the time to constantly check on what's happening with our investment, we should be more methodical about how we trade winners and losers, and recycle capital. In simple terms we need to rebalance on a regular basis.

WHEN TO STICK WITH YOUR PROFITS

We're all subconsciously aware of the fears lurking behind the old proverb that a bird in the hand is worth two in the bush i.e. it's better to have a lesser gain but certain realization now rather than the possibility of a greater one that may come to nothing in the future. Yet this precautionary way of thinking about future prospects is probably flawed if you truly believe you have a great opportunity within your portfolio, especially as that investment starts to increase in value. At the beginning of your investment, during the research process, you probably arrived at what you thought might be a sensible value for this opportunity i.e. hopefully a multiple of what you paid for it. If that analysis is correct, you should stick with it all the way through its subsequent rise. Yet I think it's also sensible to slowly start taking bites out of that success.

If you are concerned that you might have reached a plateau in the value of your asset, start selling a small bit for instance when you've hit a 100 per cent gain i.e. maybe a 25 per cent segment of your total holding, which in effect means that you've recovered half your initial investment. As an investment hits the 200 per cent gain mark perhaps think about selling another 25 per cent of your total holding, which would mean that you've now realized your entire initial sum. You could maybe take one last slice at the 300 per cent mark at which point frankly I'd stop taking any profits at all and just sit tight. In my experience, investments that increase this much in value tend to carry on moving forward in a quite relentless way, sometimes smashing past ten times the total return!

ALWAYS RUN A STOP LOSS NUMBER

My next key idea is to ruthlessly apply a stop loss procedure on **all** your investments. Quite where you set the percentage loss point is up to you, but the process should be thorough and unemotional. Here's how it could work. Any investment has three trigger or sell points i.e. percentage losses based on the original investment. At the first trigger point (say 15 per cent) you'd simply make a note to research what's causing the loss. If something strikes you as clearly concerning maybe at this point start selling. Alternatively, you may believe your initial idea is still spot on but you're simply encountering some 'market turbulence'. At the next trigger (say 20 per cent) you'd resolve to sell the investment **unless** after further research you decide that it's still a great idea, but I'd add one crucial caveat, which is that a friend has to also agree with you!! Our last trigger point is an automatic, no excuses, no second thoughts selling point – say at 25 per cent. Once an investment hits this big loss, sell it without thinking!

REBALANCE FOR YOUR DIVERSIFIED PORTFOLIO

In a diversified portfolio of opportunities and assets, you need some fairly fixed rules to help keep you on the straight and narrow. My suggestion would be to operate an annual rebalancing exercise either at the halfway year point on 1 July and/or at the beginning of the year on 1 January. Look down your list of assets and identify all those assets that have increased by more than 25 per cent in value. Sell whatever amount is required to take you back to that 25 per cent point and reinvest this money in the losing positions. With the 25 per cent gain I'd be tempted to keep half of that gain (12.5 per cent) and take profits on the rest – again reinvesting all the profits in the losing position.

Putting it all together

At a basic level investors need discipline in order to make money and their greatest enemy is usually their own ego. To combat this we need to have focus, knowledge and most importantly a plan. As with so many other challenges in this book, I think drawing up a plan and then monitoring it over time makes sense and instils a sense of emotional discipline in the reader. With investments this might consist of a list of your assets with targets set next to them – targets for desired gain, targets for income and stop loss levels where you'll sell out automatically. You should review this plan on a regular basis but not too regular a basis i.e. once every three months at most. See how the plan is going, how your portfolio is moving ahead based on your targets and whether you have any 'challenges' or 'issues'. With each problem investment, review it, analyse it and then think about selling it. And if you do dispose of the investment, always learn from your mistake.

42 Cash and its uses

> 'Money is seen as a great evil. But I've never seen a pile of cash stab someone.' Jarod Kintz

> 'Cash is king. No matter how many good opportunities come your way, do not invest all your cash. If you run out of reserves, the smallest or foolish of things may bring you down. Companies with millions in assets have gone bankrupt because they cannot make a US$25,000 payment.' Mauricio Chaves Mesén

> 'Today people who hold cash equivalents feel comfortable. They shouldn't. They have opted for a terrible long-term asset, one that pays virtually nothing and is certain to depreciate in value.' Warren Buffett

> 'The three most dreaded words in the English language are "negative cash flow".' Sir David Tang

> 'I love cash.' Roger Moore

Why cash makes sense… some of the time

Time for a confession: I have mixed feelings about cash. Of course I'd love it if anyone decided to give me lots of the stuff but overall I believe that cash is a tiny bit overrated as a financial asset. As Warren Buffett notes, cash makes people feel comfortable and I can't help but think that comfort isn't a feeling that sits nicely with those who strive to be wealthier! I've always been struck by the research on brain training for instance, which suggests that if any techniques do work at making you smarter, they probably require you to do things that make you uncomfortable, make your brain ache and are generally difficult to achieve. Stimulus and dislocation from familiar tasks, many scientists argue, is a necessary part of making yourself more 'intelligent'. I suspect the same is true for wealth. We already know that hard work is usually an essential requirement for building wealth, as is going out there and making yourself uncomfortable by taking risks. Cash works against this all by encouraging you to think that you're safe… when you're not, especially once we factor back in inflation!

My cynical take on cash is also motivated by a harder-nosed analysis of its investment prowess – which is poor to put it mildly! Remember the earlier chapter on bonds where we examined the long-term returns from holding fixed income securities versus risky equities? We used data provided by academic economist Aswath Damodaran, who examined returns over a period between 1928 and 2011. Cash makes an appearance in the shape of what are called T Bills, which are government bonds with a duration (the period over which the money is borrowed) of one year. These T Bills are in effect cash or what cash would earn if we lent it to the government for a year or less. Using Damodaran's numbers we discover that cash would have returned a measly US$1,970, equivalent to a return of just 3.66 per cent per annum over the period between 1928 and 2011. In bold, big terms equities returned over 100 times a greater return than a cash equivalent.

Oh and let's also remind ourselves of that nasty word beginning with the letter I – 'Inflation'. Over this same period (1928 to 2011) inflation would have pushed up the cost of a basket of goods and services worth US$100 in 1928 to just over US$1,300 (US$1,315 to be precise or a gain of 1,215 per cent) by 2011. So the good news is that near-cash equivalents would have generated a **real** return over this period… but only by the smallest of margins over those 82 years!

Yet I freely admit I see cash through the prism of investment and wealth creation, and it's self-evidently true that cash also serves many other primary, base purposes (not least psychological). Perhaps a more honest method is to borrow a familiar approach in this book, which is to build a balance sheet for cash, with both the pluses and minuses, debits and credits listed.

On the positive side, cash has many pluses including the fact that it is liquid, useful as an emergency reserve and does well in deflationary environments. Investors would also observe that cash has great optionality value, which means that it can be used at a later date to buy other financial assets on the cheap after markets have crashed in value and it also sometimes produces a steady income, although not a great one. Last but by no means least, it also gives us personal courage to do many other things. So in terms of practicalities I'd suggest that this list of pluses and minuses probably ends up as something approaching a draw, which should remind us that dowdy cash does have its uses after all!

In fact in this book I've already suggested two very concrete ways of deploying cash. First, we obviously all need some cash – or its short-term equivalents such as deposit accounts – as the basis of an emergency fund, which will consist of about 6 months in household expenses. In investment terms I've also suggested a sensible cash reserve. In portfolio terms this reserve for most investors over the age of 40 might consist of between 5 and 20 per cent depending on your age, market conditions and your need for income.

But there's also a whole bunch of practical questions that surrounds this issue of holding cash, not least that cash comes in many different shapes and sizes! Clearly what you choose to do with cash makes a big difference!

❸ MAXIMIZE YOUR GOVERNMENT PROTECTION

My first and perhaps most important strategy is to make full use of government deposit protection schemes for cash accounts. You don't tend to get that much for free from the government, but protection of savings and deposit accounts is one of those unmitigated free lunches that we should all dine out on! In the US the Federal Deposit Insurance Corporation or FDIC 'covers all deposit accounts, including checking and savings accounts, money market deposit accounts and certificates of deposit' up to 'US$250,000 per depositor, per insured bank, for each account ownership category'.

That insurance seems mighty generous compared to other countries, and especially the UK where the equivalent Financial

Services Compensation Scheme offers just £85,000 per person per authorized firm. The key point here is that you get protection up to a certain level and based on your usage of that banking institution's products i.e. if you run all your deposit accounts as well as other savings accounts with the same institution, you could very easily bump against the upper limits of these schemes. This alone suggests that you should diversify between institutions to maximize your protection. I'd also argue that diversification is absolutely essential once you go above those limits of US$250,000 and £85,000. Once you've smashed through these limits your protection runs out in the event of a bank failure – and history teaches us that it's big depositors who get disproportionately badly hit in bank bailouts as any wealthy Cypriot reader will now know to their cost following their own local banking meltdown.

MAXIMIZE YOUR INCOME BY INCREASING YOUR DURATION

Another simple strategy is to maximize the duration over which you'll offer up your cash via savings, deposits and money market accounts. Frankly, if you can get an extra 1 per cent or even 2 per cent by lending that cash out for anything between 1 and 12 months I'd do it. But I'd be careful at going much beyond 12 months and in practical terms if you're deploying emergency capital, I'd stop at about 6 months.

MAKE INTELLIGENT USE OF NEAR CASH ALTERNATIVES

Many wealthy investors make extensive use of money market accounts, which are equivalent to cash accounts but involve a professional manager moving money between various different structures, products and funds to maximize your income and minimize your risk. Governments around the world are reluctant to see money market funds lose their capital so that makes them fairly conservative investment ideas. Lending to the government via say T Bills of short duration is another alternative for cash investors.

Putting it all together

I'm going to conclude by making one final, slightly counterintuitive (at least within the parameters of this book) observation, which is that it doesn't make sense to take a risk with cash. Throughout this book I've argued that risk taking is an essential part of wealth creation and generally I'm something of a champion for not taking the comfortable route to success. But cash is supposed to be boring and in my experience too many investors treat it as they do their other investments i.e. something they can take some risks with to get a better return. Some intelligent use of both duration and different borrowers (governments, money market funds) does make some sense but they are as far as I would go. Do not be tempted to look at more alternative ideas that don't have government deposit protection – or not at least for your cash reserves! Taking risks with your cash is stupid and pointless, no matter how attractive the yield looks.

But I also think we all need to work harder with our cash, by looking online at different products. In particular we all have to work **extra** hard to make sure that the cash deposit rates offered by the providers of our pensions, SIPPs, ISAs and other tax-based schemes is up to scratch. Too many tax-based savings structures subsidize their low headline charges by offering rubbish interest rates on cash in the account. Don't accept being short-changed while holding cash in a pension.

43 Think global, beware confiscation

> 'The Internet is becoming the town square for the global village of tomorrow.' Bill Gates

> 'This is the moment when we must build on the wealth that open markets have created, and share its benefits more equitably. Trade has been a cornerstone of our growth and global development. But we will not be able to sustain this growth if it favours the few, and not the many.' Barack Obama

> 'What I've enjoyed most, though, is meeting people who have a real interest in food and sharing ideas with them. Good food is a global thing and I find that there is always something new and amazing to learn – I love it!' Jamie Oliver

> 'The 1980s will seem like a walk in the park when compared to new global challenges, where annual productivity increases of 6 per cent may not be enough. A combination of software, brains and running harder will be needed to bring that percentage up to 8 per cent or 9 per cent.' Jack Welch

> 'This progressive deterioration in the value of money through history is not an accident, and has had behind it two great driving forces – the impecuniosity of governments and the superior political influence of the debtor class.' John Maynard Keynes

The pensions grab

By now you'll hopefully realize that the author of this book is not one of those tin helmet Cassandras who reckon we're all on our way to hell in a handcart, powered by crazy socialist governments and the incipient bankruptcy of modern capitalism!

To me, the serious business of money, wealth and investment is too important to be left to ideological prejudices and it seems to me that both the conservative **and** progressive investor might recognize that a dose of quasi-leftist Keynesianism (involving extensive state intervention) might make as much sense on some occasions as a rigorous dose of free market austerity does on others. In both circumstances there's money to be made by the smart investor and business person and it strikes me that the place to make your political protest is at the ballot box not via your brokerage account!

Nevertheless, I think it important that we do realize one very real world threat – government confiscation of your wealth via 'pension fund reform'.

Now let's be very clear about this.

Governments already have clever and cunning ways to, in effect, confiscate accumulated wealth and high levels of income. It's called the tax system and by and large modern, advanced governments don't have to go to excessive lengths to grab a bigger portion of your wealth. Instead of confiscating your house, they can simply tax you a bit more.

But pensions represent an entirely different conundrum. In most – though not all cases – investors choose to pool their long-term savings and investments with other investors in large schemes. These pension schemes can be organized by a range of bodies including governments, employers and mutual organizations. But the point is that by working as a collective, we all benefit from lower charges, and more consistent investment administration.

Unfortunately, there's also a very substantial disadvantage with these collective pension arrangements, which is that they're very easily accessible to governments in a tight spot. Put simply, grabbing your house would usually start an outright insurrection in most advanced countries whereas a spot of 'creative accounting' with national pooled pension schemes is usually just a matter of intense controversy i.e. not a fire starter that will ignite civil war.

Governments are acutely aware of this and have come to view pension schemes as an easy target.

In this book I've tried very hard to not produce too many lists of past events but I think it crucially important that you peruse the following recent examples of state pension fund confiscation from around the world:

- **Hungary. December 2010.** In 2010, Hungary gave its citizens an option: they could move all of the private pension funds into the government fund or they would lose the 70 per cent pension payout from the government when they retired. Hungary used the money to pay current state pensions as well as paying government debt.
- **Ireland. May 2011.** The Irish government instituted a tax that taxed the capital value of private pensions at 0.6 per cent for four years to fund a government jobs initiative. Only private pensions are taxed, not government pensions.
- **Portugal. December 2011.** The Portuguese government moved assets (worth US$7.7 billion) of the four biggest banks, which consist largely of private pension funds, onto the government's balance sheet. The government acquired 5.6 billion in euros (US$7.7 billion).
- **Poland. September 2013.** Half of private pensions are confiscated by the government of Poland in order to be able to borrow more money. Bond holdings in the private pension fund would be transferred into the state pension system. The seizure was done by the government so that it could reduce its debt to GDP ratio, thus allowing it to borrow more money.

In just over two decades I've counted at least a dozen systematic attempts worldwide to grab national pension fund assets from their investors. Some plans have been defeated while others have been terribly sneaky and operated by the backdoor by for instance instituting one-off taxes on dividend payments into pension funds (the UK).

Unfortunately, I'm willing to wager that this form of national creative accounting will only get worse over the next few decades as governments wake up to the terrible realization that their future pension fund obligations are simply unsustainable. The bottom line? Governments will increasingly raid our pension pots and attempt to grab hold of our accumulated wealth by fair means or foul.

What can we do about it?

HAVE MULTIPLE SAVINGS POTS EVEN IF YOU ARE IN AN EMPLOYEE SCHEME

One protection is to not to rely exclusively on large, pooled, collective pension schemes, offered by your employee and/or the government. In the UK, for instance, we've seen the emergence of new pooled schemes such as NEST, which attempt to provide a low-cost framework for poorer savers.

This new scheme is an excellent idea and one I applaud but I'd also argue that anyone who invests in the scheme should endeavour to also build up a separate **personal** pension plan over which they have direct control. In the UK that might mean a self-invested personal pension, for instance, called a SIPP. In the US 401(k) plans offer similar benefits. Investors are perfectly entitled to operate both a collective, pooled plan and a personal one. In my judgement, governments will probably avoid making any overt attacks on these personal pension plans except by the back door of taxation. Pooled schemes will, I suspect, be much easier targets for asset-hungry governments.

DON'T RELY ON PENSIONS

In an earlier chapter we reminded readers that a pension plan is just one of a number of different tax advantaged savings structures. In the UK, for instance, you can use everything from individual savings accounts (ISAs) through to venture capital trusts. Investors could also simply avoid using tax-based schemes and invest in an ordinary investment plan, which has no obvious government subsidies and loopholes, although you will have to pay tax on any gains.

GO GLOBAL

My last strategy is to think about what's powering these pension confiscations and 'creative accounting' schemes – government balance sheets. In most cases, governments make an attack on pensions because they simply need the cash. Their balance sheets look mightily unhealthy and they need someone to help them out, i.e. you!

Pension schemes offer a great get-out-of-jail card, with relatively benign electoral impacts! Lurking at the back of this balance sheet issue is perhaps the greatest challenge for any investor who wants to build up their wealth, which is whether to place **all** your bets on your home country.

Possibly if you are an American reader, there is some logic to sticking with the world's greatest, most liquid economy, but even here I'd argue that there's a great deal of common sense to internationally diversify your investment holdings.

For investors in all other countries, I'd suggest that international diversification is absolutely essential and that we should all have at least 50 per cent of our total assets spread across different countries, markets and regions.

Some foreign property assets might make sense and it's notable that one of the fastest-growing industries on planet Earth are the free ports in jurisdictions as varied as Switzerland and Singapore, where the uber-wealthy can store their priceless works of art, collectable cars, coin and stamp collections and gold bars!

Putting it all together

There are, of course, a number of additional strategies that might help to keep your assets and wealth beyond the reach of confiscatory governments.

You could, for instance, choose to invest in gold as a physical store of value and indeed I think some investment in gold makes a modicum of sense – but only up to a point, which is probably never much more than 20 per cent of your assets (if not a great deal less than this).

I'd also argue that governments can still grab gold if they want, via the simple expedient of intervening at the small number of registered gold vaults globally. Investors can also stash their money offshore as well, especially if they're super-wealthy and can afford the extortionate professional fees that usually accompany this tax avoidance/evasion. But I'd argue that for the vast majority of readers this is a pointless exercise, and will only encourage the taxman to take an interest in your activities.

For most readers the best we can do to control the risk of government confiscation is to think, act and invest globally and diversify our risk.

44 Beware the fat pitch

> 'It's a proprietary strategy. I can't go into it in great detail.'
> Bernie Madoff on his investment strategy in *Barron's*, May 7, 2001

> 'If it weren't for greed, intolerance, hate, passion and murder, you would have no works of art, no great buildings, no medical science, no Mozart, no van Gogh, no Muppets and no Louis Armstrong.' Jasper Fforde

> 'I am afraid that our eyes are bigger than our stomachs, and that we have more curiosity than understanding. We grasp at everything, but catch nothing except wind.' Michel de Montaigne

> 'No drug, not even alcohol, causes the fundamental ills of society. If we're looking for the source of our troubles, we shouldn't test people for drugs, we should test them for stupidity, ignorance, greed and love of power.' P. J. O'Rourke

> 'I made a lot of money for my clients.' Bernie Madoff

If it's too good to be true that's probably because it is!

Unless you've been hanging out in a cave in Afghanistan I suspect you've probably heard of Bernie Madoff by now – and I have a suspicion that even a few of those cave dwellers might also have picked up on the fact that the supposed 'hedge fund' supremo was in fact a giant Ponzi scheme swindler. Now safely ensconced in a dry and warm place courtesy of the US Federal government for the rest of his life, Bernie was not the first and certainly won't be the last financial charlatan. What made him special was the sheer scale of his fraud and the astonishing degree to which he 'took in' lots and lots of very respectable people who really should have known better. And here's the rub, oft echoed in recent years by other charlatans and wheeler dealers – he made a point of targeting wealthy people. Time and time again we see wealthy people becoming a target for swindlers, up-ending an age-old tradition which held that only gullible, financially illiterate widows and orphans were targets for crooks.

The regulators, for instance, tend to distinguish between the great mass of retail investors – subject to intense regulation and compliance designed to weed out crooks, largely unsuccessfully it must be said – and high net worths and sophisticated investors who are regarded as being 'fair game'. By signing various forms and certificates you can effectively opt out of a great deal of this protection and invest in frankly anything your heart desires, which is of course a brilliant invitation to financial fraudsters to come knocking on your door.

What are their fat pitches? It doesn't take a genius to practise those sales lines in your head. My own favourites include lines such as:

- 'We offer market beating, consistent returns'– a favourite Madoff claim, with an average return of 12 per cent per annum through thick and thin the oft-quoted target for investors.
- 'Invest with us and we'll help you find tomorrow's tenbaggers' – beloved of nearly all boiler-room operators who claim to have found the secret ingredients to small cap investing.
- 'We have a proprietary system that helps us spot winners' – another favourite hedge fund trick that frequently ends in disaster.
- 'Our scheme can provide you with guaranteed, above-average income with no risk to your capital' – a favourite for dodgy advisers looking to sell schemes to older investors desperate for an income.

Yet I also want readers to disabuse themselves of another concept, which is that all fat pitches belong to crooks and swindlers. In fact, some of the most depressing episodes in wealth destruction have been at the hands of well-meaning, utterly professional people who tried to do the right thing but then made a huge series of terrible blunders. In the UK, for instance, thousands of very respectable, experienced, wealthy investors lost a small fortune through a hugely respectable insurance investment company called Equitable Life. It was for a time, in financial brand terms, the equivalent of Volvo to financial services – safe, reliable, steady. Until it wasn't and the insurer exploded.

The bad news is that it's often wealthier investors who are the target of these 'investment opportunities', which means you've got to be on highest alert if you want to avoid a catastrophic loss to your capital.

But where to start?

I'd suggest a simple three-part litmus test based around each and every sales pitch!

CONSISTENTLY HIGH RETURNS

Here's a nice and simple idea that is easy to put into practice. Ask the sales rep or financial adviser who's punting you the scheme to show you long-term returns from either the investment or the 'asset class/strategy' on which the product is based. Tell them to dig out a ten-year track record (or even longer if possible) and then get them to chart it up against a sensible benchmark like, say, the S&P 500 Index or the FTSE 100 Index in the UK. If the graph for the fat pitch investment shows smoothed returns over say ten years, heading pretty constantly upwards in a straight line, be on the alert.

This is especially the case if the returns on offer are above sensible long-term returns. To recap, I think it's entirely possible with low-risk investments such as bonds to target a return of between 2 and 5 per cent per annum over the long term, with a fairly smooth returns profile over time as an added bonus. Risky equities and other financial assets might give between 5 and 10 per cent per annum but those returns will be volatile and lumpy. What this means is that the 5 to 10 per cent return number will be an average return over time and that over a ten-year period those returns **should** encompass big gains of, say, 10 to 30 per cent in good years and big losses, which might be as much as

20 per cent in a bad year. A smoothed return from a risky asset, especially one producing 10 per cent or more, year in year out, should lead you to hit the alarm bells straightaway.

ILLIQUID SCHEMES

My next strategy for avoiding catastrophic wealth-destroying disasters is to examine what it is you are investing in. We've already discussed the trade-off between liquidity and illiquidity in another chapter. There is enormous opportunity in illiquid assets but there's also danger, namely that you can't get your money out quickly if you need to. If you're being offered above-average, consistent returns from a fundamentally illiquid asset you need to start asking lots and lots and **lots** of questions. You might, for instance, want to know how easy it'll be to access your money in an emergency. Who actually manages the asset (discussed in more detail in the next strategy) and can you visit the asset to see it for yourself?

CONTROL OF ALL THE MOVING PARTS AND THE ILLUSION OF 'NON-EXECS'

The last big flashing red sign is how the asset/investment/fund is managed. Properly regulated financial entities usually have a firm distinction between the trustees of the assets, the administrator of the fund, the actual investment manager and the underlying broker. In addition, you'll also see independent auditors, usually from the big five accounting practices, plus there will also be non-executive directors who are in place to protect the interests of the outside investor. Any practice that doesn't have this structure should instantly make you wary. In particular I'd be concerned if the investment manager completely controlled all the assets, which in effect meant that they owned the broker and the trustee and appointed lots of very worthy and busy non-executive directors who didn't have the time to properly check what is actually going on.

But sadly even if all these structures are in place, you could still be in trouble. Plenty of disastrous investments have boasted the fully regulated panoply of structures and then subsequently imploded largely because everyone was being led a merry dance by the main investment manager.

Putting it all together

I want to finish with a comment by Mr Madoff, where he boasts about his high-level contacts, especially with the big global banks. Madoff once told journalists that: 'The chairman of Banco Santander came down to see me, the chairman of Credit Suisse came down, chairman of UBS came down; I had all of these major banks.' These words should send a shiver down the spine of every reader. Wealthy people tend to have a weakness for other success stories, with the net result that they cluster around big, tent pole brands that they think they can trust. You can almost hear the line now from the potential swindler: 'Invest with us because lots of really big institutions back our investment strategy.' And in Madoff's case he had plenty. Investors included one of Europe's biggest banks (Banco Santander to the tune of US$2.9 billion), one of its oldest banks (Bank Medici at US$2.1 billion) and many of the East Coast of America's finest charities. Sadly, they all lost a mountain of money.

Too many investors say to themselves: 'If it's a global mover and shaker then it's going to be a fit and proper institution to help me with my wealth.' In my experience this is utter garbage and demonstrates a lamentable lack of knowledge compounded by lazy thinking. Respect for successful institutions is one thing, but that doesn't mean you should trust everything they do, especially if those institutions are in the business of managing other people's money. Always do your own research, never trust a brand simply because it is global/successful and always, always beware the fat pitch from someone who says they've worked with the great and the good.

45 How to fight inflation practically

> 'Inflation is taxation without legislation.' Milton Friedman

> 'It is a way to take people's wealth from them without having to openly raise taxes. Inflation is the most universal tax of all.' Thomas Sowell

> 'In the absence of the gold standard, there is no way to protect savings from confiscation through inflation. There is no safe store of value.' Alan Greenspan

> 'Inflation is the crabgrass in your savings.' Robert Orben

> 'The best way to destroy the capitalist system is to debauch the currency. By a continuing process of inflation governments can confiscate, secretly and unobserved, an important part of the wealth of their citizens.' John Maynard Keynes

The slow killer

In earlier chapters you may remember that we examined two crucial forces that impact on your wealth: compounding and inflation.

Compounding, we discovered, can be a wonderful thing over time, especially if your investments are increasing in value. But compounding also works in the reverse, with say costs (they add up over time), and most importantly with inflation. To recap, inflation describes the economic situation where the cost of a good or service, as measured by government indices with strange initials such as CPI and RPI, increases over time. These indices tend to measure a basket of everyday items that we buy at the shops or on the Internet. Over time these prices increase, eating into the current value of our money.

In simple black-and-white terms, too much inflation is self-evidently a bad thing, not least for poor old pensioners on a fixed income. But persistently high inflation is also a bad thing for all of us as it destroys underlying economic incentives, sends the wrong signals to investors and is intensely disliked by central bankers, who have a nasty tendency of swatting it down by pushing up interest rates and plunging economies into great recessions. But not all forms of inflation are necessarily 'evil', especially if those indices measuring increasing prices chug along at relatively mild levels of between 0 and 5 per cent per annum.

So in basic language, hyperinflation and persistently high levels of inflation of above 5 per cent per annum are probably bad, while rates between 0 and 3 per cent are generally 'acceptable'. Just to really confuse matters, falling inflation rates (deflation) tend to be very bad news over the long term as they imply a constantly shrinking economy.

Ok, so now we've reminded ourselves why inflation matters, here's the key secret – inflation is probably a back-door way of inter-generational wealth transfer. Older investors tend to rely on a fixed income from a pension or savings and they also can't readily increase their earnings power. Younger people, by contrast, have time on their side and the real value of their debts is reduced by inflation – most older people by contrast had very few debts! Get the message? That inflation is bad for most older people, and much less odious for younger investors. The good news is that you can do something about this challenge by looking to inflation-proof your investments or risk capital.

BUY REAL PHYSICAL ASSETS!

My first and perhaps most important strategy for minimizing the slow pain of inflation is to buy what are called real physical assets i.e. physical financial investments that have a tendency to increase in value over time by more than the rate of inflation. In this category there are a small number of fairly straightforward investments that are worthy of consideration, namely land, property and gold (to a lesser extent). Each can be physically purchased and owned and each has shown a tendency in the past to increase in value, usually by between 0.5 per cent and 2 per cent per annum on average in excess of inflation over the very long term. And if you need any evidence of this potentially positive effect take a look at the huge university endowment investment funds that are supposed to generate both an income and capital gains to pay for key seats of learning in the US and the UK.

These funds care hugely about inflation's impact and probably their single most important strategy is invest in assets that outpace inflation i.e. all they really want is for their assets and income to grow by more than inflation so they can keep paying the bills! These university funds have been aggressively buying into real assets over the past few decades with big purchases ranging from thousands of acres of forest land in New Zealand (Yale) through to a big old chunk of luxury residential property in the West End of London (the Wellcome Trust). As a very rough and ready measure, these endowments have been putting anything between 10 and 50 per cent of their total wealth into real physical assets.

BUY INDEX-LINKED FINANCIAL ASSETS

Buying physical investments is not without its challenges, even for land and property. Someone has to manage these assets, to produce an income and make sure they stay up to a particular standard expected by the market. Those 'administrative' costs may well put off many investors, in which case they might want to consider much more liquid financial assets such as bonds issued by the government that increase in value based on inflation rates. Index-linked securities are hugely popular among pension fund institutions looking to protect themselves against inflation. The good news is that index-linked government securities are easy to access, and can be bought in a diversified manner via an exchange-traded fund. The challenge for most investors – and their advisers – is to understand exactly how they work.

Index-linked gilts are still bonds issued by the government to pay for spending but their structure of payouts is very different from that of conventional bonds – with linkers as they're called the semi-annual coupon payments and the principal (the final payout) are adjusted in line with a measure of inflation called General Index of Retail Prices (also known as the RPI in the UK). This means that both the coupons (the cash flows paid out) and the principal paid on redemption are adjusted to take account of accrued inflation since the gilt was first issued – note though that the redemption price may be many years away, so prices may fluctuate on a day-to-day basis, reflecting investors' changing yield expectations.

The idea behind these innovative instruments is to protect the real value of investors' savings against the menace of inflation, which is especially dangerous for an investor in securities with a fixed income. Rather than pay a fixed interest rate (or coupon) and principal/par on redemption, index-linked gilts set the coupon and the principal repayment based around an index that measures inflation (either the CPI or the RPI, depending on the government). In essence an inflation-linked bond, the interest and/or principal is adjusted on a regular basis to reflect changes in the rate of inflation, thus providing a 'real', or inflation-adjusted, return.

BUY EQUITIES

My last suggested strategy is perhaps the most radical in that taking some risk with stocks and shares might be a smart way of inflation-proofing at least some of your portfolio. This might strike older investors – especially those in their 60s and 70s as a foolish idea because shares can go up and down in value quite markedly. And these shares are indeed risky, but if you perhaps have another 10 or 20 years to eke out an income from your pension pot, you might want to think about taking on some extra risk by investing in shares – as long as you can afford to be patient and sit tight for at least the next 10 years. In this case, investing in equities could provide real inflation protection, on two levels. The first is that the capital value of equities tends to increase by between 0 per cent and 5 per cent more than long-term inflation rates, even in the most dramatic inflationary episodes. The second key positive for equities is that many pay out a dividend, which in turn tends to increase by an average of between 0 and 2 per cent per annum above inflation rates over the very long term. This dividend yield thus provides some welcome relief for older investors, especially as it's likely to keep track with inflation.

Putting it all together

Inflation is difficult to control and once it shoots above its normal levels it tends to result in phenomenal financial distress for those on a fixed income courtesy of say a pension, an annuity or a pot of bonds that produces a fixed income. It also goes without saying that the resulting central bank panic tends to result in a sharp increase in interest rates and a sudden and savage economic slowdown. But bad things to do with inflation happen far too often and you need to think about protecting yourself. You need to be quick witted and think through your options. Hopefully, my three strategies might help you to build a more robust portfolio. But I also want you to consider two final challenges.

The first is that if you seriously believe inflation is likely to increase, sell all your conventional bonds (corporate and government) as quickly as possible. Bonds tend to perform terribly in inflationary economies. The second is a realism check – how likely do you think rampant inflation will be and how much do you want to pay for that protection? Index-linked government securities, for instance, sound like the perfect insurance policy but you can overpay for this protection. Index-linked yields might actually be **negative** and then you might discover that future inflation rates remain at low levels. The bottom line is that inflation-proofing your portfolio can and does make sense **unless** you overpay for the asset that you are buying.

46 Forever blowing bubbles

> 'Stock market bubbles don't grow out of thin air. They have a solid basis in reality, but reality as distorted by a misconception.' George Soros

> 'Once a bubble begins to form it needs sustenance. Part of the sustenance is provided by institutional parasites that make money off the bubble and have vested interests in preserving and expanding the bubbles.' Aswath Daodarin

> 'Bull markets are born on pessimism, grow on scepticism, mature on optimism, and die on euphoria. The time of maximum pessimism is the best time to buy, and the time of maximum optimism is the best time to sell.' John Templeton

> 'Being right about past bubbles does not automatically ensure that you will be right about the next.' Robert Shiller

> 'Courage taught me no matter how bad a crisis gets… any sound investment will eventually pay off.' Carlos Slim

Watching the markets ebb and flow

We all have our own strange tics, mannerisms and behavioural idiosyncrasies. As we've detailed in many instances in this book, we're not quite as rational as we believe!

At an individual level, we need to acknowledge these behavioural impulses and biases if we want to accumulate wealth. The good news is that most of these personal behaviour-based 'challenges' – which stand in the way of accumulating wealth – are easy to spot and even easier to 'manage', usually by the dint of simple planning, and rigorous rules-based behaviour.

Unfortunately, all these individual reactions to the opportunity (and risk) presented by markets can find a more collective expression in market trends, biases and ultimately manias. We've already examined one such collective, herd-like phenomenon – growth stories where investors become terrifically excited about the prospects of, say, a new technology or a new kind of company with amazing profit margins. The cheapskate, value investor tends to avoid these expensive investment opportunities but that requires discipline and nerves of steel.

Yet lurking in the background of this growth versus value argument is a much deeper and more potent phenomenon – bubbles. In simple terms, virtually any asset that can be purchased by money (with the exception perhaps of cash itself) can find itself caught up within a behaviourally induced boom/bust cycle. This can apply to national economies through to individual shares and the pattern is spookily predictable.

Using a model developed by two economists called Kindleberger and Minsky we can identify five stages. The first stage is called displacement. This is the opening phase where the trigger for enthusiasm is created, usually by something external like technology or a big market trend.

Next up we see rampant credit creation (investors start gearing up on loans issued by the banks), which sooner or later results in excessive demand for an asset that in turn grows faster than supply, pushing up prices in a positive feedback loop.

The euphoria phase is where speculation starts to kick in, and everyone seems to be involved in some form of momentum trading. The penultimate stage is called the critical stage/financial distress, which is when investors start taking profits, with insiders leading the charge. The crisis now intensifies, banks start calling in their loans and all hell breaks out.
Our last phase is called revulsion, which in turn results in capitulation. In this horrible denouement, everyone suddenly turns against the opportunity to such an extent that no one

can sell anything related to it! It's at this point that many smart investors step in!

Both individual shares and entire national markets are hugely vulnerable to this bubble/bust cycle and in nearly every single case we discover that some sort of 'growth investment' is the primary driver behind the ensuing bust, be it technology stocks in 2001, or housing in 2008.

It would of course be nice to ignore these manias but unfortunately they have a nasty way of infecting the real economy, which in turn creates economic crises, recessions and even depressions (think the 1929 boom and bust and the subsequent Great Depression).

Bubbles, booms and busts remind us of the essential risk of any financial asset, including property, namely that it becomes insanely volatile in terms of price. This comes with the territory and investors need to realize that a loss of 20 or even 30 per cent in one year can be 'normal' if you invest in a risky asset. Unfortunately, the bad news is that bubbles have a way of intensifying these mad swings, pushing markets even lower to losses of perhaps 30 per cent to 50 per cent.

This all sounds scary stuff – and it absolutely can be as you grimace at your losses on a daily basis – but there are some things you can do about it all.

TRY TO SPOT A BUBBLE

Ideally, we'd like to be able to spot these bubbles in advance, but surprise, surprise it's not easy! If a bubble were incredibly easy to spot, there wouldn't actually be any in existence i.e. everyone would know that we're about to engage in some scary financial stuff and we'd all pull back from the edge. This optimistic take on behaviour doesn't actually happen, largely because one man's bubble is another man's great growth prospect.

There are though some signs to watch out for if you want to persist in bubble-spotting.

From our earlier discussion two ideas should be immediately apparent – valuation and credit. Valuation simply speaks to the fact that a financial asset frequently becomes over-priced, and frankly unaffordable. There are many measures of affordability (in housing) and valuation (with equities and bonds) and they're all useful. The core numbers tend to focus on the relationship between an asset (a house, stock or bond) and the income it generates. In a house that's the rent, in a company that's the profits the business makes, and in a bond it's the income coupon. These can usually be expressed as a percentage (compared to the cost of the asset) and then charted over time. In stocks this turns into something called the price-to-earnings ratio, which measures the flow of earnings per share measured against the share price. In housing we look at the affordability of an average property based on average salaries. In bonds it is income yield. Once these get out of whack, based on long-term historical averages (ten years or more), we know we're entering dangerous terrain.

But we need an extra signal, and that's usually based around debt. Once enthusiasm builds we should expect to see investors borrowing more and more money in turn to fuel their excitement. Once this process of high valuation and debt creation gets out of control, you should have two key signals, which might in turn encourage you to maybe increase your cash reserves.

SPECULATE INTELLIGENTLY

Growing enthusiasm or euphoria can present an opportunity for the right kind of investor, especially one who is experienced and understands the nature of risk. Crucially, they'll have to have a speculative side to them and be willing to move in and out of a market at great speed. Two options might present themselves to this investor, at this stage. The first is to jump on board this big 'trend', gear up by using debt and make a quick killing as market momentum becomes unstoppable. Needless to say, this bullish trade might need to be terminated very quickly if the experienced, adventurous investor thinks markets are about to implode. The second option is to 'insure' the rest of their existing portfolio against any sudden increases in volatility and market panic. This 'hedging' as it's called can be done via (expensive) options that in effect make an investor a profit even if markets fall.

MOVE IN WHEN THERE'S BLOOD ON THE CARPET

My last strategy is also for adventurous types, but the idea here is more about staying aloof from the market euphoria, watching from a distance for the peak of enthusiasm and then waiting patiently for the ensuing panic to turn into what's called capitulation. Here we're looking for a financial asset to make 5- or even 10- or perhaps 20-year 'lows' in terms of price. The trick then becomes spotting the decent opportunity where absolutely no one wants to buy in. Our adventurous type then turns to their pot of cash that they've been patiently accumulating as markets become more bubble-like. This involved taking some profits and generally increasing the cash reserve as markets became too excitable and thus risky. Cash in a fearful, capitulated marketplace is a wonderful thing to have as it allows you to buy great assets at a bargain price. In my experience, the **very** greatest investment gains have been made by the steely-nerved investor who buys quality assets when markets have capitulated.

Putting it all together

Bubble-spotting can be great fun but don't become too obsessed with spotting the signals, otherwise you could end up feeding the 'glass half empty' syndrome, which is a pernicious problem whereby investors always think the sky is about to fall in and markets are one inch away from a crash. This over-cautious type might end up not taking **enough** risk and stay too long in cash. Back in the 1990s, for instance, a great British fund manager called Tony Dye believed that stock markets were getting far too euphoric and advised staying away from risky stuff. He was eventually proved right, many, many years later but by that time many of his critics had made huge profits and he was generally regarded as a maverick who was a little too fearful for his own good. The very best cure for this pessimism is to have a long time horizon for investing in risky stuff. If you're in shares you should be willing to sit tight for 20 years or more, during which time I'd be astonished if there weren't at least three or four major bouts of market volatility where prices go down by more than 20 per cent in a year. Bubbles will come and go! Be patient and sit tight and accept that you may never spot a bubble but then again maybe you don't need to!

47 Keep it simple, keep it cheap, use tracker funds

> 'The mutual fund industry has been built, in a sense, on witchcraft.' John Bogle

> 'On balance, the financial system subtracts value from society.' John Bogle

> 'Don't look for the needle in the haystack. Just buy the haystack!' John Bogle

> 'Never underrate the importance of asset allocation.' John Bogle

> 'Owning the market remains the strategy of choice.' John Bogle

Saint Jack and why you need a core of index funds

In this chapter I want to introduce the reader to yet another very famous, very successful investor – John Bogle, otherwise known to his long list of admirers (the author included) as Jack, or even Saint Jack!

Mr Bogle is perhaps one of the greatest fund managers and investment supremos in US history. He's made his investors good money but he's no showman, although he does have a loyal army of fans who call themselves Bogleheads.

As an investor Bogle rarely beats the market, and he prefers to do something much more important and powerful – stack the odds in the favour of the humble individual using small and simple practical measures. His fund management group in the US is called Vanguard and it is now one of the very biggest of its kind.

This success has been achieved by doing two very simple things.

First Vanguard keeps costs low on its funds by cutting out the sexy stuff like rampant speculation. But Bogle went one step further. He went out of his way to keep investing simple by focusing on low-cost funds that 'track' a major market index such as the S&P 500 (the 500 largest US companies ranked by their market capitalization). Bogle has pioneered a hugely powerful idea called index tracking, making it absolutely mainstream and easy to access.

At its core is a simple observation. As we're about to discover in the next chapter, it's difficult to second-guess where the market is going next if you are a professional fund manager. It's not completely impossible and there are some wonderful investors and businesses out there who do it day-in day-out, but let's just say that they are few and far between. Academic economists have long recognized an essential fact, which is that most fund managers don't beat the 'market average', which is usually the return from a benchmark index like the S&P 500. They think this is so because by and large markets get the price of a security, bond or share just about right. In the technical imagination of economists they suspect that the great tsunami of news and opinions is absorbed by the random mass of investors, which in turn moves the share price up or down just about right i.e. the market is largely but not always efficient.

If we accept this – as Bogle does – we shouldn't bother second-guessing where it might go next. What we should do instead is just buy what the market is buying. In simple terms, we'd look at that benchmark index like the S&P 500, we'd see what's inside it – stuff the market self-evidently likes because it's buying it – and then construct a fund that simply copies (or 'replicates' in the technical language) the constituents of that index. So if HSBC is say 5 per cent of the benchmark UK index, the FTSE 100, one day, our fund has 5 per cent of its entire assets in that business. If it's at 10 per cent the next day, guess what the fund has in terms of HSBC shares? Yep, 10 per cent. And so on in a methodical, almost machine-like manner. So, here's a plan for your next steps to indexing nirvana.

WORK OUT WHAT YOU WANT TO TRACK AND THEN FIND AN INDEX

Our very first step is to set up a portfolio of investments, which we then split into two parts. The first and biggest part is the core portfolio, which should be jam-packed full of index-tracking funds and ETFs. The satellite portfolio might have some very different types of funds, where you do have an active fund manager taking more speculative bets. More on that in the next chapter. Back at the core portfolio, you want to be diversified between opportunities. Maybe you'll want some equities and bonds plus a bit of cash. That might mean 100 per cent equities for a young investor but as little as 40 per cent equities for an older investor with most of the rest in bonds. Within each broad category (of equities and bonds) you also want some international diversification and some sector themes i.e. maybe a bit more focused on dividend-producing companies or on energy companies. Maybe you want more smaller companies or, by contrast, many more larger global companies. You thus work out your exact mix but make sure that in each case you figure out the 'asset class' you want (say US small caps). Our next step is to then find out an index that tracks this opportunity. Do some research on this index by Googling it and looking at a factsheet for the index (everything you need to know about it on no more than two pages). Then find an ETF or index-tracking fund that in turn 'copies' this index. Your best choice is the fund with the largest amount of assets under management (called AUM) and the lowest total expense ratio.

FIND OUT THE AVERAGE TOTAL EXPENSE RATIO OF YOUR PORTFOLIO

Why my focus on the cost and expense? Put simply, absolutely nothing in the weird and wonderful world of investment is guaranteed except that above-average costs will destroy your wealth. Let's assume that shares do grow by an average of about 6.5 per cent per annum over the next 20 years. Let's also assume I make a monthly investment of US$500 for the next 20 years, hoping to ride that tiger that's called compounding returns.

In option number 1 we invest in a fund where an active fund manager charges us the industry average, which is around 1.5 per cent p.a., which in turn means that the net return on our ordinary, average, benchmark mutual fund has gone down to 5 per cent p.a. At the end of our 20 years our investor has US$206,000. The average ETF or index-tracking fund, by comparison, charges about 0.5 per cent per annum, which would mean that we'd get the market return of 6 per cent per annum (6.5 per cent less that 0.5 per cent). At the end of 20 years we'd now have US$232,000, or US$26,000 more in capital from a difference of just 1 per cent a year in charges. I think that's a big difference and I'm hoping you do too!

Obviously our ordinary mutual fund will argue that they **aim** to produce better returns than the benchmark (6.5 per cent) by clever fund management, but as Bogle reminds us (backed up by a mountain of academic analysis) that just ain't true in the vast majority of cases! So, stick with the simpler product and save money in terms of fees. But what to look out for? The key term is called the total expense ratio, which looks at the total fees and costs charged to the fund by a management firm like Vanguard. In my own view, the lower the better and absolutely **never ever** pay more than 1 per cent a year in fees for an ETF or index-tracking fund.

THINK ABOUT USING A LOW-COST MULTI-ETF PORTFOLIO

If you want to keep life simple consider one last strategy, which is to find a fund manager that'll put together your own core portfolio for you. This means they'll have lots of different ETFs and index-tracking funds following lots of different assets classes and indices. They'll work out what they believe is the sensible mix of assets and opportunities based on your risk profile/age/time horizon. They'll then put together all these different ETFs into one simple, 'all-in' fund. The great advantage of this approach is that it makes life easy for you and it can also mean that you cut costs as the fund manager does all the boring legwork of putting these different assets into one basket.

Putting it all together

The genius of Vanguard and Bogle was to recognize that this boring way of investing presented a huge business opportunity. In essence, running this simple index-tracking fund could be done cheaply. No expensive fund manager to pay for, just a bunch of computers and a few smart people at the centre to make sure everything works properly. This allows the fund manager to cut costs to the bare minimum and then simply track what the market buys and sells. Vanguard has turned this into a vast money-making machine that has hoovered up hundreds of billions of investors' money in cheap low-cost index-tracking funds and exchange-traded funds (stock market listed funds that do essentially the same thing and have the nickname of ETFs).

Bogle has taken these insights and then relentlessly banged the drum, in books, in speeches and in person, reminding investors to keep it simple, to not beat the market and to cut costs to the absolute minimum – just read my long list of quotes by Saint Jack at the beginning of this chapter.

It's not exciting stuff to be sure but it works. And here's the thing – it'll help make you much wealthier because a) you won't be overcomplicating your investment strategy and b) you'll be cutting your costs to the bone! The genius of this 'keep it simple and cheap' strategy is to apply this thinking to your investment portfolio by making sure that in your 'core' assets you've got lots and lots of index-tracking funds and ETFs.

48 Hunting down great investors

> 'I'm only rich because I know when I'm wrong… I basically have survived by recognizing my mistakes.' George Soros

> 'I use my analysts to watch the fund's existing holdings while I look for new opportunities. It's important to do both when you're running a fund.' Anthony Bolton

> 'The other boys at Yale came from wealthy families, and none of them were investing outside the United States, and I thought, "That is very egotistical. Why be so short-sighted or near-sighted as to focus only on America? Shouldn't you be more open-minded?"' Sir John Templeton

> 'What we try to do is take advantage of errors others make, usually because they are too short-term oriented, or they react to dramatic events, or they overestimate the impact of events, and so on.' Bill Miller

> 'It's amazing how difficult it is for a man to understand something if he's paid a small fortune not to understand it.' John Bogle paraphrasing Upton Sinclair

Trust the veterans?

In this chapter I want to tentatively overturn some excellent, received wisdom! In the previous chapter we explained how a focus on index tracking, passive funds might make sense. I think the general rule is that this is true: that excluding active fund managers (this is where a professional investor manages the fund) is a great way of boosting your wealth i.e. cutting costs and cutting out an 'active' fund manager who takes too many risks is a sensible strategy. Yet there are some exceptions to this rule and in this chapter I want to touch on why recruiting an experienced, veteran manager for your investment funds might make some, limited, sense.

Now before we do that I want to first repeat the excellent received wisdom about investment funds and their managers. Most funds offered by large investment houses are not passively but actively managed, which is a sad and sorry statement of the investment world.

In the US and UK, for instance, about 70 per cent of institutional funds are actively managed and this rises to over 90 per cent for retail funds. Put it another way – of the 14,304 mutual funds currently trading in the US, 13,796 of them are actively managed. Given these numbers you'd think that these active fund managers – who charge a pretty penny for their services – add lots of 'value' i.e. they produce above-average returns.

Far from it in fact! Although some controversy still rumbles on, the majority of studies by experienced economists and analysts now conclude that actively managed funds, on average, consistently underperform their passively managed counterparts (ETFs).

Study after study has revealed a huge discrepancy between actively and passively managed (i.e. index tracking) funds. The conventional academic wisdom goes something like this: that the past isn't much use in forecasting the future, that by and large prices set by the market are sensible and 'efficient', and that it is devilishly difficult for money managers to use that past data to make any extra return. This research has even found support in journalistic circles – an article in *The Wall Street Journal* reported that the average mutual fund underperformed its benchmark by 140 basis points (1.4 per cent) a year.

So there is a consensus among academics who study this subject: active fund managers are not good at consistently, over long periods of time, beating the benchmark index (say the S&P 500). In fact, they are so bad at it, that most of the time you would be better off finding a vehicle – an index-tracking fund, for instance – that simply tracks the index.

So, game over for active fund managers?

Not quite!

There is some evidence that although good fund managers are rarely **consistently** successful they can, sometimes, be **persistently** successful over the long term. This phrasing might sound slightly weasel-like in its formulation – you can imagine a politician using this subtle difference to justify terrible performance in office – but it does speak to the fact that some veteran fund managers can over long periods of time (15 years or more) produce great long-term average numbers.

LOOK FOR FUND MANAGERS WITH A LONG-TERM TRACK RECORD

If you are going to use an active fund manager, look for a veteran with a long track record of persistent outperformance when measured against the benchmark index. Ideally what we're looking for are managers with a ten-year-plus track record, where they hog the top slots of most fund ratings systems as well as dominating the returns data for many years over at least a decade. I recently looked at just this kind of analysis with help from French fund management group Carmignac Gestion. In an article in the UK magazine *Investment Week* we looked for experienced fund managers operating in Europe, with a long track record managing their fund (15 years at least). We then crunched the numbers on performance and ratings (usually awarded by independent analysts) and looked for managers who kept cropping up in the top quartile (the top quarter of funds). Surprisingly only a very few managers were able to pull off this remarkable feat, but the ones that did also boasted some poor years when performance took a tumble. The moral of the story? Most fund managers do struggle to make the grade consistently but a few do add value if you trust them to manage your money for the long term. The key though is to find managers who've been in the job for at least a decade or more at that same fund.

Yet simple longevity isn't the only requirement. They need some other attributes...

LOOK FOR MANAGERS WITH A (CYNICAL) CONVICTION

The Internet has brought many wonderful things in its wake but one of the very best is that it can give the average investor a world of information about how a fund manager thinks. I like to back veteran fund managers where I've read interviews that clearly spell out their 'contrarian' views, their ability to take a different, alternative view about the state of the markets. That might mean, for instance, that they're very focused on value investing or their nemesis, growth stocks! Whatever the 'stance', I like to understand what makes my fund manager different in the way he or she thinks.

LOOK FOR INVESTORS WITH SKIN IN THE GAME

My last key attribute is perhaps the most basic, even venal! I look for veteran fund managers who have a persistent record of beating the market, built on a proven set of ideas about investing, where they have a huge amount of their own money invested in the fund. In simple terms I want to see them put their pension on the line alongside my own money! That means I look down the list of disclosed fund manager investments and watch out for substantial personal ownership over the past 10 to 20 years.

Putting it all together

In my experience exceptional active fund managers usually add value in one of two major respects: they're usually obsessed with minimizing downside risk (as you'd expect if they have their own money in the fund) or they are great at spotting undervalued gems that eventually shoot up in price, largely because they're willing to be patient waiting for success.

For me, these 'skillsets' mean that I tend to use these veteran active managers in the satellite parts of my portfolio, alongside index-tracking funds (including ETFs) that still sit in the core. I'd probably use these managers if they operate in a market that was a bit more difficult than the average (say emerging markets) or required very specialist skills. Alternatively, I might use them in those parts of my satellite portfolio where I'm holding money that might need to turn into cash in a few years hence. In this situation I want a more risk-aware, volatile-averse fund manager with what's called an 'absolute returns' perspective i.e. they try to make money (positive returns) through all types of markets, even if shares are falling in price. Crucially, if I were looking to add a new veteran fund manager to my portfolio, I'd always wait for those 'blue' periods, where performance is less than satisfactory i.e. those points in the cycle when fashion-conscious types are bailing out and the fund is underperforming. Be counterintuitive and bet on the veterans when everyone else thinks they've had it!

49 Taming your debt

> '[Credit is a system whereby] a person who can't pay, gets another person who can't pay, to guarantee that he can pay.'
> Charles Dickens in *Little Dorrit*

> 'What can be added to the happiness of a man who is in health, out of debt, and has a clear conscience?' Adam Smith

> 'We all think we're going to get out of debt.' Louie Anderson

> 'I'm in debt. I am a true American.' Balki Bartokomous

> 'He who promises runs in debt.' The Talmud

Living with the debt monster

Many of us have no other option than to take on debt at some point during our working career. Throughout this book we've tried to remain level-headed about this reality. Our core approach is that a problem or opportunity that is understood, analysed and measured is one that is manageable. With debt via credit cards, for instance, the most important challenge is to identify first just how much you're in the red and whether it's a problem, and then develop a plan to manage it downwards.

This chapter is about more day-to-day strategies that can be deployed in the continuing, life-long struggle with credit cards and loans.

The first part necessarily involves pinning some numbers on the beast. The average US household credit card debt in 2013 stood at US$15,270 (the equivalent number in the UK is about £10,000, which is the same once we've adjusted for foreign exchange rates). The average mortgage debt is US$149,925 and the average student loan debt is a staggering US$32,258. In total, American consumers owe US$11 trillion in debt and the good news is that this astonishingly big headline number has been slowly decreasing in the period between 2009 and 2013. Yet the most fascinating numbers for this observer is that US citizens now owe more money on their student debt (US$1.04 trillion) than on their credit cards (US$856 billion). Mortgage debt unsurprisingly towers over both at just under US$8 trillion.

Stepping back from these headline statistics, I'd offer up two observations. The first is that we are collectively doing a better job of managing our debts and slowly reducing those nasty-looking numbers but we face enormous headwinds from excessive fees and high interest rates (even during an unprecedented period of low official headline rates).

I'm also struck by the huge growth in US student debt, which poses for me at least a very awkward question – is the best way of managing down your debt levels, and improving your potential for growing wealth, **not** to go to university or college but to find more cost-effective, work-based ways of acquiring the necessary personal capital?

CREDIT CARDS MANAGEMENT

If you really must use a credit card (and they sometimes do make some sense, especially around planning key purchases), I think you should make sure that you follow some simple rules. Always try to pay off more than the minimum – paying just the minimum amount off your credit card balance each month will not only extend the time you are in debt, it will also significantly increase the interest you pay over that time. I also think it's really, really important that you don't miss a payment, ever! Late or non-payment on a credit card is an absolute credit record disaster, which means you should always have a direct debit or automatic payment plan connected to the card.

I'd also avoid cash advances like the bubonic plague! This utterly horrendous customer 'service' is actually an excuse for the banks to charge an absolute fortune and then they have the cheek to compound these charges by adding yet more interest. Avoid!

If you are looking around for a new card I'd also stress that it's not worth applying for a card you have no chance of being accepted for. In my experience, the best deals are reserved for customers with good credit scores, and failed credit card applications will have a detrimental impact on your credit score.

Last but by no means least, consider substituting your existing card with a cashback or reward card. If you are one of those sensible people who pay off your bill in full every month, a cashback credit card can be a great way to get more for your money as a percentage of the amount you spend will be returned to you once a year as a cash payment.

GETTING ON TOP OF THOSE PERSONAL LOANS

Sometimes we have to take out a personal loan in order to say help fund a car and in my experience loans are probably a smarter bet than credit cards. The fact that you have to commit to a schedule of a number of years, agree a fixed sum and accept fixed monthly payments, imposes a discipline that is much more preferable to the easy and flexible ways of the ubiquitous credit card.

One small tip – if you can obtain a cheap loan, pay off the credit card arrears, and then cut them up and never use them again.

If you do decide to go down the loan route be very 'particular' about who you choose as a lender. Always check the small print, for instance, just to make sure that you are actually eligible for the loan – we don't want a failed application on our credit record. Also remember that some of the very best buys featured in the newspapers and on adverts come with some very onerous conditions!

I'd also carefully scrutinize the early repayment charges. If you can pay off a loan early, you might find yourself hit with lots of unwanted fees and charges. Bizarrely, I'd also think about borrowing more – in general, the larger the loan the lower the interest rate. Also why don't you consolidate all your credit cards into one loan? Last but by no means least always, always fix your personal loan rate. This means that the rate at which interest will be applied to your borrowing debt, and more importantly the amount you will need to pay back, stays the same throughout the life of your loan.

MANAGING YOUR MORTGAGE

Mortgages are an essential part of modern life, unless you're lucky enough to have rich parents who can help you avoid the whole expensive business. For the rest of us we have to find the best mortgage to suit our needs. That forces us into finding a deposit, and then finding a mortgage product with the right interest rate – and a willingness on the part of the bank to lend to us. My advice is to always fix your mortgage interest rate unless rates are really very high. If you do opt for what seems like a cheap tracker mortgage, make sure you set aside the 'savings' from that low rate and use that money to accelerate the repayment on your mortgage. More generally, I'd suggest trying to repay your mortgage with your savings where appropriate. Also, one last piece of practical advice – don't be seduced by a mortgage deal's headline rate alone. Many mortgages boast unacceptably high fees that can often be reduced by a spot of forceful 'negotiation'!

Putting it all together

I want to leave the reader with two thoughts. The first is that you can manage your credit rating in a very similar way to managing anything else to do with your money i.e. improve it. For instance, failed applications leave a footprint on your credit record, which will count against you should you make subsequent applications. That means you should avoid frivolous applications for credit. Also, every year or so check your credit rating, especially if you plan to go out and apply for a new loan in the next few months. Scrutinize all the comments on your file and be ready to challenge anything you think is unfair.

My biggest message though is a familiar one, which is that small (positive) numbers can make a big difference over time via the wonders of compounding i.e. cutting small amounts of excess interest rate cost can make a material difference to your total wealth. Let's accept that the average cost of credit is between 15 per cent and 18 per cent per annum – that means that the average household in debt in the US is probably spending around US$2,000 a year in interest payments, give or take a few hundred dollars each way.

Assuming that the government stats are right and the average US household income is about US$53,000 per annum, that means that getting on for 4 per cent of our average total income is being spent on paying interest (though in reality we actually end up compounding this interest).

If that same average household eliminated all its debt, and then reinvested that money (US$2,000 p.a.) in an average shares-based investment plan (with returns averaging about 6.5 per cent p.a.) for the next 20 years, they'd accumulate US$80,000 in capital at the end of the term. Even if we managed to cut that interest rate number by a third, we'd still be looking at a capital pot of US$26,000. These numbers sound smallish on paper but an extra US$25k or US$50k made via this credit-card savings strategy might be enough to double the total lifetime wealth of most average US households!

50 Be creative

> 'Creativity is allowing yourself to make mistakes. Art is knowing which ones to keep.' Scott Adams

> 'A business has to be evolving, it has to be fun, and it has to exercise your creative interests.' Richard Branson

> 'Nothing great was ever achieved without enthusiasm.' Ralph Waldo Emerson

> 'Your culture is your brand.' Tom H. C. Anderson

> 'Creative thinking is not a talent, it is a skill that can be learnt. It empowers people by adding strength to their natural abilities which improves teamwork, productivity and where appropriate profits.' Edward de Bono

Grab the opportunities, shape the challenge!

My very last chapter represents a call to action. For many years now a mental barrier has been erected between the supposedly razor-sharp worlds of business and money and the 'softer' world of creativity. Businesspeople and wealthy types were supposed to be tough as old nails and focused on the bottom line while creatives were focused on doing new stuff that was terrifically exciting and usually didn't make much money.

Here's my very last Secret. This divide between money and creativity is now artificial and if you are at all serious about building up your wealth, you desperately need to be creative.

Not necessarily in the sense that you have to go out and draw amazing paintings, merely in the narrower, opportunistic sense that money, business, wealth is increasingly becoming the art of the possible.

In virtually every other chapter in this book we've seen that the world we're living in is changing yet again, with openness, energy, positivity, connectivity and technological awareness all becoming vitally important not just for survival but also for prospering. What is empirically true beyond doubt is that those who are enterprising, opportunistic, creative, and constantly striving through hard work are more likely to accumulate wealth.

Big corporates have also woken up to this profound change. One small example of this trend is that outfits like Google, 3M and DuPont now expect their workers to spend as much as 20 per cent of their time thinking creatively about new business opportunities. And what's true for the main workforce is also increasingly true for the corporate elite. IBM recently asked 1,500 CEOs to list the most important leadership characteristics, and creativity was ranked higher than integrity, intelligence and a global mindset. What's changing in the world of business?

I started this chapter with a number of quotes from leading businesspeople, investors, scientists and creatives. They all emphasized the joy of creation and discovery, the enthusiasms of culture, and the constant need for 'emotional intelligence'. But I think two well-known personalities can sum up what's changed much better than I can.

The first is the comedian John Cleese (from Monty Python), something of an expert on both success and psychological insight. According to Mr Cleese, 'we all operate in two contrasting modes, which might be called open and closed. The open mode is more relaxed, more receptive, more exploratory, more democratic, more playful and more humorous. The closed mode is the tighter, more rigid, more hierarchical, more tunnel-visioned. Most people unfortunately spend most of their time in the closed mode.'

But how does this challenging way of thinking translate into investment, professional and business success? Richard Branson, an insanely influential entrepreneur (he's the innovator behind the Virgin brand in case you weren't aware) sums it up beautifully thus: 'I love creating things. I sometimes compare, maybe slightly presumptuously, an entrepreneur to an artist. You have a blank piece of canvas, and you're trying to make people's lives better in a particular area, so you're filling in every aspect of that canvas. It's great fun trying to take on, say, a big goliath, especially if they've become a bit fat and a bit bloated, and do it a bit better than they've done it. Give the public something which they can enjoy, and you can be proud of creating. I have great difficulty in life saying no!'

Branson is a genius at using creativity to generate what's called collision points, intellectual exercises where he takes thinking from two different worlds and then tries to mesh them together in a business mash-up. More to the point, he then uses these insights to take **risks**, by starting something new that will hopefully create wealth.

I would contend that if you want to accumulate wealth and respect and success, you need to be constantly on the hunt for new ideas, for new ways of working smarter, better ways of developing your personal brand. Some of that is simply about being opportunistic (networking, working for inspiring, disruptive businesses) but we also need to be brave and creative, take risks and try to create something new.

SEARCH OUT NEW EXPERIENCES AND PERSPECTIVES

Move out of your comfort zone and try something new on a regular basis i.e. maybe think about working in a different industry or field every few decades. Within your normal world of work or business (or even investment strategy) systematically challenge everything that's important to the way you operate now. Also work with others to nurture ideas that initially seem flawed – explore whether they lead you somewhere significant. And remember that the best way to harness the creative mindset is to take away restraints in the beginning of any process of discovery and renewal.

THINK DIFFERENTLY

Challenge yourself by setting personal goals to brainstorm, foster and develop ideas. That means you'll need to find time to think. One simple idea could be to spend 20 minutes a day brainstorming new ideas, or spend one day a month or quarter working offsite in a different environment than your everyday office.

STRUCTURE YOUR CREATIVE THINKING

There's a rather dangerous myth lurking around about creativity. It consists of the notion that great ideas suddenly emerge in a puff of brilliant inspiration and then sweep through the world, changing absolutely everything! Nonsense. This way of thinking stops us from recognizing that any creative process (starting a business or developing an investment plan or working out a life plan) needs to be thorough and well planned. There's no getting away from my underlying utilitarian assumptions that a challenge well understood and mapped out is one that is conquered. The creative process involves an ongoing, painstaking, development of fresh perspectives and the nurturing of initially small ideas in order to gradually create something significantly innovative. True ingenuity needs structure and analysis as well as brainstorming sessions and whacky ideas generation.

One practical suggestion is that you keep track of all your new ideas and innovative thinking. Maintain a monthly review – call it a portfolio review of sorts – of all your new thinking and meticulously chart your progress over time. This 'archiving' of good ideas will serve as a fantastic reference tool for your later thinking and best practice. More than a few times I've looked back at my 'development' lists from a few years back and had a sudden revelation about a new twist on an old problem.

Putting it all together

I want to finish this book by saying that creativity is the real secret to success in our 'post-modern' world. We operate in markets powered by continuous creative destruction powered by the drum beat of disruptive technologies. We live in social worlds where connectivity and communication celebrate ingenuity and confidence and depth of knowledge. Crucially, we work in businesses where creativity is now seen as an essential for career advancement, but only in a structured way. And what's true for corporations is doubly true for entrepreneurs. If you honestly believe that you'll build a fortune by not doing something brave and new… well, you're quite simply deluding yourself.

Last but by no means least, even dry old investors need to think about how they can be more creative. Don't stick with the old assumptions, watch for new patterns and new opportunities. Most importantly, this openness to change means you need to think and behave differently. In a very structured way you need to be emotionally intelligent, learn and listen and be willing to make mistakes. Take advice, listen to new theories and then work out how to act decisively. Be brave and take risks.

Discover the secrets behind greatness

SECRETS of HAPPY PEOPLE — Matt Avery

SECRETS of CONFIDENT PEOPLE — Richard Nugent

SECRETS of WEALTHY PEOPLE — David Stevenson

SECRETS of SUCCESS AT WORK — Nigel Cumberland

SECRETS of INFLUENTIAL PEOPLE — Steven Pearce

SECRETS of CONFIDENT COMMUNICATORS — Diana Mather

SECRETS of RESILIENT PEOPLE — John Lees

SECRETS of HAPPY RELATIONSHIPS — Jenny Hare

SECRETS of THE NLP MASTERS — Judy Bartkowiak

For more information visit:
www.secretsguides.com